Architectures of the Unforeseen

Architectures of the Unforeseen

Essays in the Occurrent Arts

Brian Massumi

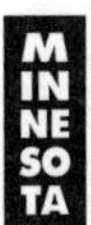

University of Minnesota Press

Minneapolis

London

The author would like to acknowledge the generous support of the Social Sciences and Humanities Research Council of Canada.

Earlier versions of portions of chapter 1 were published in "Interface and Active Space: Human–Machine Design," in *Proceedings of the Sixth International Symposium on Electronic Art* (Montreal: ISEA, 1996), 188–92; and "Becoming Architectural: Affirmative Critique, Creative Incompletion," in *The Innovation Imperative: Architectures of Vitality,* special issue of *Architectural Design* (UK), ed. Pia Ednie-Brown, Mark Burry, and Andrew Burrow, vol. 221 (January–February 2013): 50–56. Earlier versions of portions of chapter 2 were published in "Flash in Japan: Brian Massumi on Rafael Lozano-Hemmer's 'Amodal Suspension,'" *Artforum International* (New York), November 2003: 37; "Floating the Social: An Electronic Art of Noise," in *Reverberations: Philosophy, Aesthetics, and the Politics of Noise,* ed. Michael Goddard, Benjamin Halligan, and Paul Hegarty, 40–57 (London: Continuum, 2012); and "Espresar la conexión, arquitectura relacional / Expressing Connection: Relational Architecture," *Vectorial Elevation: Relational Architecture No. 4,* ed. Rafael Lozano-Hemmer (Mexico City: National Council for Culture and the Arts, 2000), 183–208 (a bilingual English/Spanish translation by Susie Ramsay). Chapter 3 was published as "Making to Place: Simryn Gill, in the Artist's Words Refracted," in *Here Art Grows on Trees: Simryn Gill,* ed. Catherine de Zegher, on the occasion of the 55th Biennale of Venice, 185–237 (Sydney/Ghent: Australia Council for the Arts/MER, 2013), reprinted by permission.

Published by the University of Minnesota Press
111 Third Avenue South, Suite 290
Minneapolis, MN 55401-2520
http://www.upress.umn.edu

ISBN 978-1-5179-0595-8 (hc)
ISBN 978-1-5179-0596-5 (pb)

A Cataloging-in-Publication record for this book is available from the Library of Congress.

Printed in the United States of America on acid-free paper

The University of Minnesota is an equal-opportunity educator and employer.

25 24 23 22 21 20 19   10 9 8 7 6 5 4 3 2 1

Contents

Introduction

These essays are not "about." They are writings-with. What is perhaps peculiar to them in relation to other practices of writing-with is that the impetus behind them was felt as an impact, at once contingent and obligatory: anything but a well-reflected choice to enter into well-mannered dialogue. They had more the tenor of a fortuitous encounter tantamount to a capture: a latching to an alien creative practice of my own process of philosophical concept-making, at very particular points of contact. Points of contact is not the best way of putting it, because it connotes two already-made forms rubbing up against each other and sharing something of their contents across a boundary. What I am talking about is at a very different level, the level at which things are in the making: where what they can do and where they can go is a pressing, open question. This is the level of unruly constitutive problems, using the word "problem" in the positive sense of a galvanizing tension imparting an impetus for a process to take shape. A constitutive problem energizes a coming trajectory with formative potential, but not without also lacing it with imperatives acting as enabling constraints that will orient its unfolding without predefining it. A region of problematic overlap is a better way of putting it than a point of contact. Two processes, strangers to each other, can intimately overlap in a problematic that is constitutive for both, without coming in any way to resemble each other in form or even sharing content. Practices do not share content. They fashion their own, reciprocal to their singular taking-form. They may perturb each other or attune, interfere or resonate, cross-fertilize or contaminate, but each will ultimately incorporate the formative potential in

vii

their own problematic way, so that the overlap is also a forking. This is what Deleuze and Guattari call *aparallel evolution*: the intimate art of keeping a formative distance.[1]

Both the niceties of conversation and the agonism of debate are anathema to this: they are mediations. They presuppose constituted terms entering into interaction in the capacity of what they have been, from the perspective of where they now stand. Aparallel evolution, on the other hand, is an event. It stages a relation that sweeps its terms up into its own dynamic perspective, from the immediate standpoint of how they might now mutate. This may well involve dialogue (as it has with the essays in this book), but only as a condition for the shifting into gear of a process surpassing dialogue's conventional communicational function.[2]

My own work has been in aparallel evolution with the three practitioners written-with in this book for varying durations. In the case of the first two, the duration is long, very long. A chance introduction to pioneering digital architect Greg Lynn in the mid-1990s riveted my attention to the problem of the abstract as a *practical* issue. The virtual, in Proust's formula taken up by Deleuze, is "abstract yet real." So what, practically speaking, is its mode of reality? How can a design practice avail itself of that reality not only as a resource but as a force, for its own creative process? Given that the digital is in no way synonymous with the virtual, understood in terms of formative force, what exactly is the relationship between them? In what way does the dynamic form in which a design process incorporates the abstract reality of the virtual as a creative growth factor change what we can think and say about form-generation? How does it change what we mean by form in the first place? What is the relationship between a design process that alters what we mean by form and the design products that emerge as a result of that alteration? May a process availing itself of the reality of the virtual contrive to carry the charge of the virtual into its product? In what (dynamic) trace-form? Under what conditions may a product convey into the world at large the abstract but real formative force from whose impetus it emerged, from within a particular precinct of practice? Thinking this knot of questions through Lynn's architectural design practice, goaded on by his rallying cry of "animate form," impelled my work in directions it might not otherwise have taken. It enabled it to gestate concepts it might not otherwise have birthed, as it followed his process in aparallel accompaniment over many years, punctuated by intermittent discussions and crossings of paths as well as more concerted overlaps such as a two-week studio residency at his offices in Venice, California. I cannot purport that the encounters inflected Lynn's trajectory in return. The fact that the inflection remained virtual on one side, however, in no way detracts from the abstract reality of the processual encounter. The thinking that oriented Lynn's coming into his own practice had a philosophical virtuosity, evidenced in his writings of the 1990s. In its emergent stages, his work was in intimate relation with the kind of process-oriented philosophy that also moves my work. It was too absorbed in following through with the impetus of that encounter, pressing it into the invention of its own practical dynamic, to need a second hit of it. What it needed was to spin its own formative line and tangle, leaving my process to similarly spin off, orphaned by Lynn's while irreversibly correlated to it, a wasp in the abstract embrace of an intimately distant orchid. Encounters actually unmet, non-encounters of the virtual kind, are also events, after their own manner.

In the case of Mexican-Canadian digital-media artist Rafael Lozano-Hemmer, the inflection has at times gone both ways, and the duration is even longer, beginning at the end of the 1980s. My early work on the politics of everyday fear formed part of the background for one of Lozano-Hemmer's works, discussed in chapter 2. A young Lozano-Hemmer had actually had a hand in the fear project as a member of the collective that formed around the project in its embryonic stages. Later work of mine on amodal perception factored into a subsequent project of Lozano-Hemmer's, also analyzed here. Collaborative encounters happened.[3] The problem that Lozano-Hemmer's work crystallized for mine concerned the distinction, already mentioned, between interaction and relation. Here was an "interactive artist" vehemently repudiating that label, insisting that what he was really doing was "relational architecture." And here was an artist whose early projects were held up as a paragon of site-specific art claiming that they were anything but site-specific, even as they occupied the public square and drew materially on the history of the place. And here was a pioneer of electronic art who never defined his own process in terms of the technological medium of the digital. What is "relationship-specific" art, as Lozano-Hemmer also calls it, as opposed to site-specific art? What is a practice of urban art that takes-place locally but refuses to be confined to that locality? What does the taking-place of relationship-specific art say, not only about the concepts of site-specificity and locality but also of medium-specificity? How does it challenge the very nature of what we take a medium to be? Another knot of questions, another aparallel accompaniment, more goadings and gestatings, inflections and conceptions, in the processual intimacy of a formative distance. Where the overlap with Lynn's work brought me into an encounter with architecture, through Lozano-Hemmer the encounter with architecture opened out into the urban environment and its relationship-specific overspilling of its own locality.

With Malaysian–Australian photographer and installation artist Simryn Gill, the duration was more constrained: roughly a month. But it was a month that offered an opportunity to make the kind of processual fellow-traveling I had experienced with Lynn and Lozano-Hemmer a planned practice, distilled into a procedure suited to the time frame available. I proposed a series of recorded discussions where Gill would describe her process, what moves it, and what concepts she mobilizes in order to move with it. Key terms would surely stand out in the discussions, proposing themselves as formulae: terms that both trouble and potentialize the work, standing for problematic nodes around which Gill's practice bestirs itself and takes shape. I would take these constitutive problems up into my own writing, in the exact terms in which Gill articulated them. I would then nudge them into a becoming-philosophical. By that I mean giving them the kind of consistency native to philosophic practice. This must involve something very different from reported speech in faithfulness to a dialogue. In this case, dialogue was entered into as a well-reflected choice. What would come of it had to be contrived to processually surpass that point of entry. Choice had to be tricked into contingency, dialogue bumped past mediation into relational encounter.

By consistency of a practice I mean its constitutive texture: the way in which the creative factors entering into its constitution come-together, co-compose, and fuse into the emergence of a produced effect that stands by itself and for itself, in its own manner. Each art practice has a consistency uniquely its own, and the consistency of an art practice is very different from that of a philosophic practice. The consistency of a philosophic practice is defined by the reciprocal presupposition of its component concepts. That is a fancy way of saying mutual embrace. The work of philosophy is to craft concepts into a weave where each has meaning only as a function of the concepts around it— and *all* the other concepts are around it. Each is implicate in the others, and all the others are implicate in each. In other words, the vocation of philosophy is to invent a systematic holding-together of concepts. This is stranger than it seems at first. "This requirement" of systematic reciprocal presupposition, White-head warns, "does not mean that [the concepts] are definable in terms of each other; it means that *what is indefinable in one such notion cannot be abstracted from its relevance to the other notions.*"[4] The conceptual weave is a dynamic open system. Each concept's embrace of the others' relevance amounts to an implicate *movement* of thought carrying the concept beyond the limit of its own meaning, into the collective texture. The fact that every concept envelops that movement in its own way, and they are all doing it together in concert, makes the system a maximally consistent conceptual expression of thought's capacity to carry itself to the limit of the definable, where it edges into the unthinkable. Thought unbounded—by dint of mutual relevance, taken to the highest power. In the essays that follow, it will be asserted that the "medium" of a practice is the manner of event it occasions. The medium of philosophy, by this definition, is mutual relevance at the limit of verbal meaning.

Staging a problematic overlap of a philosophic practice and an art practice leaves neither unscathed. The problematic nodes of the artworking embed enabling constraints in the philosophic writing. These are like proto-conceptual eggs, cysts of coming concepts that hatch alien tendencies in the philosophy whose maturation in the writing propels the philosophizing toward a change in consistency. There can be no application of a conceptual framework: in philosophy, the systematicity is emergent. From this perspective, the status of the art practice for the philosophizing is that of a *non-philosophical* field immanent to philosophy's becoming.[5] The problems that are creatively geared into by the artistic practice, and condition its process toward its own taking on of consistency, are *transduced* into philosophic problems entering into the constitution of a new philosophic expression. Problems leap from one process to another, like jumping genes. From the other side, the status of the philosophic practice for the artworking is as a coming-to-conceptual-expression of proto-concepts already stirring within it and itching to condition its process more fully. The philosophical expression of these constitutive problems can potentially fold back into the art process and modulate its subsequent adventures. Transduction can go both ways. It wants to go both ways, to different effect on each side. It is aparallel evolution. At its most powerful, it is a becoming-different-together, in processual overlap and mutually transformational feedback.

There are risks. The artist will see her words escape from her, into the defiles of philosophy. Her constitutive problems will hatch anew and mutate, then mate with other problems plying the philosophic field. For philosophy does not have newborn innocence. It is haunted by its past consistencies. Despite philosophy's possession by its own past systematizations, it retains a transductive openness. However steeped in its own history, a philosophic practice retains the ability to overlap with constitutive problems belonging to a non-philosophical field. This can only be because the problems in-forming that non-philosophical field were already stirring in the philosophy, after its own manner. It was itching for it, just waiting for the contingency that would trigger its scratchings. As Raymond Ruyer says, you can only imitate what you are already almost capable of inventing.[6] What is at issue is indeed a kind of imitation, a kind of mimicry, where one process inventively takes on the problematic curves of another's incipient gestures. Through this transductive relation, philosophic writing becomes a kind of ventriloquism, in which it is not always certain which one is speaking. That uncertainty was consciously taken on board in the essay on Gill as an enabling constraint. Gill's own words were taken up into the writing in a way that made it impossible to attribute any given formulation unambiguously to one or the other of us. In the lead-up to the essay's original publication in the 2013 Venice Biennale catalog for the Australian Pavilion, this drove the copyeditor mad. An all-out war over pronomial propriety and the owning of speech ensued.

The fact that you can only ventriloquize what you are already almost capable of inventively mouthing means that the processual transduction between art and philosophy can only work if the philosophy already has an appetite for the problems. The philosophy must feel an impetus of its own to incorporate the formative force of the problems into its becoming, as if it already carried at its very heart a precursory imprint of the non-philosophical outside. Under that impetus, as the appetite satisfies itself, the problems unfold into a properly philosophic expression and take on a new consistency—one that might well seem monstrous to the artist. It is in these terms that Deleuze spoke of his relation even to other philosophers. Given the absolute singularity of their respective consistencies, philosophical systems are processual outsides to each other, even though they ply the same domain of activity. Their community in the same institutional discipline is a false filiation. What they belong to is only their own passage to the limit of the thinkable, in processual overlap with the non-philosophical fields for which they have an inventive appetite. Philosophy as a discipline is a *discipline*, not philosophy. Philosophy is transdisciplinary by its very nature. It not only retains the ability to problematically overlap with non-philosophical fields, it is only on the condition of doing so, in defiance of its disciplinary history, that it lives and breathes. Deleuze spoke of wanting to beget a monster with his philosophical interlocutors. But it was essential to him that were it possible for them to encounter it from beyond the grave, they would nevertheless be moved to recognize the ill-begotten issue as their own mutant offspring. His main concern, he said, was that the philosophers he philosophized from would not be set turning in their graves. In this case, the concern was that the artist, still very much alive and kicking, would not collapse into a heap in the studio. The hope that the creative practitioners whose work I was writing from would still be able to recognize themselves, in some unthinkable way in the becoming-different of their process as it transduces into philosophy, was a guiding concern. In the case of Gill, it was explicitly part of the procedure. We agreed that if she opened herself through the discussion, I would take out from my ill-begotten text anything she couldn't live with. There were in fact things that troubled her, but in the end she affirmed the trouble and went with the mutation, unheaped. She embraced her own becoming-different—which, after all, is what her art is all about. Even though it was less formalized in the case of Lynn and Lozano-Hemmer, the transductive approach and the concerned ethics of monstrosity it involves were very much a part of those encounters all along.[7]

The risk on the philosophical side is a certain loss of control. As they hatch, the encysted problematic nodes can exert an unexpected pressure on how the conceptual weave evolves. The conceptual tools for their successful texturing are not at the tip of the ventriloquist tongue. Since the initial formulation of the problems is found in the non-philosophical field, bristling with enabling constraints native to that environment, they will carry notional rugosities that rub the becoming-philosophy in what feels like the wrong way. But the "wrong way" has to be allowed to become relevant, to the limit. This requirement produces more problems. A cascading problematic movement takes hold that sweeps the philosophical writing into turbulent directions it would not have otherwise chosen for itself. The hapless writer finds himself grappling with issues he hadn't anticipated. It is not out of the question that, under the problematic force of the current, he will find himself saying things he never imagined he would say—and perhaps is not even certain he agrees with. But personal belief and ownership of thoughts is not what is at stake. What is at stake is the generation of surprises of thought: the sudden setting into the weave of what was all but unthinkable, finding a foothold for itself in the world where it can exert a force as a goad for further thought and other practices, in follow-on transductions potentially to come.

In chapter 1, the encounter with Lynn's work cascaded from the problem of the reality of abstraction to the problem of the body. Where is the body in animate form? The question is a common one often raised in a tone of accusation against Lynn's work, dismissed as a mere formalism from which the body is absent. The body, however, was a central concern of Lynn's in his writings on architecture of the 1990s. In keeping with the problem of abstraction, this was an *abstract body*. Whatever could that be? And why does the very word "body" disappear from Lynn's vocabulary in the 2000s? Where did it go? The central concern of his designs and writings seems to shift to the surface. Surface, after all, is a squarely (or in this case, curvaceously) architectural concern. What is the relation between body and surface? What else shifts when the body surfaces? The essay strives to follow the vicissitudes of Lynn's evolving practice through these shifts. Since Lynn himself has never enunciated the shifts in so many words, the more concertedly the philosophizing follows his process, the more monstrously it drifts from anything Lynn would ever say. The more problematically overlapped the processes become, the more fork-tongued is the outcome.

In chapter 2 on Lozano-Hemmer, the problem of the relationship-specific in contradistinction with the site-specific raises the follow-up problem of the status of the historical references, cultural codes, and social conventions activated and played upon in the work. This inevitably raises the issue of language, and of mediation in general. Lozano-Hemmer's work is predicated on the bodily involvement of participants, in an immediacy of shared experience. And yet they speak. Can the language be construed not as a mediating structure but as a directly bodily involvement? Is participation, then, an *im*mediation, even in the use of language?[8] If the specificity of what happens is in the relationship, then the event of participation is not confined to the individual body any more than it is confined to the locality. Does that mean that it involves a collective body? What sort of thing is that? Is there a transindividual level of language corresponding to it? If we say yes to these questions, how does that change what we understand by culture? By the social? Is there difference between them? If so, what is it? And what is their relation to the political? Thorny, forky problems all. In the case of Lozano-Hemmer, it seemed more feasible to attack these problems through an intensive engagement with a limited number of works from a particular period rather than follow the full length of the processual arc of the work, as was attempted for Lynn. The chapter, as a result, does not reflect the full breadth of Lozano-Hemmer's prolific and ever-ramifying creative production; rather, it concentrates on certain pieces from the earlier years of the "Relational Architecture" series. The philosophical movement circles obsessively, with increasingly complex contrivance (some might say casuistry), around the question of the cultural and the social. This was a problem transmitted to it from Lozano-Hemmer's early work. It is not one my philosophical work would have freely chosen to confront head-on, absent this transduction. It finds itself saying things it would not have otherwise, and that may not be transmissible to its own future variations, obligated as they will be by other encounters.

The constitutive problem in chapter 3, on Gill, is place. More precisely, it is the inhabitation of place as a *translocal* practice. Gill might also be said to be practicing an art of the relationship-specific as opposed to the site-specific. The phrase of Gill's taken up to serve as the chapter title, "making to place," says as much: her art is not a making *in* place but a making *to* place, in the way we say that we tap to a rhythm. In Gill's case, however, the process hones down to focus on a single body, its solitudes and forays. Here, the thorniness is around the notion of identity that is so habitually applied to single-body solitudes and forays, as well as the role of biography as constructive of identity. For a practitioner of philosophy who systematically errs on the side of pre-personal and even impersonal intensities, this could be very problematic. The artist's practice and her discourse about her practice are anchored in her biography. But then . . . her stated concern is precisely *not* to anchor her work in her biography. It is to find processual freedom for her work by "floating" her identity. Her working through her biography is in order to float it beyond itself. The alternative would be to be a slave to the historical and geopolitical determinants, and the way they pin an externally constructed identity to a body and its life's path. History and geopolitics and the way they biographically determine an identity have to be controverted—converted by the artworking into factors for becoming. They have to be counteractualized as enabling constraints for creative freedom. This must be done in a way that charges the individual body with the force of the collective, minus its power to fully determine itself in line with its history: with a singular twist. This twist on the problem of biography delineates a problematic region of overlap between the appetite of process philosophy and the process of the art, which the essay has to work out in its own manner, in the voicing of conceptual taking-form it stages.

No, it's not "about." It's not about Greg Lynn, Rafael Lozano-Hemmer, or Simryn Gill, as biographical entities. It's not about architecture, digital art, or installation art, as disciplines or genres. It's certainly not about art history: how those biographies embed themselves in and contribute to the progressive development of their disciplines. At no time do I perform the gesture, considered de rigueur in academic discourse, of "situating" the practices I encounter with respect to these extrinsic determinant frameworks. Never do I judge the aesthetic quality or social/political value of the work according to criteria external to it. And when I've said "I" in this introduction, it's not with pronomial propriety and a claim to ownership. It's not about any of that.

It's "with." It's the "with" of processual fellow-traveling, in the mode of immanent critique as I understand it: the aparallel evolution of processes entering into mutually constitutive overlap, the better to transductively diverge again to further their own singularity. If it's about anything, it's about becoming-different-together in a relationship-specific movement courting the limit of the thinkable.

In a word, this is a speculative undertaking. On the philosophical side, it is when the conceptual texture reaches the limit of its consistency, where the mutual relevance of the concepts reaches a pitch of reciprocal presupposition, that the working-through of the constitutive problems is at its most intense and the movement of thought returns to its own singularity. Each concept is carried beyond the limit of its own meaning, into the collective texture of what is indefinable in the others, and all together. At this collective limit, they flicker out of the overlap with the non-philosophical practices with which they have worked in symbiosis, to resonate intensely together at a distance, in a fit of self-reference. In that intensity of self-reference, the descriptive, or exo-referential, function of the writing blinks out. Philosophy lifts off from its non-philosophical field, into self-immanence.

At these points, I can already hear the reader protesting, *But the art work doesn't* actually *do that!* Perhaps it doesn't. But it is no less true that it has released the aparalleled *potential* for it: the proof being that it has come out in the writing. If the writing has been successful, the speculative, as such, *takes effect* in it. Philosophically, that is what it is ultimately about.

Architectures of the Unforeseen

Form Follows Force

Greg Lynn

ENTER PROCESS

It is a working assumption of the architectural practice of Greg Lynn that the instruments of design are not incidental to the creative process. They are not neutral tools through which a conceptual program passes on its way to realization. "Throughout the history of architecture, descriptive techniques have impacted the way in which architectural design and construction have been practiced."[1] The tools contribute to the definition of the trade, partially determining its outcomes. Their practical action cannot be entirely subtracted from the final design form.

The implications of this are wider than generally recognized. The means of creative production cannot be relegated to the status of outside elements belonging to biographical or historical "context." If the means of production enter into the definition of the product, they are nothing less than factors of creation. The "instruments" of an artistic discipline are internal variables of the creative process. They are generative factors, intrinsic to artistic form: formal co-conceivers. Face it: no achieved architectural design has ever leapt fully formed from the Chronos-skull of a gloriously autonomous creative "author." An architectural idea meanders through many a channel of technique, each of which inflects it, before pouring into the concrete ocean of the surrounding city. The most static of built forms embodies a fluvial movement, of its own making. In progress, a building's only context is its own formative process—to which nothing with which it streams is extrinsic. Only after it is constructed does a design idea stand still enough to have an external context. Before, it has only growth factors.

The question of form alluviates into one of *formation*: form generation. "Morphogenesis" it is: *enter process* (check your God's head at the sluice gate).

Lynn points out that there is an inherent abstractness to the most basic instruments of architecture, which has always maintained a privileged relation to geometry and will necessarily continue to do so. Architecture's traditional focus on the classical geometry of the basic Euclidean figures and Platonic solids has had to share the limelight in recent decades with topology. Topological design techniques had to wait for the computer for their full deployment. First introduced into architectural practice in the late 1980s, as the cost of computing power came down, their use became increasingly widespread, if not ubiquitous.[2] For Lynn, a pioneer in topological design techniques, this development cannot be neutral to the concept of architecture. He exhorts designers interested in rethinking the history and changing shape of their discipline to attend to their instruments. This requires a willingness to engage with the abstractness of the computer-assisted design space: its specifically topological abstractness. Yet more specifically, its topological abstractness as accessed by animation software of the kind used in film, as opposed to the traditional CAD used to digitize the familiar architectural drafting process. All of this entails a radical change in perspective.

GETTING TOPOLOGICAL

Rather than treating discrete forms composed of isolatable elements, topology deals with continuums. Topology will take a traditional geometric form, say a sphere, and torture it. It will twist it and turn it, stretch it and compress it, until it turns into something else entirely, say a horseshoe. The topological figure itself is neither the sphere nor the horseshoe. It is the *continuity* between them. The continuity is of a transformation. The transformation is a *deformation*. The Euclidean form you end up with is secondary to the deformation. It arises as an *effect* of a transformational process. Topology concerns continuities of deformation more directly than static form.

You could, of course, reverse the process and regain the sphere. Regained, it no longer appears as the point of origin it might be taken for. It is now an effect as well, of the deformation from the horseshoe. It has been sucked from its apparent position of Platonic preeminence into the same continuum, of which all traditional form can now be seen to be derivative.

There is no reason to stop there. You can always continue the continuum. You could go on deforming in either direction, past the demoted sphere or the tortured horseshoe. You could twist and turn some more, stretch and compress, on to any number of other forms. The thing is, they all belong to the *same* topological figure. They are all effects mutually included in the same transformation. Their relation to each other is one of *mutual inclusion* in one and the same process. The process itself *is* their mutual inclusion. It *is* the continuum that sucks them in, one and all. There is another word for "mutual inclusion." The relation of the overall topological figure to any of the forms that can be extracted from it is that of *immanence*.

The word "extraction" is important. You can only get something particular out of the ongoing transformation by wrenching it from its immanence in that process. The topological figure is in principle *endless*. It could just as well go on forever, generating an infinite number of forms. To end up with any particular form, you have to extract it from that ongoing. You have to stop the process. A classical geometric form is a topological *station*.

Considered as a stationary effect of the topological transformation from which it is extracted, the classical Euclidean form will be seen to bear *traces* of deformation. It may be seen as *expressing* in static trace-form the dynamic immanence from which it derived.

The topological figure may be thought of as the form of all the forms that express it. But it is not a "form" in the same capacity as they are. They are *forms of expression*. It is a *form of transition*. If the topological figure is not in any of the particular forms that stand out from it, then it can only be in between them. It has only transitional reality. It is a space of pure transition.

This is a decidedly odd space. Outside any of its stations (in which it is outside of its processual self) it has only twists and turns and stretches and compressions. That is to say, it has *no shape* of its own. It is defined by *vectors* of transformation rather than figural components. In addition, it is *unbounded*. It can go on endlessly, in any of the three dimensions of Euclidean space and the two dimensions of time (being reversible). Further, it can be zoomed up or down. It has *no inherent scale*. Being endless, shapeless, unbounded, and scaleless, it cannot be said to have position. Being endless, shapeless, unbounded, scaleless, and *positionless*, it cannot constitute a univalent type. It includes any number of geometric types. It mutually includes them: it is *hypertypological*.

Its stations, the classical Euclidean forms that can be extracted from it, do belong to a type or class of geometric entities. The sphere is a discrete member of the set of spheres: a particular instance of its ideal class. The topological transformation doesn't subsume its formal expressions under an ideal type. Rather, it *effects* them. In crowds. It proliferates them. Classical Euclidean forms are included in the overall topological figure in the sense that they *populate* its process. Their mutual inclusion is their population of the same generative process. That transformation has no invariant features. Having no shape that is proper to it, it has no figural *properties*. It has no properties except the plastic parameters of its own continuous inclusion (of the de-form).[3]

Another way of saying this is that the topological figure is utterly *singular*: wholly and only its own process. It is a singular populated by particulars. So it is a *multiple* singular. Having no properties or invariant features, you would also have to characterize it as in some way *generic*. The topological figure is a strange figure, unlike the usual logical entities with which we are in the habit of thinking. It is a *multiple singular-generic*.

It gets even stranger when you consider that although it is unbounded, it is *not unlimited*. I have referred at several points to the "same" topological figure. Given its anomalous, untypical nature, how do you tell when it is no longer itself? The answer was staring at us from the beginning: the identity of a topological figure is defined by its continuity. Cut it, and it ceases to be itself. Puncture it, and it is not what it used to be. For example, if you take the all-suffering sphere and punch a hole through it, you get a torus or tire shape. You can twist and turn and stretch and compress the torus and get a coffee cup. You have entered a different topological space inhabited by a different population of forms. You have a new multiple singular-generic teaming with members of the ideal classes of coffee cups and tires.

It is important to note that the limit is not a formal feature. It is an *event*—an accident befalling the transformation. Like the figure itself, the limit has a *time-like* element. It is also shapeless, scaleless, and positionless. It cuts the topological figure off in a *vague* time-like space of its own process. Like an atom of continuity floating in the void. Where is it in that space? Once again, it is not in any one of the forms expressing it. It *passes through* them all. Between any two classifiable forms populating it are stretches of formal *mutation*. But the topological figure as such is not in those stretches either. If you stop the process in between, you get a mutant Euclidean form. But even in the mutant, the topological transformation, in its process, its continuity, has already passed on. It is in no particular station or transition. It is irretrievably *recessive*. Wherever it is seen to be, it has already passed. It is formally elusive. Not only logical or abstract, but always effectively elsewhere: *virtual*. Its transitional reality is a virtual reality.

Now if you ask what space two different topological figures share, you'd have to imagine atoms of continuity in the same virtual void. But lacking scale or position, they couldn't be spatially distinct strictly speaking. It's a misnomer to call their mutual inclusion a "space." Although in their immanence they are not spatially *distinct*, they are still *differentiated*. The image you end up with is of tirelessly (and coffee-cuplessly) differentiating atoms of continuity in a state of virtual *superposition*. Like dynamic *monads* swirling about in the same animated abstractness.

Characterizing the topological as I have, there is no choice but to say that if the figure is or is in a space, it is an *absolute* space of formal transformation: positionless; unclassifiable and therefore incomparable; only in its own ever-recessive process; pure immanence. It is perhaps best to call it an *absolute movement* instead of an absolute space, given its vanishingly durational nature.

Infinite and unbounded . . .
Unbounded but limited . . .
Limited but absolute . . .
Abstract and real (because effective) . . .
Virtual.
Process.

GOTTA LOVE IT

It is easy to see the fascination this might exert in a field like architecture, whose practitioners traditionally valorize static form, typologically considered, and the concretization of an exacting program. And here you have an utterly strange logical creature that is all deformation and movement and vaguely recedes into the most ungraspable of realms. If you have a contrarian streak, or if you're just plain curious, you gotta love it.

Lynn loves it. There is a palpable sense of joy and even abandonment in his discussions of topology.[4] Yet love it as you might, if you want to design with it you have to figure out how to instrumentalize it. You have to domesticate the beast to some extent. Lynn unironically regards his topologically enabled computer as a not entirely house-trained "pet" introducing a degree of "wildness" into the designer's "domestic habits."[5] When you instrumentalize the topological creature, you find yourself loving that instrument. This is one of the things that stands out most in Lynn's design practice. He enters wholeheartedly into a relationship with his tools. He joyously embraces what are traditionally considered incidentals, mere practicalities, and welcomes them to the life, and heart, of architecture. As we will see, this embrace extends from the incidentals to the outside: to what are usually considered extrinsic constraints on architectural design, or even downright obstacles. That is how the many extra-instrumental things a historian of architecture might see as external "contextual" influences are apt to appear to the practicing architectural author. Obstacles: all that cluttery stuff out there that leaves unsightly sedimentary traces in the purely conceived forms of authorial prerogative. Dirty little things, like zoning, budgets, prevailing tastes, preservation movements, the weather, engineering considerations, clients with an irritating tendency to have preferences, gravity, people who live or work in buildings, so annoyingly often in ways contrary to their program. Messy little things, like the world.

Architecture, for Lynn, is affirmative. It will embrace its incidentals and its outside. In other words, it will be attracted to its own limits. Like the topological figure, the identity of architecture will describe itself as an endless movement to the limit. Its identity will occur to it, as a limit-event—deferred. Like the topological figure, architecture will affirm itself as its own continuing deformation, as absolutely its own continuous variation. It will affirm its process, as a work in progress. It will still be the "same" discipline, generically speaking. Because it won't be cut off, from the world at large or from its own past processings. Lynn makes no self-aggrandizing claims to the "revolutionary," "radical," or "avant-garde." To those in the early years who greeted his technology-happy practice with mutterings of "anti-architecture" or the "death of architecture" he calmly responds, No, *it continues*. Sorry, no apocalypse here. Just the same multiple singular-generic going on. Something architectural is doing, although you will never know what it is to your exacting satisfaction (its identity deferred, by the very doing of it).

"Like" the topological figure . . . Lynn embraces a becoming-topological of architecture. As they say, you become what you love. (Pets have their dangers.)

Much of the uneasiness that surrounded Lynn's work had precisely to do with the affirmative approach by which the architect enters a zone of indistinction with his or her instruments. Lynn's work aroused a tremendous amount of anxiety and even anger over what was repeatedly characterized as an "overenthusiastic" and "uncritical" embrace of the computer. No less than Peter Eisenman railed that architects like Lynn who adopt an affirmative posture are trying to mire the discipline in their own "cybernetic hallucinations."[6] Nothing so dramatic as an apocalypse. More like an adolescent indulgence. From where Eisenman stands, architecture seems to have gamboled off on a digital acid trip. Where Eisenman stands, interestingly, is in many respects very close. He is himself a pioneer in the use of computerized topological methods in architecture;[7] stylistically Lynn's designs are often considered to echo Eisenman's, and Eisenman mentored him into the profession. For all of that, in the final analysis Lynn and Eisenman must be seen as inhabiting different worlds, different architectural monads.

What most irks Eisenman is precisely what Lynn rejoices in: the processual indistinction between the creature and the creator. Failing to maintain the separation between the powerful new tool of the trade, the trade itself, and the creative artist amounts for Eisenman to a delusional abdication of architectural authorship. To be used responsibly, the computer-assisted topological figure must be kept at arm's length, on a self-reflective leash. Its proper employment is as a mediating device inserted between the "authorial subject," the authored architectural "object," a "receiving subject," and the "interiority" of architecture as a discipline, in such a way as to maintain their distance from one another even as it brings them into contact.[8] The point for him seems to be that the contact remain external and regulated, so that the authorial subject may "overcome" and "access." In other words, a critical distance must be maintained. The contact will be a mediated interaction rather than a becoming. Despite protestations to the contrary, walking the topological dog will be a dialectical exercise—a deconstructive "dialectic without synthesis," as the motto goes. Architecture will include its outside only as "signified"—as already "written" into its interiority prior to any interaction. The outside is understood as a signifying "discourse" that has always already left "traces" on the inside anterior to any event. The anteriority of writing is used to deconstruct the interiority of the discipline—dramatically, as an overcoming assertion of subjective "autonomy" (from "history," from the "social," from "repressed memory"). By Derridean sleight, Freud's "mystic pad" firmly in hand, the architectural master can have his interiority and deconstruct it, too. For present purposes, the main point is that in this perspective anything of any import that occurs architecturally will be on the order of signification (if the man with the leash has been known to bark, don't worry, it's only metaphorical).

As we will see, in Lynn's practice things are too unregulated and get too involuted to maintain a signifying remove. The whole notion of an "interiority" of architecture falls away in *operative*, or in Lynn's vocabulary "performance"-based, continuity with its outside (technical, historical, social, personal, gravitational, whatever). What traces there are, are in effect (*following* the process).[9] Deprived of the anteriority of an interiority of architecture, the critical practitioner is barking at the wind: there is nothing to deconstruct.[10] The inside of architectural form is not anterior. It is consequent to a technique of extractive construction, lovingly deployed: more craftily jerry-rigged than gloriously begotten. Kiss dramatic mastery goodbye. The world is on a continuous gambol through the in-between of forms. Go out and take a topological walk with it. If you can't dramatically overcome tradition, you might as well follow process (and love it). Trace away, mouse happily in hand (or more like it these days, finger caressingly on trackpad).

If Lynn's architecture is hard to distinguish stylistically from that of either Eisenman or other architects, modern or contemporary, it is of little concern for Lynn. If you follow process, architectural differentiation is no longer fundamentally a question of styles and their typology. Lynn has no need to assert himself on the stylistic level. For him, it is no longer a question of genre but of the generic (the hypertypological).

Generic process: where topology rather than standard typology is key, conventions of style are as incidental in the same way as the computer tool. Both are anterior only in the sense that they come to the design practice as a found object. Repeat: style is an incidental or outside element of the architectural design process. Formed styles and styled forms have been deposited outside, in the world, and stay there unless and until they are mutually reincluded in architectural design's ongoing, as one growth factor among others. *The architect does not operate from within the tradition but in continual reencounter with it.* The architect is not in the tradition: she is *in the world*. The worldly design reencounter is not a dialectical interaction at a signifying remove. It is an unmediated fusional event, sweeping up contributory elements in the same effective transformation; the same unbounded, as-yet-unclassified becoming; the same "uncritical" or participatory, proliferative differentiation.[11] Architecture's tradition occurs to it, indistinctly, like its deferred identity (in fact, its perpetual, self-transformative generic reencounter with its disciplinary inheritances *is* its serially deferred identity). So a discipline grows: by drops of form-taking, precipitating from the process of fusional iteration plying the in-between of forms, to add themselves to the world's ongoing. Rather than a dialectic without synthesis: an *addition without a sum*. Certainly without a prior structured whole eternally subsuming its parts, as tradition traditionally figures. Serial addition without a sum: that could be a motto for affirmative architecture.

Open question: By what device do things incidental and outside come to be included in the process? How, from a gambol, does a building grow? How is the topological beast part-tamed?

FORCE, FIELD, NATURE–CULTURE

It is actually quite simple. The preceding discussion of how the topological figure differs from a classical Euclidean figure was all about deformation. Yet in that discussion there were no deforming forces (other than the force of thought). To instrumentalize topology in mutually inclusive fashion, you simply program deforming forces, with an abstractness and elusiveness equal to the "space" of the figure. In other words, you use the computer to actualize the "absolute dynamic void" that was described earlier as the space or movement of topology. Of course, since that "space" was virtual, absolutely recessive, when you bring it up on-screen and actualize it, it is something else. The abstract space of the screen is a virtual *double*. You have *added* an *analogue* of the virtual to the actual. It is very important to be clear about where the virtual isn't. The virtual isn't on the screen. It isn't in the pixels. It isn't in the code. It isn't in the machine language. All of these are actual. They are technological "stations." The virtual is what *runs through* them. The virtual is what *passes* when the program boots. It is what *happens* when all these elements operatively fuse into a running event.

What you bring up on-screen bears an oddly analogical relation to the virtual passing through it. "Odd," because the virtual is unclassifiable, comparable only to itself. But in order to program it, you have had to assign it a look, and having a look it inevitably falls into comparison. The virtual is no longer itself to the precise extent to which it resembles how we think of it and, in thoughtful resemblance, becomes comparable to other things. Rendering the virtual is an analogical procedure. However, the analogy produced is essentially *without resemblance* to its model. Another way of putting it is to say that the resemblance is precisely what is artificially produced.[12] You have added to the world a semblance or double (a "simulation") of the virtual through which it oddly returns to itself, on the run, in its always self-differing. For the virtual, returned, has passed through and been conditioned by what it isn't. The traces left by its return—the shapes generated on-screen—will record an essential non-resemblance to its ongoing. The shapes are what the virtual looks like after it has passed on. They are its visible wake. They are its optical end-effect.

Overall, the process is of a self-differing addition of and to the virtual: virtual proliferation, in the passing. The fact that *the virtual is only accessible through analogical procedures*, and that for the concept of simulation to be useful it must be borne in mind that *simulation is not the virtual* but rather *simulation is of the virtual*, are extremely important asides. But they are beside the main point here, which is how things enter mutually-inclusively into the design.

Once again, you begin with forces. You begin by thinking of the building and its eventual site in terms of the forces operative in and around them. Remember, you cannot see a force. Only the effects of forces are visible. Forces are actually accessible only in traces of the deformations they effect. Forces are invisible realities. It is like them to recur. So they are not all in any particular exercise of their effective power. They are singularly recessive; iterative and therefore also generic; variational and thus multiple. In a word, forces *are* virtual. They are the natural expression of the virtual. So you simulate them. You double the natural expression of the virtual by the most artificial of means.

For example, you might simulate gravity. Gravity, of course, is not the only kind of architecturally operative force. Say you are designing a bus terminal. There are other attractive forces at play. The flow of traffic past the terminal, into which the arriving passengers will tend inexorably to be swept, is one.

Another important aside: this urban "force" forces a rethink of "nature." Nature, from the affirmative perspective, is anything encountered by creative procedure which may be procedurally construed as having been already in operation. Here, "already-operative" is one pole of the base definition of nature. Nature, from this angle, is the also-ran. It is the processual "given": whatever is "found" by a process under way as evidence of another process having run; whatever is encountered by a process as effectively other than its own; whatever comes to it as from across a dynamic gap; whatever it operatively takes itself to be cut off from and whose operative inclusion must therefore be prepared. The "givenness" of nature is the outside "anteriority" of other runnings, grasped procedurally from the angle of their actual effects, their literally encountered physical traces (not their metaphysical–metaphorical supplementarity). To return to an earlier point, it is only in this sense of givenness that style and disciplinary tradition are of the "nature" of architecture as practiced. That "nature," however, naturally extends beyond the given. The forces that have produced the traces constituting nature as given are iterative, and through their repetition are apt to produce novelties of effect that go beyond the given. This is the other pole of "nature," included in the very definition of force: the tendency to surpass the given, in new, emergent forms.[13] The architectural process, as operating in an open field not bounded by its disciplinarity, enthusiastically takes up "nature" from this angle. Its own "cultural" activities are but this "nature," furthered.[14]

There is a common critique of Lynn's work that it is "naïvely" complicit with "naturalism." This objection must be tempered. The opposition between the natural and the artificial, as commonly understood, is not in any way fundamental here. Neither is the dichotomy between the naïve and the contrived. They may well be fundamental to other operations, particularly ones that style themselves "critical." But here, the artificial is affirmed as being as natural as nature by any other definition. There is considered to be a generic (processual) indistinction between nature and culture. Taking in the givenness of indistinct nature(–culture), and forcefully bringing it to another surpassing of itself, requires the most artificial of means. The given only figures in the process as *prepared* for this surpassing. Naturalism (the genre) and naïveté are not the issue. The issues are virtual process and its procedural expression across an operative nature–culture continuum, with respect to which divisions between the two are derivative stations. Like all static forms, seen or conceived, their separateness is on the level of effect. It is *produced* (and endures only as forcefully re-produced). Our static metaphysical sense of the natural and the artificial as discrete formations needs to bend to a pragmatics of virtual processing and its generic vagueness—understood as *reproductive* of distinction (productive of new difference). If this generative, iterative perspective also bends our sense of the isms we have grown anxiously accustomed to opposing, so be it. Relax, let down your genres. Leave your battle stations. Follow process.

In Lynn's project for the Port Authority Bus Terminal in New York (1995),[15] it goes like this. You prepare a site simulation. You translate prominent features of the site as abstract forces. This produces a dynamic map filling the screen. Noncoincident forces occupying the same space fill it with gradations. For example, you could program as regions of attraction the flow of traffic on the street in front of the terminal that arriving passengers will want to merge into and the gravitational pull that will draw them to street level. You program where the terminal stands as a region of repulsion, as a region for leaving. You end up with a gradient force-field composed of basins of attraction, a basin of repulsion, and a transition space where attractions and repulsions shade into and out of each other. In a gradient field, there are no strict divisions. Regions are vaguely bounded by thresholds of interaction belonging to more than one region. The threshold zones' mutual belonging varies in degree,[16] according to the relative strength of the influence that the basins radiate at particular points and of the interference patterns arising from the overlap of their resident forces. The site, thus mapped, is an open, differential field. It is characterized by a gradient continuity of tension—a variegated tensile continuum—rather than sharp boundaries and discrete features. If a Euclidean space could be likened to a still shot, the gradient field programmed for the screen is the spatial equivalent of a dissolve. It is differentiated not by the frame and the cut but by fadings-out that are simultaneously fadings-in. The usefulness of the cinematic comparison is limited, however. The field is differentiated invisibly. It is not yet a question of visual form but of unseen degrees of *intensity* (defined as the differential co-presence of forces that cannot cancel out each other's operations without remainder, and therefore must be understood as integrally co-operating in the determination of any effect that may arise).[17] The field is *proto-formal*: a topological field.

Intensely prepared as a spatial dissolve, the screen is now ready. All it needs for something to come to pass . . . is something to come to pass. Throw an abstract object into the openness of the force-field. Something happens. What has been proto-formally prepared is an event. Throw in a spherical particle assigned a certain mass: it will move. The tension of the field plays out as movement. Intensity, in the event, translates extensively as movement. The particle will waft from basin to basin, sometimes hesitating at the thresholds between. In most cases, it will end up being captured by the strongest basin of attraction and fall into entropic quiescence.

The shape of the particle should not mislead. The particle does not fundamentally figure as a form. It is programmed for activity: as a counterforce to the field. Its shape is a token of its force, the rigidity it needs to resist the field's dissolve, to resist being dissolved into the field. Its visible form is an expression of the invisible force of resistance it opposes to the continuum. The particle is endowed with a second force in addition to its rigidity factor: "mass." The strength of the attractive and repulsive influences the basins exert on the particle, and the way in which it will be affected in the transitional zones where they shade in and out of each other, are functions of its assigned mass. Ratchet up the mass, and the way it moves will change. The velocity and path of the particle, the nature and extent of its movement, expresses the interaction of the gradient force-field with the sub-force-field of its mass. The movement is a visible expression of the *relation* between the resident forces of the field and those of the particle: its optical effect. Motto: FORM FOLLOWS FORCE.

Both the gradient field and the particle are themselves internally differentiated: they are already relational (a consolidated alliance between rigidity and mass against an open differential of attractions and repulsions). The relation of which the movement is the visible expression is a *relation between relations* (running abstractly, prior to and outside the actual relations of the physical site-to-be). Operatively, what you see as a geometrically discrete particle moving against a background is an unfolding continuity of complex relation. The relationality is not itself visible. The form and its path of movement expresses invisible interactions of forces. The Euclidean geometry of the particle is secondary to the playing out of this abstract intensity. "Playing out" should be underlined: it takes time for the relationality to render its effect in the particle's observed movement. This has to run. It must unfold. It is irreducibly durational. The architect is no longer designing primarily with visible form. She or he is designing with *duration, rendered visible.* The time-likeness of the topological space of transformation has expressed itself in duration.[18]

"Duration" is another word for the virtual on the run, in the direction of the emergence of the new. Visible form is now in the service of the virtual. Its calling is to *actualize* the virtual in movement: to *render* it dynamically (so very different from representing it). Architectural design is not simply using a new tool, that of "virtual" technology. It is keying directly into the reality of the virtual, in all its self-differing continuity and elusive abstractness. Architecture is rendering itself a technology of the virtual.

The virtual can become the elusive object of a technology because it is itself as produced as it is given. Although it is not "in" any particular form expressing it, neither is it separable from its renderings. It is not outside and abstract in the transcendent sense. It is transpiring. It is the eventfulness of form: what repeatedly runs through it. It is only marginally better to think of the virtual in terms of information than it is to mistake it for Platonic transcendence. The virtual is not informational input or output. It is relational *throughput.* Since it cannot runthrough without leaving traces of its passage, without taking formal effect, the virtual is as dependent for its return on the re-generation of form as form is dependent for its dynamism on the intensity of the virtual. Codependency. The virtual and its actual expression through form are wed in a symbiotic rhythm of return and regeneration.

If the process is rhythmic, then in order to double it technologies of the virtual must be iterative in their procedure. To iterate is precisely what the virtually inclined architect does in design practice: tweak and repeat. Change parameters and rerun. Reassign mass, vary the topology of the field, and see what happens. Tweak and see: technologies of the virtual are experimental practices.

Expert at "reading" what is "written" in visual form, the critical architect is required to be painfully literate. The virtually affirmative architect,[19] on the other hand, is encouraged to be abundantly iterate. The critical architect, feeling tradition-bound and hating it, is challenged by perceived strictures (given structures). The affirmative architect, operating with joyful abandon in an open relational field, is challenged by the plethora of invisible procedural possibilities to surpass the given. This leads to a novel problem, one that is entirely different from that of being bound by tradition. It is a directly processual problem, what in computer parlance is called the "stopping problem." The regenerative process can be repeated endlessly, to different effect. So how do you know when to stop? Which effect is the "right" one? What criteria can you apply to a process that is so incomparably open and elusive that it continually defies set categories? How do you judge something that offers no self-justification other than its own runaway appeal? Granted, you love it. But can you stop tweaking already and choose?

MULTIPLY AND VARY (CLOUD AND BLOB)

Not yet. So far, we have little more than a speck wafting around on the screen. That hardly qualifies as startlingly new, let alone a bus terminal. The whole thing also seems so programmed and mechanical. The force of gravity it accepts into the very heart of its modeling seems to be the epitome of determinism. How could such a recalcitrantly Newtonian force "surpass the given"? It is hard to see why Lynn persists in calling the process "animate."

As the most cursory glance at the history of Newton's laws of motion show, however, the determined behavior of gravity has been less than exemplary. If you have two bodies—two gravitational basins of attraction—the interaction is calculable. The movement expressing their relation is regular and predictable. With three bodies, something happens. The interaction between three relational subfields is mathematically incalculable and empirically unpredictable. A margin of indeterminacy enters the interaction. The interference patterns between the basins of attraction create thresholds of undecidability. When one of the bodies approaches a threshold, it is impossible to know its subsequent path with certainty. Gravity is exemplary after all: it is the textbook example of "deterministic chaos." That term refers to the fact that relational-field effects ("resonance" in Poincaré's vocabulary) can be counted on to undetermine what by formal definition are the most predictable of things: natural forces.[20]

The programmed gradient field described above comprises more than two relational subfields. There is always a possibility that when the particle approaches a threshold zone it will fly off chaotically rather than settling entropically into the strongest basin of attraction. Or it may hesitate at the threshold just enough to settle into a weaker basin. This can be clearly seen on-screen if instead of throwing in one particle, you throw in a whole mess of them: a particle cloud. The interaction gets impossibly complicated, because the masses of the mess of particles are interacting with one another as mini gravitational fields in addition to each interacting with the ambient gradient field. When the rigid little creatures collide they bounce off one another in gaseous abandon. Every parameter is completely determined, yet the outcome retains an element of chaos.

At the same time, a pattern emerges. This is because the law of large numbers takes over. Statistically, many more particles will make their way to the strongest basin than will fly off unpredictably. The precise path each particle will take toward its probable entropic destiny will vary, so that although the overall pattern may be foreseen, its exact contours cannot be. The form can only be vaguely predicted, and remains fuzzy on the edges. When order arises out of resonance, even the most exact determination of process parameters renders "anexact" form.[21] It is the element of unpredictability and the persistence of processual vagueness that allows Lynn to speak of the formal end-effect as "animate," even if it has run out into a largely stable pattern.

The manyness of the mini fields in a particle cloud means

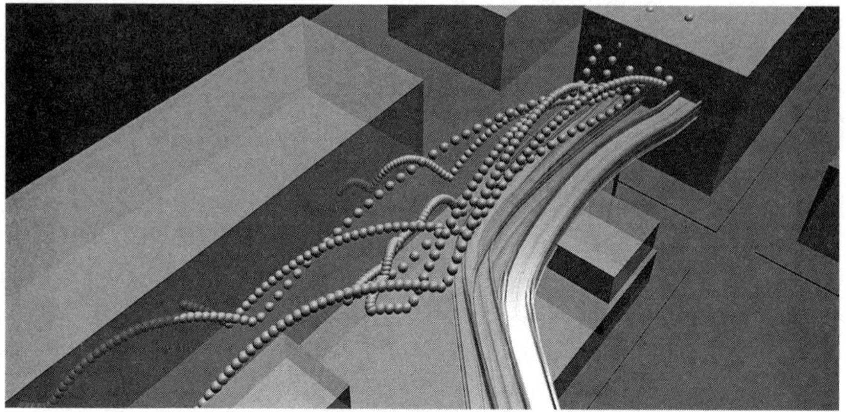

Phase portrait. Particle cloud modeling exit ramp, with street-level basin of attraction. Port Authority Gateway Competition, 1994. Greg Lynn Form.

that the chaotic effect of order out of resonance can be achieved with just one ambient gradient field, modeling for example the earth's gravitational influence. The particles' rigidity factor can be relaxed to give them extra chaotic bounce. The architect can take the resulting anexact cloud shape and extract a useable Euclidean form from it. This can be done as simply as by taking a freeze-frame and cleaning it up. Another procedure uses an animation "sweep" technique to produce a "phase portrait" of selected particles' trajectories. This consists in capturing images of a particle at regular intervals over the course of its movement, superimposing the stills on the same frame, then repeating the procedure for several particles, and finally superimposing the portraits.[22] The resulting form is useful because, by the very nature of the process of its patterning, it automatically embodies gravitational effects. The Euclidean translation of the anexact chaotic form is *pre-engineered* for gravity. It is fit, for example, to be an exit ramp. It must be emphasized that the usefulness comes out toward the end. The process leading up to a functional result is not itself functionally determined. It is intensively determined, through resonance and rerun. It is *proto-functional* in the same way that it is proto-formal.[23] The functionality *emerges* in the same movement as the form itself, both as expressions of a relational process resembling nothing other than its

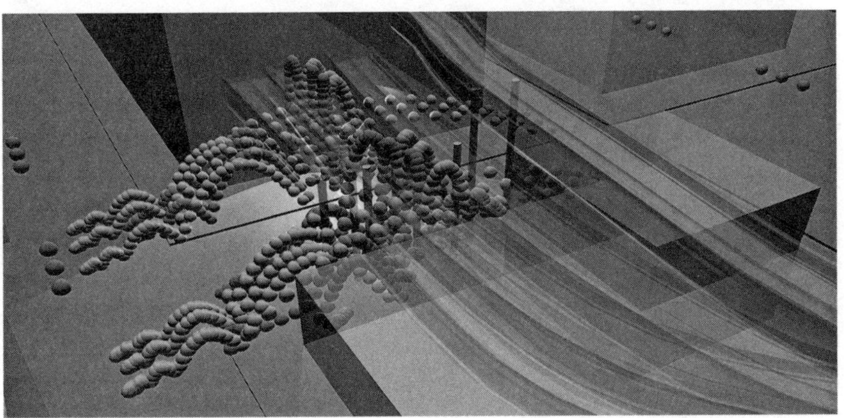

Phase portrait. Particle cloud modeling Fifth Avenue exit.
Port Authority Gateway Competition, 1994. Greg Lynn Form.

own process, its own iterative intensity. FORM AND FUNCTION
FOLLOW INTENSITY.

One of the upshots is that the universal architectural constraint of gravity has been *internalized as an enabling condition
of the design*. Instead of feeling his creativity constricted or con-
tradicted by it, the architect welcomes gravity into the design
process and plays variations on its resonance-readiness. The
constraint of gravity becomes a positive contributor in the creation of new form. Any number of gravity-resistant forms can be
generated simply by varying the parameters and doing a replay.
Which end-form will be chosen? It is in the selection—out the
far end of the process—that issues of style and reading may enter
back in. The selection may well be made by the architect, in
cognizance of the genres of architecture and their history, as a
function of her allegiances and aversions, or her will to distinguish her work. Although, it is just as likely that the *client's* taste
and (perhaps) ignorance of and inability to read architectural
history will intervene. In that case, the architect can still inflect
the outcome by taking the client's reaction and stated preferences and re-generating the form until a mutually acceptable
mutation of designer and client preferences emerges—something
recognizable enough from both sides that it "passes," but not
so recognizable as to be confined simply to being one way or

another. The design process can internalize another universal architectural constraint almost as easily as that of gravity: that of social *negotiation*. In fact, the closer the design process comes to alluviating into concrete, built form, the more negotiated it will become. For example, contractors may feel that pre-engineering leaves something to be desired. No problem: tweak and rerun again. *The process continues.*

Its continuability is so open-ended that even the "completed" building will have to be considered essentially provisional. It could just as well have been any number of other buildings, if the programming and negotiated reprogrammings had, by chance of chaotic circumstance, run slightly differently. The building retains an element of the generic, even in its concrete particularity. The finality of the design is by nature *deferred*. There is no one moment where the architect can stand back from the process and say, I, creative master, have spoken in my form; read what I have said. The design process is less an external conduit for the artist's creativity than the artist is a conduit for creativity of the design process. Every constraint that gets internalized, from the very first run, is a literal coauthor of the form: another of its intrinsic growth factors. The process takes on a certain *autonomy* of expression. The architect admits his inability to control exactly how the form will emerge and what it will "say" when it does (how it will be "read"). The architect is less a godly creator than a deskbound shaman abstractly summoning powers of virtual transformation through the medium of the computer, coaxing them to express *themselves* in a particular form.

From one perspective, this autonomizing of the design process is authorial abdication. From another, it is simple honesty. What architect works alone? Isn't every architectural signature—like that of the cinematic auteur—scrawled over the group efforts of a corporate body: "The Office"? Isn't the necessarily collective nature of actual design organization an enabling "constraint" on individual authorship from ground zero? Shouldn't buildings have credits?[24] And what artist can ever really control the fate of the creation once it is loosed upon the world? There is ultimately no controlling the effective events a building will cooperate in producing when it is itself a basin of attraction or repulsion in the wide-open fields of the city and the countryside.

Is not the only truism of history that it will continue? Is not the only historical certainty change? The critical desire to impose a particular reading, or even the general approach of reading, for all the archival savvy that may inform it, can be argued to be profoundly anti-historical. The most anti-historical thing one can do is demand that anything *be* historical in a determined way—that anything *be* anything determinate—for longer than a provisional freeze-frame, for longer than a rhythmic beat in a cycle of return and regeneration. If history were not always in the process of re-becoming itself in a way that brings all historical being integrally back into question, it wouldn't be what *it* is: the playing-out of all the world's relationality; the widest chaotic expression of the infinitely complex intensity of the most encompassing of unbounded fields (the earth or cosmos, understood as nature–culture at its broadest). The instant you assert an ideal of creative control, as soon as you try to impose a program in the traditional sense, you are working to stop the ongoing process of worldly self-expression that is becoming of history. You are trying to make a private station of it—a freeze-frame with your individual signature written all over it. Okay, so you admit it won't be the actual end-all of human history. Still, you feel that your creation should at very least have the staying power of a lasting monument to your personal genius (even authorial subjects can be modest in a pinch). The affirmative artist, for his part, stops in the name of a next beat. He makes a stay, that the collective rhythm continue. Affirmative architecture affirms even (especially) the provisional nature of its own products. As Greg Lynn set out to build what would be his first completed building, the Korean Presbyterian Church in Queens (in collaboration with Michael McInturf and Douglas Garofalo, 1995–99), he was advised by the client that it would likely be torn down or substantially redesigned within three or four years because the congregation was increasing so fast it would soon outgrow it. He loved it (although it hasn't happened yet). This is not to say that an affirmative artist cannot be immodest, ambitious, or even downright egotistical, or that a critical architect necessarily has those traits. It is not really a question of character or personal qualities at all. It is a question of quality of process. Personality traits are on a level with everything else: processual parameters among others, adding spice to the expressive autonomy of the chaotic world-soup of design.[25]

In a way Eisenman was right to cry abdication. After all manner of constraints have been internalized into the process in the capacity of coauthoring growth factors, it is impossible to say exactly who is responsible for what. Each internalization of a constraint has added a determination. But each determination is only a part-determination. In the long run, the determinism of the process is chaotic, retaining an inexpungible element of openness. The architect's reruns are part-decisions contributing to a process that is in the long run self-directing. The artist is a collaborator in a process of virtual expression that he can intentionally inflect or modulate but never completely control. As a willful individual, he is to the overall design process as his wafting on-screen particles are to their gradient field. His will is like a sphere: a surface rigidity silently bespeaking openness of relation. Creative will is a conscious bubble expressing in its apparently linear ordering a complex interplay of forces encompassing of any actual instance of decisiveness. Design is cloudy: a relation of relation between populations of cofactors taking more-or-less chaotic shape. The collaborative role the individual architect plays in the collective shape-taking is more a processual symbiosis subject to chance-driven evolutionary pressures— piloted by a self-regenerating internalization in the process, by the process, of its own external constraints—than the mastery of a program or design object.

Here come the "blobs." The cloud-massing particles discussed so far were not topological figures. Their shape was invariant. What was topological in the sense discussed earlier was how their collective relation to the gradient field played out. Lynn's trademark blobs directly figure topological transformations.[26] A blob is a flexible sphere radiating a quasi-gravitational field of influence. The force of the field varies according to the blob's surface area and assigned "mass." When two or more blobs enter into proximity, their fields of influence interact, forming a zone of relation or reciprocal transformation. Depending on how their relation plays, they will either inflect each other's surfaces amoebically in unpredictable ways, or fuse into a single super-blob. From the topological point of view, Lynn notes, a sphere is but a lonely blob: a blob without influence, isolated from neighboring forces.[27] Once again, classical geometric figures can be considered isolates or extractive limit-cases of topological transformations.

Now put a gaggle of blobs in a gradient field and let the program run. The blobs will stretch around one another like amorous slugs. Some will fuse, forming plurichambered bulbous structures or tubulations. What collective shape arises from their deformational congress cannot be predicted with accuracy. The blobs do not only mutually deform. Their reciprocal transformation is itself inflected by the surrounding gradient field. Relation of relation. Interrelation to the second power: greater complexity, increased unforeseeability. Stop the program. The visible shape you are left with is a processual emergence from the relationally unforeseen.

Suppose the shape is earmarked to become a house. But suppose the client doesn't want to live in the stomach of a highly unforeseen amoeba. Perhaps, for reasons the architect will never comprehend, the client doesn't figure his life in a geometry of slug love. Say the client wants a house of a certain generic floor plan. An H-plan, for example. This was the external typological

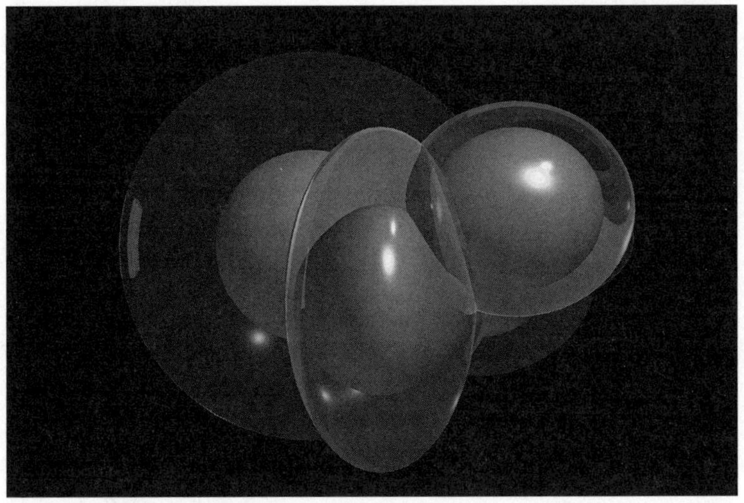

Blobs with zones of influence, mutually deforming. Greg Lynn Form.

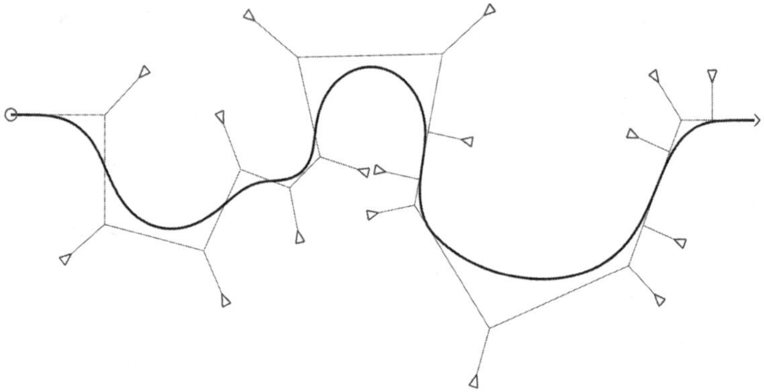

Curvilinear spline figure showing weighted control vertices. Greg Lynn Form.

constraint placed on Lynn's *House Prototype in Long Island* project (1994).[28] Lynn realized that blobular stretching and fusing, or other too-random form-generating procedures, could be *limited by addition*: by adding another relationality. Blobs were attached to an H-frame made of "splines." A spline structure is composed of linear segments attached end to end to form a "skeleton." Unlike a Euclidean line drawing, the spline figure is active. The points of intersection between skeletal segments have virtual strings attached to them. The strings are vectors pulling on each intersection in a different direction, with variable strength. The static figure is in fact a holding pattern formed by a tensile equilibrium between vectorial forces differentially applied through the length of the frame. If you vary the strength of one of the vectors, the influence propagates throughout the entire skeleton. The frame moves like the X-ray of a mime. Although compositionally the spline frame is linear and segmented, the *movement* that propagates through its structure is continuous and curved. The *activation* of the tensile relation between linear segments describes a topological transformation. Splining activates a Euclidean figure in a way that generates topological effects.

In the Long Island House project, the virtual strings attached to the intersection points of the splinar H-frame connected to "site forces": attractions or repulsions in the gradient field modeling the plot on which the house would be built. Again in response to client preference, the site forces primarily concerned visibility. A large tree and the line of sight to the ocean were programmed as forces of attraction. A neighboring house blocking the view of the ocean and an existing driveway were forces of repulsion. The connection of the skeleton frame to these forces actively translated features of the site into form. To be more precise, they translated *values* attached to site features into iterations of proto-architectural form-generation. The values entering the process, it must be emphasized, were not the architect's. The architect's contribution came in the way a formal typology and hierarchy of values imposed by another's desires were integrated into the developing design process. Love those blobs: they seem to have attached themselves to certain edges of the frame. While the frame is busy formally propagating translated site influences, the blobs are at it again, doing their thing. But their range of amoebic mutation was now limited by their value-laden splinar mooring. Their neighborly abandon is moderated in a way that successfully renders it proto-functional: the tubularities that the blobs become in congress will be architecturally rendered as transitional spaces between the inside of the relationally activated frame and the influential outside of site-specific values. The project, however, is never built. It remains a proto-house, its growth stopped short of actual architectural rendering.

In Lynn's approach, *what the architect works with during the design process is not an architectural object*—yet. It is a

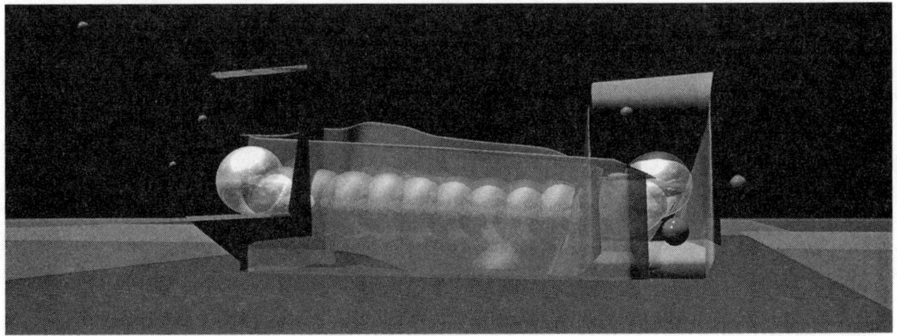

Blobs interacting with spline H-frame to model site forces.
House Prototype in Long Island, 1994. Greg Lynn Form.

proto-formal, proto-functional, abstractly real evolutionary entity. It is proto-architectural until it is actually built. Animate architecture posits *a difference in kind between proto-type and finished architectural form*. The proto-type is its own abstract reality *becoming-architectural*. The prefix "proto-" is misleading. The proto-type isn't an already-architectural object of a certain type waiting passively on-screen to be realized in steel. It is already actively real and still in process: it has the virtual reality of what was earlier characterized as a hypertype. Here, "hyper-" can substitute for "proto-." Looking at Lynn's design projects, it is difficult to make sense of them as determinate kinds of building, house, or terminal. They still have to be rendered recognizably architectural. This happens gradually as (or if) they pass into construction. They are architecturally type-cast in passing: in continuation of a process that changes its nature as it goes. The evolving, hyper-typological, proto-reality of the design entity is what makes it necessary to speak of the design process encountering its own discipline as its outside, as it does with other contributory factors. The design process encounters its discipline as an external cultural constraint or natural given that it variationally internalizes—as part of the same passage by which it comes to be internalized by the discipline, as part of its own continuing variation (double becoming).

But isn't this true of any design process, topological or otherwise? If design were architecturally predefined, how could designing change architecture? How would architecture itself ever evolve? It would be trapped in the vicious circle of its definition preceding itself, only ever to become what it already is. The very fact that architecture has a history necessitates the paradoxical view of the design process as a real becoming integratively outside the history it changingly enters. What is new and different about animate architecture is neither its virtuality—its self-immanent proto-reality—nor its co-variational emergence. What's new is that it admits to and nurtures them. That it admits to being just emergent (rather than always already defined). That it brings out its coming out. And revels in it, taking cheer in its own creative incompletion. Never does Lynn claim to be the end-all.

The cheer of becoming, open-ended, challenges architecture at large to review its disciplinary being. This is not a question of revisionism. It is not a question of opposing one version of architectural history to another. The issue is the very manner in which architecture, as a discipline, has a history. Bringing out that issue is the affirmative version of critique (practiced, as always, in passing). Incompletion and continuation are two sides of the same coin. Taking cheer in its own incompletion is a way of topological design reiterating: it continues. Architecture does not only have a history. It has a future. Change ahead.

FOLDING IN ARCHITECTURE

When Lynn launched the rallying cry of "folding in architecture" he was not referring to a new style. "It is important to maintain a logic rather than a style of curvilinearity."[29] Although topological design technique facilitates curvilinear form, there is no necessity to its dominating any final architectural rendering. As Bernard Cache has also vigorously argued, there is no intrinsic connection between topological design technique and any particular look.[30] "Folding in architecture" connotes not a style but a dynamic "logic," a quality of process: "the formal affinities of [topological design projects] result from their pliancy and ability to deform in response to particular contingencies."[31] The folding "in" architecture is a contingent "folding-in" of the architectural outside.

The quality of process in question has been amply characterized already. The process is serial. The seriation is of events. The process redefines itself at each event-step. It is evolutionary. Each event along the way is a more-or-less chance encounter, between its own internal variables, or between its internal variables and external constraints. The design process evolves most decidedly by integrating external constraints, converting them into internal growth factors: folding them into its self-generative activity. The process is additive. It is capable not only of multiplying versions of its formal results ad infinitum but also of indefinitely increasing and varying the internal variables it eventfully combines toward each result. Welcoming of intrusion from outside, it is "pliant." Which is not the same as "compliant" in the normal sense.[32] It doesn't conform to external constraints. It folds them in—to its own unfolding. It uses them to vary its results, to creatively diverge. The integrative process of divergent variation is autonomous in spite of—because of—its responsiveness to the encountered necessities of the outside. Both in terms of its internal disposition and its outward responsiveness, the process more fundamentally involves a composition of relations than of forms or elements of form. The composing of relations runs: it takes time. The process is durational: open-ended. Static form is its productive fallout.

Referring to cheery responsiveness to external constraints, Lynn labels his approach "opportunistic."[33] A less self-deprecating term for the quality of its process might simply be "generous." The infolding approach invites the desires and values of others, among other alien "constraints," to feature as positive occasions for growth. This is a welcoming approach to design, constitutionally accepting of what lies outside its control, tending from the very beginning toward productive engagement. Folding-in architecture is as directly an ethics as a design endeavor: an ethics of engagement.[34]

"Adventitious" would be a less value-laden term. It describes a divergent manner of growth connoting chance encounter: "arising or occurring sporadically or in other than the usual location" (said of buds).

THE BIOMORPHIC HYPOTHESIS

If Lynn's architecture were misconstrued as taking for its guiding principle a style or formal aesthetic, it would doubtless be characterized as *biomorphic*. It is in fact a common perception that Lynn sets out to produce architectural forms conveying biological metaphors. His designs do seem to burgeon or exfoliate, amoebate, or grub. But it is entirely missing the point if this metaphoricity is taken to characterize the design process. That the process does not exclude metaphorical associations is attested to by the regularity with which they are voiced by viewers. But if the process gives rise to metaphor it is by nonmetaphorical means, as a by-product of its relational operation. Any metaphorical associations that may set in between a topological design and a preexisting biological form are produced resemblances, in the sense discussed earlier: derivatives. When a metaphorical reading begins, it is a sure sign that the process has stopped. It has been taken up by or flipped over into an entirely different process, one based on formal assimilation rather than formative differentiation.

A particularly instructive example of this occurred at a public presentation several years ago of a very early draft of a small portion of this essay.[35] A famous psychoanalytically inclined literary critic in the audience became visibly agitated by the carryings-on of the blobs on-screen. When the question-and-answer period came, his hand shot up. In a tone that announced that the coming comment would trump the entire presentation, he pronounced, "But of course, they're breasts." But of course. Why hadn't I noticed? Why hadn't I realized that Lynn was not pragmatically enacting an impersonal creative process but was only acting out a melancholic repetition-compulsion to return metaphorically to his own all-too-human beginnings? Why had I been taken in by all this techno-topological mumbo jumbo? Multiple singular-generic, my foot (or is that swollen foot?). It was all so simple, so clichéd, so abject and unaffirmative all along. I had been deceived by Lynn's self-deception. Partners in disavowal, caught out by the penetrating critic.

But then: perhaps I hadn't noticed because there were five blobs. Is it disingenuous to remark that breasts tend to occur in pairs? A literary critic may *wish* they came in fives. Disavowal . . . or wish-fulfilment? Whose "performance envelope" is showing now?

Metaphor is on the tongue of the beholder. Metaphors are produced adjacent to, and in uptake from, the form-generating process.[36] They occur where a visual apprehension of a sameness in the generated form authorizes an assimilation between that form and another already-constituted form. Metaphor starts from a pregiven form from which it extracts identifying properties, like curviness. The form is recognized on the basis of those properties as a particular case of a general class, taken as predefined. A second class of forms is seen to exhibit the same properties, albeit combined with other properties not exhibited by the first form. The partial overlap of recognizable properties enables a transference to be effected between the forms whereby the functions of one are attributed to the other (in this example, functions of an Oedipal nature). The functions also are taken as predefined. Once the transfer is established, it can be refined and expanded through linguistic associations underwritten by the symbolic structure of a signifying system. The symbolic structure, once again, is pregiven.[37]

It takes little effort to see how different this metaphorical process is from the topological design process, for which no form is pregiven. The starting point is force, rather than form. The forces are multiple, cohabiting an active space. They figure in that space as differentials composing an intensity rather than exhibiting an identity. To be more exact, they prefigure in that space, because they are proto-formal and proto-functional. No set of visible formal properties or determinate function can be assigned to them as yet. These will come of the process of the intensity's playing out. The form of that playing out—the continuity of topological transformations involved—is hypertypological. That is, it is constitutively multiple and irreducible to a general class. Neither can its constitutive multiplicity be reduced to a plurality of particular cases belonging to general classes. It is not particular-general but singular-generic. What defines the nature of the figure are the transitions it effects toward its own mutual inclusion of potential forms. The process does not labor in the domain of function; it moves in the realm of potential. Virtuality is its element. The figure is not fundamentally functional, symbolic, or signifying. It is purely operative. It has no inherent properties, only parameters of movement and transformation. Likeness—sameness, identity, resemblance—are not of its nature. Its nature is in transformation. It is only at the end, after the process stops, at the point at which a freeze-frame is extracted and the topological figure falls out of its immanence to its own playing-out, that any of the formal characteristics that ground the possibility of metaphor take root. Taken as a stand-alone form, its marking by the process is interpreted as an expression of architectural style against the background, no longer of its own formation, but of the history of the discipline.

It is here that a certain biomorphism will be noted. The forms Lynn generates do suggest organic metaphors, not all as loaded as the suckling critic's penta-breast. Lynn doesn't deny this, and at times will play along with it, as when he presents his design for the Yokohama Port Terminal as architectural "sushi." Other designs might suggest foliations or invaginations, pseudopods or flowerings, budding and couplings. Metaphors happen.[38]

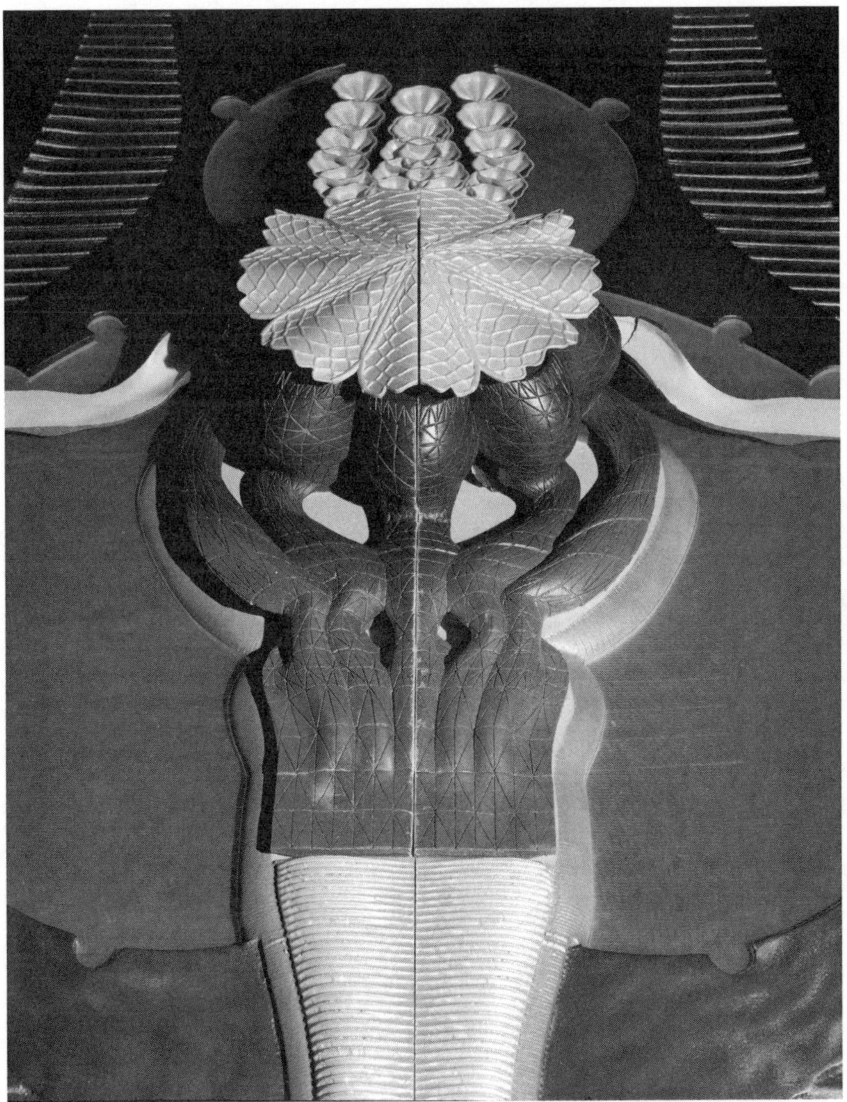

The Ark of the World Museum and Visitor Center, Costa Rica (2002–3). Greg Lynn Form.
This is the only project conceived biomorphically, in conscious imitation of biological forms.
Its style is convergent with, not the model for, Lynn's other topological design projects.

That's the point: metaphors happen; they are derived. They are by-products of the exuberance of the topological form-generating of the process, taken up at the point where that process stops. They mark one of its limits. They are a cutoff point of topological figure-formation. The key concept, worth repeating again, is that Lynnian resemblances are produced. They are produced by a process which in no way resembles its product—but may operatively echo it. The resemblances are "not attributable to some reduced simplified type but [are] rather the result of dynamic non-linear interactions of internal directives . . . and the generative fields that are configured by a flexible and adaptable system of integrating differences."[39] What biomorphism may be seen is the result of an operative analogy between how nature generates form in the wild and the nature of the form-generating process in the studio.

Earlier, Lynn's design process was qualified as "adventitious," as said of buds. This does assert an identity of sorts. But it is not fundamentally between buds and buildings. It is less that buildings are budlike than that the processes from which both buds and buildings grow proceed adventitiously in like *manner*. In other words, Lynn's architecture is "animate" in the sense that it marshals for architectural design some of the "same" relational growth processes—those native to generative fields plied by flexible and adaptable systems of integrating differences—as have led to the proliferations of life. It runs with the same exuberance of variation and evolutionary abandon as is everywhere apparent in nature outside the studio. The concept of identity at issue here does not hinge on visible resemblance. It is not a formal identity. It signifies nothing. It runs (away with itself). It is an asignifying *operative identity*. Operative, or processual, identity has its own logic. It is not subject to the formal likeness-driven classificatory thinking underwriting metaphor. By the same token, it is free of imitation. The concern is not to imitate biological form any more than it is to produce metaphors of it. "Building are not organisms but merely provisional structures that are already multiplicitous."[40] The concern is for the de-form, as it happens: the multiple, the singular, and the generic, in differential continuity and continuous differentiation. Imageless, ongoing, iteratively divergent and divergently emergent.[41]

TOGGLING POTENTIAL

Lynn's refusal of metaphor sometimes comes across as a refusal to think beyond the design stage. What of the completed design? What of the built form? When he sidelines metaphor, and with it symbolism, stylistic allusion, and signification—so dear to so many twentieth-century architects—is he abandoning the building to its literal functioning? When all is said and done, does he end up a default modernist in topological clothing, allowing form to meld with function yet again? Is there any way the "station" extracted from the topological design process can retain something of the relational dynamism and multiplicity of the process that generated it?

Entirely in character, Lynn uses a geometric concept to tackle this problem. The thresholds discussed earlier between basins of attraction and repulsion in the active topological field are termed "separatrices." A separatrix is a curve featuring in a dynamic interaction of different orders of forces whose difference plays out across a threshold to selective effect. In the cloud example, the co-operating forces of mass and rigidity made visible in the spherical form of the particles interacted with the topological field in such a way that the particles separated themselves out by crossing thresholds into different basins. Their distribution could not be predicted in detail, on a particle-by-particle basis, but it nevertheless followed a certain probability pattern. The selection effected at the separatrix carries a margin of indeterminacy that does not preclude stability. The stability, however, is not foundational. It arises from a dynamic process after a certain duration, and for a certain duration. A stability of this kind is called a "metastability." A metastability emerges. It has the character of an event. It cannot erase the indeterminacy of its generative process or expunge the specter of ultimate instability that goes with it. Still, it has probability on its side. For this reason, it remains stable within certain parameters, or within a "performance envelope."

Metastability is exactly what you want when you board a sailboat. You don't want the boat to have a hull whose functioning is invariant. If the hull didn't respond variably to the motion of the waves and wind, the chaos of the sea would be directly transmitted to the boat, readily capsizing it. The process of designing a hull has to integrate contingency-sensitive variation into a single end-form. "The abstract space of design is imbued with the properties of flow, turbulence, viscosity, and drag so that the form of the hull can be conceived in motion through the water. . . . The design space is conceived as an environment of force and motion. . . . The virtual force of the environment in which it is designed contributes to its shape."[42] This is done not in order to make a hull that changes shape—any more than animate architecture seeks to construct buildings that move (a reductio ad absurdum often thrown at it). The aim is to wrap the potential for a multiplicity of responses into a single form. Depending on how the forces of the environment hit the hull and sails, the spine will toggle the boat into different postures or "points of sail." The spine operates as a separatrix between postural "basins" of attraction, adapting the boat's movement, at each buffet, to the environing turbulence. As a result the boat will be metastable: its motions will describe sailings more regularly than sinkings.

"On the hull's surface, multiple points of sail are . . . resolved in the form itself . . . multiple vectors of movement are stored in the object itself as potential energy."[43] The constituted form itself is understood (and used) dynamically, from the point of view of potential for variation. The form's variational responses to contingencies of force are carryovers from the active space of the topological design process. They are abstract design dynamics that have entered into the object and are "stored" in it. What is potential energy if not a remainder of virtual movement in actual station? A surcharge of multiplicity imbuing the simplicity of an unchanging form? A surplus of variation animating a single spline? Something of the process has been effectively packed into the product, making it concretely multiple-singular. It doesn't matter so much what the hull looks like as long as it meets generic expectations, in both its multiplicity and its singularity. No matter what it looks like, there will be visual and linguistic associations. Granted. But they will have nothing to do with the operative identity of the design process, as it has successfully carried over into its product. The carryover of potential energy is an invisible thread of connection bringing the constituted form back into continuity with its formation. The product still doesn't resemble the formative process. But then it doesn't resemble its own potential energy either. Or its own performance, for that matter. What shape is a toggling? The continuity of process remains invisible and without resemblance, even as it takes actual shape. Its rendering visible is never without remainder, and it is the unseen remainder that is of the essence.

What is the analogue of a sailboat's hull for a building? Perhaps the use of interactive materials whose performance changes in response to variations in light or temperature. But isn't that missing something? That kind of dynamic variability operates in the absence of anyone in or around the building. A building without human bodies is like a sail without a wind. Is there a way of making the process continue in relationship with the turbulent forces of the human body? Potential energy may be a mode under which virtuality passes into the actual. But it is not the only one. In fact, it is arguably the lowest degree of the virtual in the actual. The potential it packs into form is restricted to variations on extended movement, lending itself to a necessarily limited number of selective postures. How can that envelopment of potential be reintensified? For example, what virtual powers might be accessed in connection with the human body's forces of perception, sensation, and expression? Is there a way to build in potentials for variation that fold out in other ways than extended movement? That imbue form with even greater dynamism and multiplicity—without falling back on metaphor and its resemblance-trafficking co-conspirators?

THE CONTINUING PROBLEM

The stopping problem is a continuing problem. If you answer the question of when, why, and how to stop the process running in order to render a form, you are immediately faced with the problem of how to make the process continue again across its stoppage. When you want station, you are faced with a runaway process. When you want to continue the process, you are confronted with a static form. No one ever said that animating architecture would be easy.

Other ways of posing this problem: In what way do topological events of iterative variation inhabit the actual building, in interrelation with human matter and its movements? Does the building in some way do what made it? Does it effectively continue in its own creative process?

A partial answer to these questions was provided earlier, when it was said that even the built form in a sense stands incomplete. Tinged by the contingency of its making, lacking a self-aggrandizing sense of its own monumentality, it invites redesign or razing, remaining receptive to further processual infoldings. But this modesty, this openness, is addressed only to the small band of people with actual authority to influence decisions: basically, design, planning, and construction professionals as well as the client. What of the crowds of people into whose lives the building enters, those who pass into it or simply pass it by? Can these questions be asked on their behalf? To do so is to ask that problems normally approached in terms of programmed function, with aesthetic or signifying extras, be reapproached processually: that the question of good form make a turn to becoming.

Lynn built the beginnings of a response into the Korean Presbyterian Church in Queens. For reasons that will become clear, this evolutionary branch of his practice, relaying process into reception and perception, seems largely to have dead-ended. What Lynn and his collaborators did was to design the ceiling of the main sanctuary to act as a visual version of the hull of a boat. The idea was that a single form would envelop more than one optical effect. The lighting was recessed between a series of fins running laterally across the ceiling, and tilted toward the pulpit. When the congregation enters the sanctuary near the pulpit, they are bathed in the light. The parishioners who move toward the back of the room to find seating may sense the angle of the light becoming more oblique, its quality more diffuse, the higher into the seating and the farther away from the pulpit they get. If they were to watch the ceiling as they filed toward the back, they would notice that at a certain point the fins seem to flip closed like a shutter. From the back, the ceiling appears smooth and the light is noticeably concentrated on the pulpit, but more subtly than by a spotlight. Since the lights themselves are out of sight, it is as if the pulpit glows with its own illumination. This inspirational effect was achieved by using iterative topological

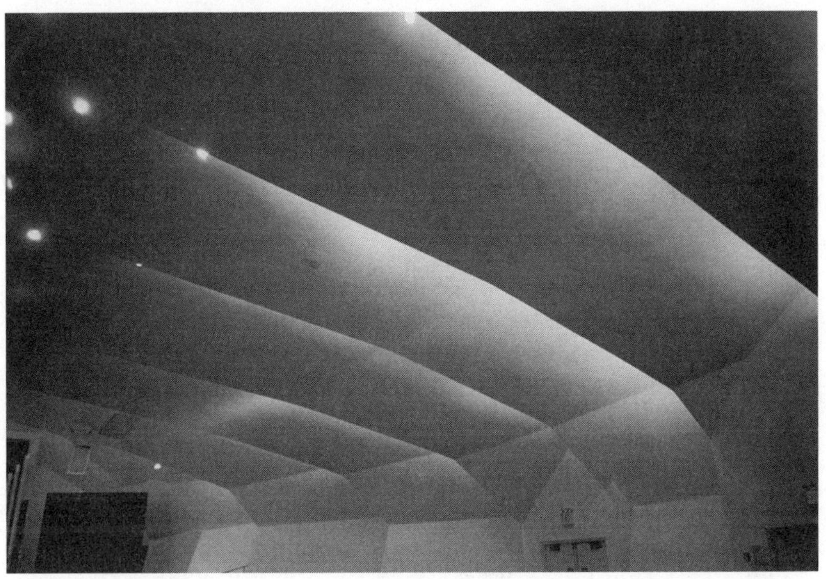

Ceiling fins acting as perceptual separatrices. Sanctuary, Korean Presbyterian Church of New York, Sunnyside, Queens, 1999. Greg Lynn, Douglas Garofalo, and Michael McInturf.

deformations to seriate the fins. The relation between the ceiling fins and the room can be understood as the relation between a topological figure and an environing, gradient force-field processually "identical" to that of the active design space from which its form was extracted. The paths of circulation into and around the room and the more- and less-desirable seating areas are variably weighted basins of attraction. The pulpit is a basin of repulsion for the parishioners' circulation, but a basin of attraction for their vision. The flip of the fins that occurs for a certain probability distribution of people entering the room and ascending the steps into the higher seating areas is a separatrix toggling between two "points of illumination" in much the way the spine of the boat hull toggles between points of sail on the high seas.

The built sanctuary-form succeeds in continuing the process. The fin operator intensifies a formal design element by imbuing it with perceptual "potential energy." This imbuing of the actual with a virtual co-presence of potentials is quite real. But it is also quite limited, in ways entirely appropriate to the circumstances. The lighting effect focused on the pulpit lends the minister a God-like air. The toggle between points of illumination simultaneously toggles the mood of the members of the minister's flock, from the aggravation of making their way through the city to the church, then parking and finding a seat, to the exaltation of the service. It transitions the parishioners into a state of receptivity to the inspirational narratives and associative chains the sermon is meant to reawaken. The fins do double toggle duty, switching not only between perceptual effects but also between the perceptual level and the symbolic. This is indeed potentializing. But to a low degree of virtuality (like the hull), since it does not trigger a becoming. It confirms, or at most intensifies, the conventional definition and function of the space as a place of worship. It makes the church more "like" what it is (in contradistinction to the factory it was, and whose memory is preserved in the retrofitting design strategy). The operations of the fin separatrix, in its crowded religious gradient field, addresses established genre more than the generic in the emergent sense.

It is noteworthy that the optical effect built into the Korean Presbyterian Church triggers a symbolic association of just the kind against which Lynn so carefully defends his design process as a whole. The symbolism takes the form of an optical effect. Like all optical effects, its appearance stands out from the conditions of its appearing. Its pops out from its production, to occupy a separate plane from it. Here, it pops out of the singular-generic into a genre; from operativity into symbolism; from experimentation into belief; from the generativity of process into perception experienced soulfully; from open field conditions mobilizing the never-before-seen of the virtual to subjective reception confirming the already-felt. The ceiling fins, from this point of view, are a kind of gearshift mechanism between vastly different compositional planes.

Architecturally, this is not uninteresting. The appearing of the optical effect is an event, and as such activates the architecture, and does so differently than architectural gestures that invite "reading" or "critique." The eventness overcomes the ornament–structure dichotomy that traditionally frames architecture, since what appears is a unitary stand-out effect fulfilling its own (symbolic) function and (non-architectural) aesthetic value. There is no application of a decorative element to a functional structure. The optical effect's function and aesthetic value are indissociable from each, inhabiting the same plane of their eventful standing-out.

Lynn's gesture of building something like what he is building, and building for the people who use the building—his modestly allowing a symbolic becoming-Christian of his own steadfastly ungodly design practice—is a manifestation of the processual generosity alluded to earlier. It would be pure arrogance (not unheard of among architects) to build in defiance of the clients' perceptions of their own needs. At the same time, this processual generosity in some ways amounts to a processual abdication. The generative process gearshifts out of itself onto another plane, of a very different nature, where it culminates in a reproduction of the already-felt rather than continuing on its generative way. In the optical effect of the ceiling fins, the architectural process in-folded right out of itself. Emergence peaks out of itself, perceptually. This is one way of dealing with the continuing problem. But to judge by the subsequent evolution of his work, Lynn felt that this way, if generalized in his work, would lead to an impasse.

It is possible to imagine similar gestures that could succeed in continuing the process generatively and not lead to the same impasse. For example, Lars Spuybroek experiments with building in strategic patches of perceptual vagueness that require an active, embodied response that triggers a kind of wayfinding through the built environment in the course of which new perceptual orientations, enveloping a potential for emergent functions, arise.[44] Arakawa and Gins also make use of vagueness, suspending the perceptual cues that normally anchor the body's orientation in the built environment. Their Bioscleave House, for example, is built in such a way that there is no perceptible line of demarcation between floor, walls, and ceiling. Neither are there windows affording a view that would situate the house in its exterior milieu, offering vanishing points and a horizon line necessary for perspective. The elements of the interior architecture are conceived as "landing sites." These are affordances that partially resolve the vagueness of the surrounds, not into regions of clarity but into sites of ambiguity: just resolved enough to evoke the potential for a response without prefiguring which response, for what function. This polyvalency is meant to break the mold of habit, and invite the body to improvise on its manner of inhabiting, reintensifying its experience of the built environment. The idea is to create the conditions for the emergence of new modes of life arising relationally, between the body and the surrounds. The architectural process continues in the betweening. There is no longer a body in a building, but a body-building(-life): an integral "architectural body" wrapping the differential between the body proper and its built environment into a single, continuing process of becoming, more intensely alive again. Reanimate architecture.[45]

Both of these solutions to the continuing problem are predicated on an appeal to perception, foregrounding the embodied nature of perception and striving to overcome the duality between the embodied subject of architecture and the materiality of the built environment. The work of Spuybroek and Arakawa and Gins demonstrate that it is possible to imbue form with greater dynamism and multiplicity, reintensifying the architectural end result with intensities of ongoing potential, without falling back on any constitutive role for metaphor, symbolism, or signification, and without predefined function taking form-generating precedence. But this will not be Lynn's way. After flirting with this path in the fins of the Korean Presbyterian Church, Lynn lets it drop like a deflated blob. It is as if he wishes to avoid, at all costs, anything that might steer architecture toward something resembling phenomenology.[46] Any appeal to perception, embodied or not, however integrally in-betweened, is, it would seem, to skirt too phenomenally close for comfort. This has contributed to a widespread judgment leveled against Lynn's work, one that is without doubt the most commonly stated reason among his detractors for dismissing his work: that he is a "formalist." A corollary to this judgment is that he lacks a concept of the body, or even that he is coldly, digitally, methodically anti-body, a kind of fundamentalist of geometrical reason. This is a misdiagnosis.

What Lynn is against is not the body but the subject, understood in any foundational way. And as the foregoing discussion of his concept of animate form should have made clear by now, he is not a formalist but a processualist. What animates his work is a commitment to a process of becoming-architectural that is its own dynamic subject: a subjectless subjectivity one with its running; driven by its own ongoing infolding of formative forces; constituted by that very movement, which it can only recursively call its own.

Lynn, of course, does not deny the existence of the subject. The openness of his process to in-folding outside growth factors that include client preference and even belief is proof enough of that. But that is all the subject is to his process: one growth factor among many, all of which differentially populate the generative field of the design process. As we have seen, Lynn's own subjecthood, his own authorial agency, likewise figures as growth factor for the in-folding. Any constitutive or foundational appeal to a subject, embodied or not, understood in Cartesian terms as sovereign author of its actions or in phenomenological terms as a transcendental field, would vitiate the processual autonomy of the architectural process as self-running, for emergence. It would water down the animateness of animate form. It is precisely because Lynn is *not* a formalist that he needs a concept of animate form—a concept of form that is processual through and through. "Animate" form has none of the characteristics of form in the usual sense: having a general or ideal existence lying outside process; being fully determined and categorizable according to inherent properties; appealing to the recognition and operating according to resemblance based on those properties; serving as a mold for a matter separate from the mold, such that formation is applied from without in an exercise of transcendent ordering reproducing the same, rather than arising immanently from within the playing-out of a generative field of difference producing yet more difference. It is for the same processual reasons that Lynn rejects the subject-path and that he is not a formalist.

Lynn declines to follow the perceptual path as his main avenue, for fear that a foundational subject might contrive to return through topological architecture's backdoor, vitiating his move toward animate form. Where he goes instead is toward *surface* on the one hand and *performance* on the other. Either way, bodies are most welcome—provided a non-Cartesian *and* nonphenomenological notion of what constitutes a body can be conceived and operationalized. Lynn does not lack a concept of the body. In fact, the reconceptualization of the body was a central concern of his all along, as evidenced in his very earliest writings. The title of the collection of his essays from the 1990s makes this centrality clear in the very placement of the word: *Folds, Bodies and Blobs*.[47]

THE BODY TOPOLOGIC

The choreographer William Forsythe once defined the body as "that which folds."[48] Lynn would surely concur, adding an extra topological twist: a body is that which continually in-folds for continuous out-folding. The example of a body that Lynn develops most extensively in his writing is instructive—and not a little surprising. It is of a stadium wave: the tidal movement of waving hands that sport fans collectively produce to intensify the excitement of the game.[49] In what sense is this ephemeral dynamic form a body?

The first thing to remark is that the stadium wave is a gesture, and that it is expressive (of excitement). The second thing to remark is that its expression is self-propagating: it feeds off of its own momentum, producing what it expresses. Each roll of the wave folds the impulse inherited from the last and relays it forward, the expressed intensity mounting toward a crescendo. Who is the subject of the wave? There is no one. A single individual is not capable of starting it. More than one is required. The wave originates *between* existing bodies. It occurs when a number of bodies collectively launch themselves into correlated movements of their hands, in a kind of unspoken alliance that coincides with the event of the wave's taking effect, and does not survive its run. There is no subject of the wave, other than the event of the wave itself. This is a *body-event*: one only with its own taking dynamic form.

The wave is a singular effect arising from no one cause. Every effect has some kind of cause. But some causes are more-than-one. These cannot be localized, in one subject or at one particular point in space. The cause of the stadium wave is by nature distributed, akimbo the in-between. It is simultaneously here and there in the originating group, in the intervals between those existing bodies, all at once. The existing bodies are not acting as separate bodies. They are acting as correlated wave-formation factors. Their vitality enters selectively and partially into the wave. The participating individuals do not enter into the wave as *who* they are. Their identity is not important to the wave or what it expresses. In a full-stadium wave, even the participants' identity as fans of their particular team is suspended, as fans of both camps may act in concert to pump up the atmosphere. What the participants are is *how* they are, together, for the wave-making. All that is relevant is their concertation as formative factors for this event. They do not figure in the event as individual persons or identified bodies. They figure purely operatively, from the precise angle of their wave-making activity. They only figure in this capacity, in pro-wave efficacity. They are proto-wavers, in much the same way blobs are proto-architectural elements. They are elemental forces for formation, correlating into a composite movement. Each individual's gesture movingly fuses into the dynamic form of the wave. One wave, many bodies. From many subgestures, an integral overgesture. A singular *"fusional multiplicity."*[50]

Elemental does not mean foundational. Elementarity is relative to the composition at hand. The stadium wave is composed of proto-waving subgestures. These are also caused, and their cause is, like the wave, composite and ultimately nonlocal. But the wave cares nothing for this. It takes them up into its own formation as the elementary units proper to its own constitution. The forces entering into the composition of these pro-wave elements are many and heterogeneous. The participants' self-identification as fans is among them. Even though that identity as such is not taken up into the wave as a formative factor proper to it, it was part of what brought its proto-wavers to the stadium. It is among the forces that have produced the conditions for the wave-making. The cultural codes and conventions of fandom also number among the conditioning forces. As does the presence of the cameras that prime the expressive fires of the fans by providing them a channel for the propagation of their gestures' effect beyond the stadium to the millions of fans watching TV at home, not to mention the media commentators who whip up anticipation. The list could go on indefinitely. There is an infinity of contributory factors, of vastly different scales, straddling the vastest of distances. These factors cannot be counted, and the particular contribution of each cannot be precisely separated out. They overlap and interpenetrate, diffusing into an open field whose exact size or contours are indeterminate. The best way to describe them would be in terms of *differentials*—the differential between fans of one team and those of another, between fans and nonfans, between stadium fans and home fans, fans and commentators, camera feeds and viewing in situ, to name just a few—and *intensities*—levels of fan loyalty, vivacities of participation, and the number and variety of media feeds, each with its own reach and powers of attention-grabbing and passion-stirring. An open, differential field of intensities. That is what peaks in each gesture of each fan who lends him- or herself to the wave-making. That infinity of contributory factors is integrally enveloped in each wave-forming subgesture of each proto-waving fan. Like the wave itself that they compose, each of the wave's composing elements are a fusional multiplicity. The fusional multiplicity of the stadium wave as a whole folds-out from the elemental folding-into its composing subgestures of the infinite, open, differential field of sporting intensities, multiply peaking.

One of the main ingredients in this event has not been mentioned: the giant in-stadium screens. These provide instant feedback to the fans in the stadium of their own enthusiasm, so that it feeds on itself. This affective feedback mechanism is directly collective: it reflects the fan's concertation back into its own continuing. Using the stadium wave as exemplary of what a body is raises a fundamental question: Can there be such a thing as a *body without a surface*? The notion of an ephemeral body is not terribly brain-teasing. But a body without a surface? If such a thing did exist, why would it be relevant to architecture? Isn't architecture traditionally defined precisely as a play between volume and surface? Here, there is neither.

ABSTRACT SURFACE

The presence of the in-stadium cameras highlights the affective dimension of the event. Affect provides a way of answering the question of whether there is such a thing as a body without a surface. The answer is no. At least, not concretely. The dynamic form of the stadium wave is a self-propagating rhythm, not a surface in any usual sense. But it does agitate something: affect. Its rhythm rolls and rises: affectively. The wave has the shape of an enthusiasm.[51] Affect is the *abstract surface* upon which the wave inscribes itself. It is into affect that the myriad formative factors of the open field of conditions in-fold. The affect then eddies on itself, through the feedback provided by the in-stadium cameras. The eddying doesn't stand in place. It energizes the unfolding of the wave's continuing formation. This is not a standing wave. It is a wave that rolls affect in, to roll itself over and onward, in the process transmitting the affect to bodies not participating actively in its production.

Next question: can there be a wave without *matter*? Again, the answer is no. But this is a trick answer. The matter of the wave is not the hands of the wavers, as it might be tempting to say at first impression. It is not exactly hands that form the wave. Rather, it is their expressive gestures. It is only because the hand motions are already in the gestural register, and the gestural register is already in the key of affect, that the wave is the body-event that it is. The hands lend themselves to the affective effect—and disappear into it. Watching a stadium wave is not to watch a bunch of hands waving. It is to see their integral effect, directly in the key of affect. The matter of the body-event is affect itself. Affect is the *intensive matter* of the event. It constitutes the abstract surface registering the integral intensity of this singular event, bringing to affective expression the differential intensities of the contributing factors actively folding in to it.

If you focus on the hands, you cease to see the wave. The hands as such are a disjunctive multiplicity, while the wave has the integral continuity of a fusional multiplicity. You can't have one without the other. But that doesn't make them the same. There is a minimal difference between a bunch of fleshy hands and their collective shape of enthusiasm. But this minimal difference makes all the difference. The activity of the hands enters into the wave through their gestural ability to agitate the abstract surface of affect. But the hands themselves do not enter into the wave. The wave folds their activity into its own composition. It does so only by taking off from their form, in order to come into its own. The event *takes off from* hand-matter, folding into intensive affective matter, which is the register in which the event effectively expresses itself.

The stadium wave occurs at the limit of the physical body, where a dynamic form detaches from the outline of the individual body and is directly actualized on an abstract surface. The materiality proper to the hands, flesh and blood, *doubles* the affective matter of the event, on another level. As Bergson noted, "The surface film of the body that constitutes the visible body is apt to double itself, one of the two copies remaining with the tactile body. But the fact remains that there is a body that is detachable from the body that one can touch, a body without interiority, weightless, and that is transported instantaneously to the point where it is."[52] Bergson was talking about the reflection of the unitary body in a pool. Here, a crowd of touchable, gesturing physical bodies double themselves en masse. An abstract double detaches from one and all, instantaneously transported into a fusional multiplicity that is directly seen, as the affective matter-of-fact of the event, appearing right where it is—effectively all over, globally distributed—as a weightless abstract surface without interiority, affectively felt through the eyes without being touched (or touchable). "Our body," William James writes in a related comment, "is the palmary instance of the ambiguous. . . . We can treat it as physical or as non-physical according as we take it in the narrower or in the wider context."[53] The body is "ambiguous" because it is two-sided: physical (touchable) and non-physical or abstract (untouchable, if still feelable); individual (proto-wavers) and collective (wave-effect); narrower and wider; elemental and integral; several and fused; given bodies (giving their activity to the wave) and a becoming-body (taking that distributed activity into itself, where it is).

The body is duplex: that which folds itself double. The fusional multiplicity of the collective effect stands out from and doubles the individual bodies forming it, without *physically* separating itself from them. Rather, it abstracts itself out of the in-between of them, into its own dynamic form. It couches itself in its own intensive matter, which overlaps with the physical *activity* of its fleshly bodies, while distinguishing itself overall from their elemental forms. The becoming-body of the wave brings

the multiplicity of flesh-and-blood bodies to a singularly eventful, affective expression, on and as its own register of the real:
intensive, expressive body-event.

THE ARCHITECTURE OF BODY-EVENTS

Now imagine that all the hands are covered by a thin membrane.
They are holding up a diaphanous tarp. When they wave, the
membrane's surface ripples, deforming into the rolling of the
wave. The dynamic form of the event would be the same. But
now a concrete surface—the tarp—is doubling the abstract surface that doubles the collectivity of the wave's formative elements. Doubling doubled again. The concrete surface shares the
same dynamic form as the abstract-surface wave, which it makes
actually visible. The membrane doubles the abstract form of the
stadium wave with a sensible form whose rhythm and patterning is identical to it. Even though this dynamic form is shared,
there is still a minimal difference that makes all the difference:
between the nonsensuous and the sensuous. This is the difference
between intensive matter (which is nonlocalizable, as an all-over
effect) and extensive matter (which, concretely extending over
an area, has physical location). The affective matter of the wave
is redoubled by visible matter. The nonphysicality of the body-
event concretes. The touchable membrane covers the event,
contributing its own physicality to it. That physical resurfacing
interposes itself between the formative factors of the wave—the
crowd of stadium fans—and the home fans populating the wider
context of the media environment.

Now, shift focus. Think of an architectural surface, a wall,
say. Everything that was said of the stadium wave can be said
of the events that compose themselves in and around the walls
of the building. Inside the building lies the open, differential,
intensive field of inhabitation, composed of an infinity of conditioning factors—habit, desire, physiological needs, convention,
furnishings, equipment, embedded media systems, and so forth
ad infinitum. Not just hands, but a mixed bag of elements of
all natures. Outside the building lies another open, differential,
intensive field, of the urban. This field is composed of factors
such as zoning, patterns of circulation and frequentation, noise,

community facilities, collective equipment, policing, and norms of interaction. Another mixed bag, many-handed and more. *The architectural surface folds these open fields into and out of one another*, producing all manner of body-events on the abstract surface of *habitation*. This folding in and out is the intensive matter of architecture. Walls, roofs, and floors compose the extensive surface visibly doubling the abstract body-events of inhabitation.

The elements in the open fields lying on either side of the walls are so various, the complexity of their interactions so complex, that each field taken in its own right, and both together, in their folding into and out of each other, exceed the visible. The concrete architectural surface lends its own visibility to this excess over the seen. The concrete surface stands in vision for the dynamic form of this fielding and folding. Its static form is the visible instantiation of the dynamic form of architecture, of its animate form. The concrete architectural surface expresses the multi-dimensioned, many-fielded, formative forces of architectural body-events in three dimensions—just as the particle clouds, blobs, and splines of Lynn's design process expressed the many-dimensioned formative forces of the design process on his 2D computer screen.

In the case of the architectural surface, the membrane, though physically static, is *active*. Its physical form co-organizes the body-events that occur in the fold between the fields. As with the hypothetical stadium wave tarp, the concrete surface doubles an abstract surface. It is the sensible index of an eventful becoming-body that as such is nonsensuous. The body-event occurs once again on the affective register—now of inhabitation rather than fandom. Unlike the stadium wave, the concrete form does not physically present the dynamic form of the abstract body-event. The configuration of walls, roof, floors does not have the same rhythm and patterning as the body-event—which is so many-dimensioned as to defy geometric expression in itself. In this sense, the concrete architectural surface is a disjunctive expression of the fusional multiplicity for which it stands. Architectural body-events are made visible in concrete architectural form, while having their own form different from the concrete form. It is because of this disjunction that it is possible to consider the concrete architectural surface "formally." By that I mean separately from the dynamic form of inhabitation; in extension, as a standing geometric configuration bracketing the intensive matter for which it stands, in its very making visible of it.

Architecture-related events are typically categorized as falling into the domestic-inside and the urban-outside. But the architectural surface, understood in this way as the dynamic form of a becoming-body event made visible in concrete form, is not just a divider between an inside and an outside. It is not just a separatrix but an active membrane. Walls, roof, and floors establish a *regime of passage* between the open fields on either side of them. When you go in or out, you toggle between domestic and urban events. The separation between the two domains is not airtight. They trail affectively into each other, mutually modulating, interfusing. When the sound of a storm or the noise of a passing car passes the membrane, or an internet feed or radio transmission infiltrates, the domestic-inside and urban- and media-outside bleed together. They fuse, paned on a window or cabled through a wall. When you storm out of the house at the speed of a domestic spat, the becoming-body of that abstract event concretely swings on the hinges of the slammed door. The architectural surface is a *transducer* between the open fields, in the fold between which architectural body-events take shape. Through endless iterations of going in and going out, through the many panings, cablings, and hinge-swings and all manner of other passages, it brings affective effects fielded inside the walls into fusional continuity with affective effects fielding outside. The folding together of the fields forms a duplex: a single, two-sided transductive field of intensity. This is the affective matter of architecture. The dynamic form of architecture stands intensively in (and out of) its concrete form.

In the complexity of this process, novel effects can arise, through resonance or interference between the fields. On-the-fly improvisations may produce new variations, playing on the fusional multiplicity of conditioning factors that peak into architectural gestures of inhabitation. Body-events that cannot be clearly demarcated as either domestic or urban can emerge from this. A building's program can be supplemented—outdone by itself—by these emergent expressions. Architectural-body events (or architectural body-events) are always happening at any rate, each in their own way, on their own scale, duplexing their own crowd of formative elements. Their novelty may be more visible in nonstandard architectural constructions, but they also occur in buildings belonging to traditional architectural genres, such as the sports stadium or single-family home. Body-events can take off anywhere—and do so in profusion, on all scales.[54]

ABSTRACT EXPRESSIONISM OF THE BODY

All of this changes the terms of architectural design. The dialectic between volume and surface becomes secondary, displaced by the formative play of differential factors in open fields. The divide between the interior and exterior is no longer as fundamental, displaced by transductive relations between open fields. The fundamental concepts of architecture are no longer architectonic by nature. They are naturally processual instead.

This is another way of saying that architecture must be defined in the first instance in terms of proto-architectural forces, from which architectural forms proper are processual precipitates: derivatives. When a built form precipitates from the design process, dropping into the open fields of life, the "derivative" reactivates, becoming a derived force. Its now concrete surfaces become transductive membranes actively modulating architectural body-events of inhabitation. In a way, the "continuing problem" discussed earlier, the question of how the design process feeds its fielding of its elemental formative forces forward into the built environment, is a non-issue. The process cannot but restart. At the first laying of a brick or application of drywall, it's up and rerunning, enjoying an active afterlife. Across the interval of construction, it has transduced from a proto-architectural design-event to an architectural event proper.

The stadium wave is an architectural body-event that does not have an inside or an outside, only a rhythm appearing on an abstract surface. In this sense, it retains its proto-architectural nature, at the price of exhausting itself in its own ephemerality. It has an architectural becoming, with no concrete architecture become. It is embryonic architecture. Mature architectural forms, architectures in the finished, standing sense, take becoming-architectural to a concrete conclusion, doubling the abstract surface of expression with a material surface (a surface of another matter). In all cases, becoming-architectural involves a coming to integral expression of a multiplicity of formative forces differentially inhabiting open generative fields. The expression is always on an abstract surface, which in certain becomings-architectural (the kind that are actually built) is doubled by a concrete surface. The abstractness of this surface of expression as such qualifies Lynn's architecture as exactly what he says it is: not a formalism but an *abstract expressionism.*[55]

Now return to the screen of the digital design process as earlier described. The screen is also a concrete double of the form-taking events passing through it. Properly speaking, these events occur on the abstract surface of topological transformation—purely abstract affectings and being affected, folding into and out of one another geometrically. The resulting animated figures are visible doubles of *abstract bodies.* A blob is not a metaphor for a body: *a blob is a body.* It is an abstract body, visibly expressing itself in pixels, arising from an interplay of abstract formative forces operating in a virtual differential field. The abstract body is the manner in which the virtual field—which in and of itself is recessive in relation to experience, as discussed in the opening sections of this essay—comes out into experience. It is the actualization *of* the virtual: the nonsensuous image of that which has none.[56]

Architecture has all manner of body-events, on any number of levels and scales. Essential to the architectural design process are techniques for transducing form-making, or form-taking, becoming-body-events from one level and scale to another. Each transduction moves the process to a new *associated milieu* (a different duplexing of open generative fields). The supreme abstractness of the digital phases of topological design process enables architecture to in-fold into its abstract surfaces all manner of formative forces from all manner of generative fields, digitally rendered virtual, thence to unfold them again, across an interval of construction, into body-events occurring on other levels and scales.[57] The running of the digital is the most intensive architectural matter of all.

Gilbert Simondon, the philosopher of relational individuation whose thinking is most thoroughly topological, speaks of the human body itself in terms of transduction.[58] Within the envelope of the body—or the "film" of the skin, as Bergson called it—lies a hierarchy of nested levels of innumerable proto-actors collectively composing the physical body. Each level constitutes a subsurface producing integral effects proper to its own level. These effects constitute expressive subgestures doubling the multiplicity of the proto-actors populating that level, or stratum. The sub-integral effects feed up the strata, peaking in affective expression-events, issuing in the whole-body overgestures that we recognize as our actions. Hunger, for example, integrates a multitude of micro-events, physiological and psychic, and both in interfusion, in the global action of seeking or denying oneself food. *Perception* is the dynamic form doubling the body's actions as a whole.[59] It is the abstract surface of inscription for whole-body affect and action, in their expressive connection to each other, summing up in a single issue the teeming undergestures that percolate through the body's constituent levels.

The surface of perception is an abstract membrane. Bodily subgestures fold out across it, into the overgesture of action. At the same time, in lockstep, the process folds back in-across, in an affective reflux returning the action to its source, readying another go. The folding-in takes the form of memory and habit, and their joint production, anticipation, all affectively tinged and weighted. Memory, habit, and anticipation bathe the entire multilevel architecture and all its component proto-actors with differentials of potential. The differentials are between the affective tinging of various elements and the way that variable weighting tips the traces of present, just past, toward the future. The differential between the past and the future is the primary differential. It marks all of the elemental proto-actors, defining them as tendencies, needs, or desires—future-facing dynamics conditioned by the past. These come in crowds, in tension with one another. The differential between the tensions energizes the coming iteration. The next whole-body step is the working out of their tensions. Their resultant expression vectorizes life's generative field, orienting its coming issuings into action in the ongoing expressive movement of variation that is life. These energizing, vectorizing differentials are abstract formative forces: a differential sets in between. It has no form but that betweenness, which is nonsensuous. It has no concrete form. It is purely abstract; so abstract that the formative activity is largely nonconscious. These differentials compose the virtual field of emergence for life's taking integral dynamic form. They in-form the generative field's issuing, across its many levels and multitude of components, into iterative action-sequences globally addressing the continuing problem proper to life: how to act so as not to die; how best to live.[60]

Part of the significance of Lynn's stadium wave example is that it opens the possibility of understanding self-organizing body-events which occur on the abstract surface of perception as fundamentally architectural; even if they are ephemeral and purely abstract, doubled by no concrete surface; even if they are hosted by an architectural construction. Architectural constructs can host architectural body-events of the embryonic kind (the as-yet unconcretely doubled kind). These embryonic architectural body-events can be spontaneously self-organizing. Although stadium waves have settled into the stuff of cliché, they most likely originated spontaneously before becoming conventionalized.

This brings up an important point: architectural body-events, even ephemeral, are subject to *capture*.[61] This is the processual definition of *program*. An architectural program is a blueprint for the capture of a species of architectural body-events. Architectural *genres* are preplanned forms of capture. The processual point is that even when architectural body-events are captured, for example when stadium waves come to be preplanned, consciously led and organized by pre-designated instigators, they still must *take*. However planned they may be, their proximate origin is always the affective uptake of the fans' collectively fanning the fandom fires. They don't always take. And even once started, they may fizzle. If they take, their unfolding always has an element of contingency. They may travel to the opposite side of the stadium before winking out, for example. But then again, they might circle all the way around. They might bifurcate into two waves, and the two may cross paths. When this happens, they may move through each other to continue on their way, or run interference with each other and fall into chaos. However clichéd it has become, the dynamic form of the stadium wave continues to exhibit self-organizing dynamic-form-generating potential. In their ability to "choose" to take or not, to continue along different paths, to converge and diverge, to resonate or interfere with one another, stadium waves display topological vitality that is not unblob-like even though its visible manifestation and the field of its emergence are entirely different. The same is true for an architectural construction realizing a program in a given genre of building.

Lynn's proposition is less that topological architecture is a new kind of architecture. It is that architectural process is topological, always and everywhere, from generative top to bottom, field to field, program to genre. As a design practice, it is always in the business of in-folding forces of its outside, feeding on generative field conditions more radically open than any exterior defined relative to a structurally defined interior. The discipline of architecture is naturally allied to complex, self-organizing phenomena of a proto-architectural kind, regardless of what discipline or domain they are native to.[62] Explicitly topological architecture is just this natural tendency, of infolding for folding-out, coming into its own, enabled by new tools and abetted by alternative geometries. The topological in architecture is "facilitated" by the pet tools of the digital but "not simply reducible to" them.[63]

Lars Spuybroek generates his own modes of practice that are also explicitly topological, in alliance with proto-forces of the architectural outside. Unlike Lynn, Spuybroek retains a central concern for the perceiving body in its transductive relation to its environment (as witnessed in such projects as *Vision Machine* and his later theoretical work on sympathy).[64] Spuybroek's transductive process of architectural design continues the continuing problem in an original way: by folding the proto-architectural expressions of digital form-generating into and out of materials-based analogue computing. Spuybroek's architectural practice extends topological design techniques into the analogue world it supposedly left behind. Although Lynn's and Spuybroek's practices are very different from each other, their processes are fellow travelers in the sense that they both pursue, each in its own way, the transductive deployment of topological thought. Both constitute abstract expressionisms.[65]

The divergences are a function of the angle of attack. As the foregoing analysis of the body was meant to demonstrate, the concrete surface of architecture and the abstract surface of perception are reciprocals. They fold into and out of each other in many a manner, fusing-forth integral effects, lived as body-events—without in any way blurring the essential difference between abstract and concrete surfaces. It goes without saying that we do not confuse perception with architecture, or vice versa, even though they bodily interfuse. It is perhaps because of that nonconfusion that we don't appreciate often enough the nature of their processual embrace—its dynamic abstractness. Embracing topological architecture is not a question of choosing the coolness of form over the thickness of lived experience. There is no alternative between concrete and abstract. That way of construing it, and the associated deprecatory accusations of formalism often addressed to architects like Lynn, miss the point entirely. The point is that the abstract and the concrete go processually together. The sensible, concrete surface of architecture and the abstract surface of perception, waving with intensive affective matter, on which architectural body-events nonsensuously register, are *two facets of the same topological figure*. They are in as intimate an embrace as the two sides of a Möbius strip.

Lynn's work converges toward the surface as his privileged angle of attack. Spuybroek focuses on perception (as do Arakawa and Gins). That difference in approach imparts an angular momentum to the respective design practices that makes all the difference when it comes to their techniques and the terms in which the problem of design is posed and theorized. In the course of Lynn's practice, the question of the body segues into a concern with the problem of the surface. The concern for the surface in turn segues into a concern for how surfaces perform. For Spuybroek, on the other hand, the question of perception unfolds into an exploration of material potentials, guided by the problem of intensive matter.[66] Lynn's move to surface and then through surface to performance circles the design practice back toward questions of functionality. Spuybroek's work does not of course ignore function, but because of his perceptual angle of attack, function comes wrapped up in the material qualities of experience carried by the ebbs and flows of intensive matter, rather than streamlining into a vector of performance.

But we have gotten ahead of ourselves.

SURFACING DESIGN: INTRICACY IN ACTION

It is after the construction of the Korean Presbyterian Church that the problem of surface becomes the organizing node of Lynn's work. The word "body" all but disappears from Lynn's vocabulary in the 2000s. The body-event continues to figure, but largely implicitly, wrapped in surfacings. Body-related questions of perception, even of aesthetics, are by no means absent. They resurface in new ways, although not entirely divorced from the traditional concepts of form in the history of architecture. But as always, form is subjected to a decidedly processual twist whose dynamic it is important to understand in order to appreciate Lynn's adventitious relation to the discipline whose interiority he never respected, but which he never rejected.

Focusing on the problem of the surface brings with it enormous advantages for a topological architecture. A surface can undergo topological transformations to yield proto-forms that can be scaled and adapted to feed forward into any genre of architectural construction, house, office, station, tower, kiosk even. Lynn's projects extend to all of these genres—and beyond (even so far beyond as extraterrestrial habitats).[67] His design practice from the turn of the millennium encompasses interiors, art installations, household objects like tea sets and cutlery, furniture, boats, and high-performance vehicles. This breadth of design activity is not an eclecticism. It is not a leaping hither and thither at whim. The diversity inheres. All of these divergent lines of development unfold from the same source, which is not an origin so much as a generative matrix for the continuous production of variation.

As we have seen, the primary design elements are virtual forces. The virtual forces co-compose as differential fields. Architecturally embryonic topological figures arise from the differential fields' playing out. Across their iterations, these proto-architectural figures run into emergent architectural forms.

The programming of the fields and their algorithmic runnings in-form these emergences with performance envelopes that pre-engineer them, function-ready, for transductive relay into the urban field. Taken together, these formative factors constitute the generative matrix of digital topological architecture. None of the formative factors in themselves—virtual forces, differential fields, topological figures, proto-architectural figures, or performance envelopes—has the property of scale. Nor are they fundamentally answerable to formal types, conventional styles, or predefined functions. They are proto- all that. In themselves, they are proto-polyvalent.[68] Form and function emerge through them, and are only then captured by genre typology and style. In themselves, they are pluripotent: they carry variations amany, enveloped in potential unfoldings. They are the form in which diversity of form operatively inheres.

All of the varieties of design object encompassed by Lynn's practice inhere in this singularly multiple matrix. Lynn does not skip around eclectically. He systematically returns to this generative field. By tweaking procedures, modulating enabling constraints, and adjoining new channels of continuing—most notably automated milling using computerized numerical control (CNC)—the process is iteratively reoriented toward outcomes answering to the exigencies of specific genres and their requirements in terms of program, or functionalized performance. It is because diversity inheres in the matrixial field that Lynn's design practice coheres in its diversification. In fact, his practice exhibits more consistency, processually speaking, than is typically the case. The focus on surfaces increasingly assumes the responsibility for orienting the playing-out of the cohering diversities' matrixial consistency.

We are speaking, of course, of curvilinear surface. A curvilinear surface, in the process of becoming-architectural, is neotenic. Even lifted out of the series of topological iterations to which it belongs to feature as a stand-alone figure, it retains many of its proto-formal embryonic characteristics. It has a natural tendency to resist such traditional properties of architectural form as the frontality of the façade, the structural dichotomy between vertical load-bearing and horizontal elevation, the encasement of a volume by an assemblage of figurally and structurally discrete elements (walls, floors, and roof with clear lines of demarcation between them), modular massing by the accretion of figurally and structurally discrete elements, the rigid volumetric division of inside from outside, the dressing of a surface with cladding, and the overdressing of ornament. All of these distinctions can be topologically smoothed over into lines of continuous variation, making every element a dependent variable in integral co-composition.[69] This erases what is perhaps the master distinction undergirding not only the typical understandings of architectural form but almost all classical and modern practices and philosophies of form as well: the structural contrast between the part and the whole.[70]

The keyword for surface in Lynn's approach is *intricacy*.[71] The way in which the relationship between the waving hand-elements of the stadium wave and the wave's own dynamic form was described earlier provides a gateway to this concept. The wave, it was said, folds the activity of the hands into its own going on. The dynamic form of the wave folds the multiplicity of its constituent sub-wavings into its own occurrence. The overwave's continuous propagation takes up the diversity of the hand-wavings into itself, smoothing over their discreteness. The multiplicity of the hands, the individuality of each absorbed in its own gesture, is resorbed into the singularity of the wave. The wave as a whole arises as a *fusion* of its parts. On their level and in their own materiality, the hands remain discrete. But what is seen, in all immediacy, on the abstract surface of perception, is the global effect of their integration. The unfolding of the effect effectively guides the continuing of the wave's formation, as audience members follow its movement and fall in with it. The effect is felt, nonsensuously, in the register of affect. And it is felt as in some way beautiful. It is an aesthetic effect. The important processual point is that *the aesthetic effect of the wave is not separate from its formation*. That is to say, it is not separate from the *technique* by which the wave is composed (in this case, "entrainment"). Not only do the parts fuse into their whole, but *the aesthetic plane collapses into the activity of the formative field*. The point of collapse, where aesthetic effect and form-generation fuse, is on a par with the deployment of technique.

"Intricacy's visual sensibility emerges from technique rather than figuration or content."[72]

This entails a very different relationship of part to whole than the way it is usually conceived. The part–whole relationship is no longer a structural contrast. It is a contrast, but not between the parts as such and the structure of the whole they compose through their local, part-to-part functional connections. The contrast, rather, is between the singularity of the *detail* and the stand-out integral *effect*. But wait: "There are no details per se. Detail is everywhere, ubiquitously distributed and continuously variegated."[73] What is seen is the everywhereness of the variegation. It is the details' manner of coming-together nonlocally that is seen. It is the interfusion of details that is seen— their fusional multiplicity—rather than any structural contrast. The contrast between the details and the integral effect subsists, but *at the same time,* it disappears into the fusion-effect. This is what is meant by intricacy. As mentioned earlier, you see the overform of the wave at the price of unseeing its details. But the wave wouldn't be there if its details weren't proactively lending themselves to its appearance.[74] The local elements composing the wave are seen only in effect. However, they can reappear for themselves with a shift in attention, in a toggle from the plane of the effect to the plane of detail. There is a constitutive "*flicker* between discrete elements and smooth figural flow."[75] The integral perception of the wave envelops this flicker as its condition of emergence, blinking it out into its own surfacing. There is no deep structure to the wave. It consists entirely in its own effective surfacing.

These principles of intrication came together for the *Predator* art installation, a collaborative project between Lynn and the artist Fabian Marcaccio. Fusion was operative in several ways, feeding itself forward through the process, riding on technique. "Two disciplines," painting and architecture, "were digitally fused" into the flow of the installation's taking form.[76] The first step was the printing of a large-scale painting on a clear plastic sheet. Procedurally, this is the application of decoration to a surface. But processually, it goes beyond, toward the fusional, because the translucency of the sheets visually melds the color pattern with its substrate. A complexly curvilinear invaginating figure was then topologically designed. The folding of the figure on itself extruded a volume from the surface. Surface folded into structure, flatness folded out into volume, fusing the two dimensions into each other, completing the overcoming of decoration. The surface was then decomposed into over 250 sections. This was done to decrease the manufacturing costs of the final form by dividing it into segments that could be easily milled and handled. The design process flowed directly into the manufacturing process by means of CNC, as foam molds were milled from the digital files. The sections of painted sheet were then vacuum-heated to fuse to the form of the molds. The resulting figural elements could then be assembled into a concrete 3D construction of the topological figure of the installation. To say that the figure was "assembled" is inadequate. The fitting together of the figural elements did not just add up to a structure. "The interrelations between elements [became] intricate."[77] Beyond a structured aggregate of elements, this produced an interfusion: the "harmonic and dimensional interdependency of components one to another."[78] It is in this interdependency that the figure consists. The figure takes off from its concrete conditions of emergence into its own harmonically co-composed appearing, one with the mutual belonging to each other of its contributory elements, to collective effect. This is the final, perceptual fusion crowning the technical accomplishment of the form. The concrete figure doubles itself with an abstract surface embodying the intrication of its elements in the event of perception.

Traces of the manufacturing technique—the tool paths left by the milling—remained engrained in surface. These reactivated at the level of the perceptual figure's taking off into itself as additional factors of its formation. "The geometry of these tool paths is intricately related to the shape of the surface so that undulations in the pattern highlight and reflect the undulations in the form itself. In this manner an intensive decorative pattern emerges from the shape itself."[79] There is indeed a certain decorative dimension to the perceptual effect—a novelty in Lynn's work that came into effect with the *Predator* project and remained an ongoing interest from that point onward.[80] But this decorative dimension is "intensive": it inheres in the cohering of the elements. It cannot be separated from the effect of their inter-dependency. It does not stand as a discrete element that has been applied. It co-inheres, integrally in-folded, adding not a discrete feature but rather a holistic "highlighting." What it highlights is the effective relationality enveloped in the figure's fusional mul-tiplicity. The decorative perceptual effect here is not working for itself. It is doubling genesis, making the intricacy of its many-fusioned emergence felt.

Rather than an add-on, the decorative effect is an integral overexpression of the intensity of the relationality of the figure's matrixial genesis. If it "adds" anything, it is an overtone unfold-ing from the same in-folding constitutive of the figure as a whole. The decorative dimension is an extra-effect of the figure's inte-gral expression. What it highlights is the sense of the abstract surface's doubling of the concrete surface. It brings the figure's taking-off from its concrete conditions out further, abstractly extending the abstract surface into the space surrounding the concrete surface deployment of form. In a word, it adds "atmo-sphere": an affective expression expressing the expressiveness of the abstract surface, at once immanent to it and emanating from it. Affective atmosphere is what Walter Benjamin would call an "aura," or what Whitehead would call an "affective tonality."[81] It extends the expressed interfusion of the elements into a perfu-sion of the surrounding space. It is an aesthetic extra-effect, an affective emanation that some call beauty. It is not reducible to form, but rather adds to it an *epistratum*. It epistratically diffuses the intensity of the process of the emergence of form into the sur-rounding space. This adjoins to the concretized form an atmo-spheric associated milieu whose appearance is at once purely perceptual (an abstract surface) and at the same time inhabitable (spatializing; affectively aesthetically diffusing into a milieu that can be moved through).

The decorative effect of the machined tool paths is most wrapped up with color (yet another fusion). The process has returned, in processual analogy (as opposed to imitation and metaphor), to something that is found in "almost any plant or animal pattern," namely: "a correspondence between a change in surface and a change in pattern and texture. The pattern is neither simply projected nor applied, nor is it gridded and extrapolated.

The pattern and texture is intensive to the shape. This fusion of shape, color, and texture into a synthetic and mutually expressive continuity has been our ambition for the use of color and materials ever since."[82] This new extension of expressive continuity into a play between color and machine-tooled texture has been deployed in Lynn's work across the board at every scale, from the Alessi tea sets to the building complex of the Ark of the World (2002–3). The co-belonging of these projects to the same architectural matrix is betokened in the official name of the Alessi designs: the *Alessi Tea and Coffee Towers* (2003) and the *Alessi Coffee and Tea Piazza* (2000).[83]

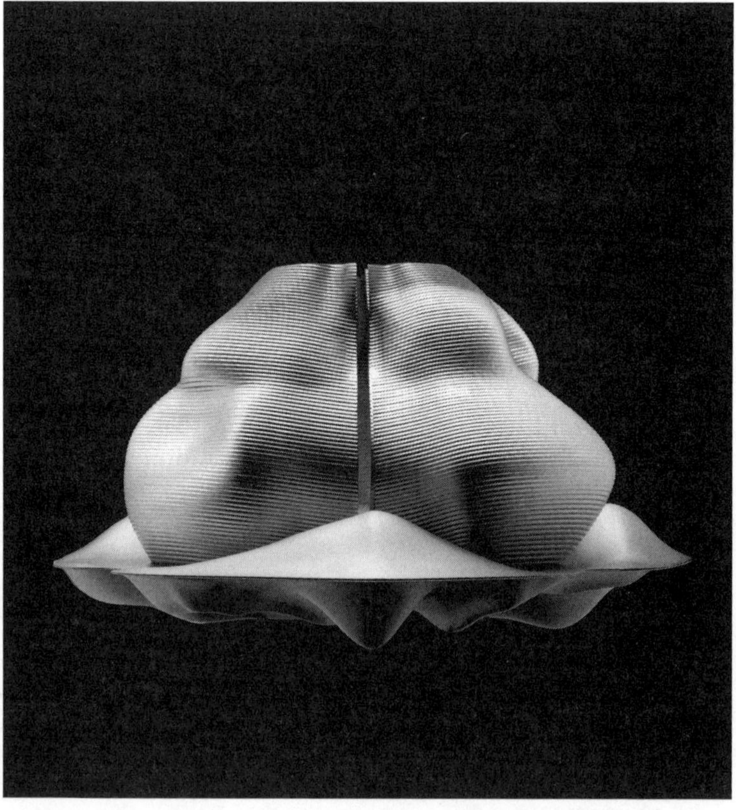

Alessi Tea and Coffee Towers, 2003. Combining color variation and machine tooling traces to produce surface intricacy effect, as in the *Predator* installation.

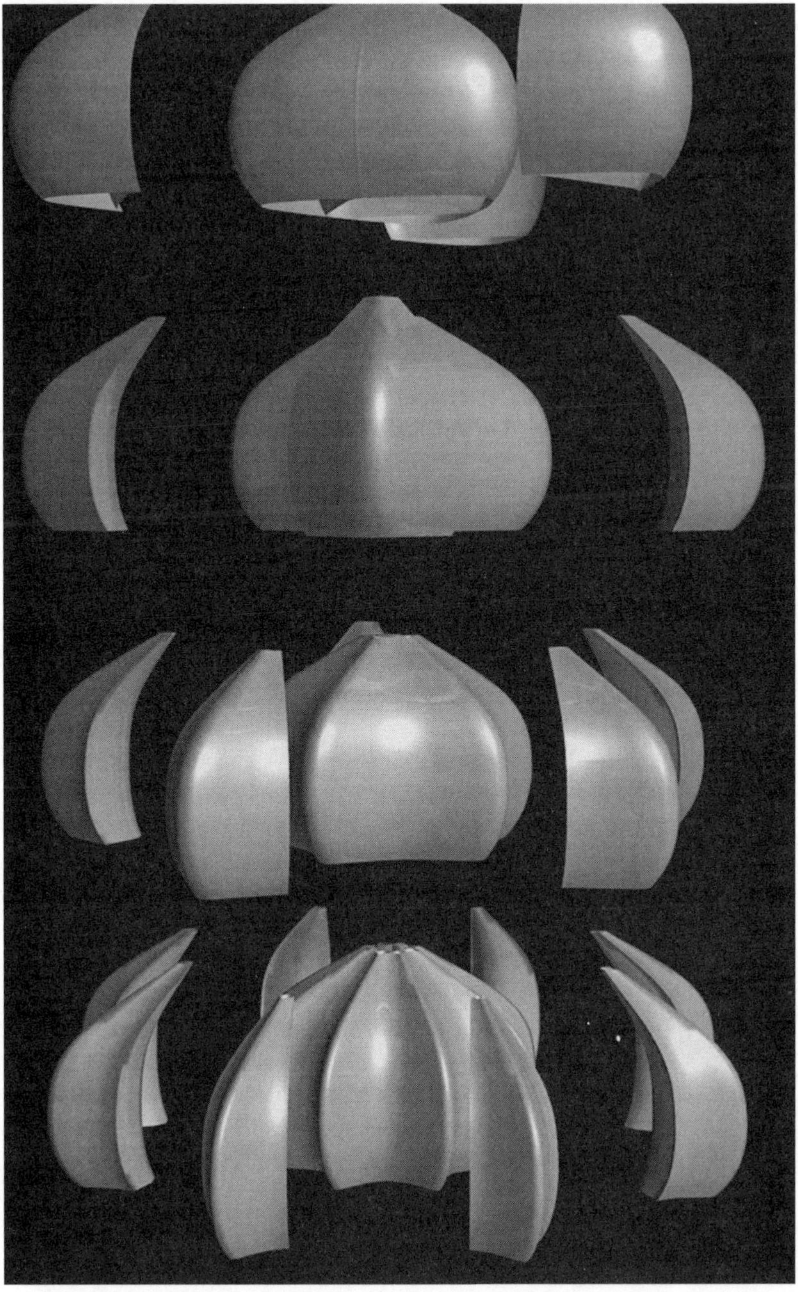

Alessi Coffee and Tea Piazza, 2000. Cluster of coffee and tea items of different size and geometry generated from a matrix of curves, using a similar technique as used for the composition of the *Predator* installation.

The extra-effect of affective atmosphere related to the use of color carries out its own function, of a sort. It operates as an *attractor*—not unlike the basins of attraction wooing the on-screen particle clouds of other projects. This is where the perceiving body, the individual body of inhabitation, reenters—in multiples. After all, this is an art installation, offered to the public for its passing inhabitation. Crowds cloud around. The perfusing of the surrounding space by the "decorative" affective effect creates a pull toward the figure as a whole. Pulled in toward the figure, the attention of the perceiving body flickers to the level of detail, bringing out the intricacy of the composing elements' interdependency—but momentarily losing the overall effect. The attention then flickers back to the figure as a whole, only to be lured by the next pull of the intricacy of the compositional activity of the details insisting on itself. This is also a flicker between the figure's concrete emplacement as the seat of detail, and the holistic diffusion-effect of the figure's affective filling of the surrounding space. The effect is a certain animatedness, in which the body of the visitor shares. The body is led, pulled on a flickering leash, into an ongoing oscillatory exploration of the figure. The body moves, around the figure and into its invaginations. In the course of this exploratory ambulation, the figure incrementally unfolds its integral expression in an improvised variation. This will occur differently for each individual body, creating something like a probability distribution, in part determined by the predilections and attentional habits of the attendant bodies. The figure's perceptual peaking will be composed and recomposed by the milling of the bodies. Through the crowd, the singularity of the figure forms its own multiplicity, any number of versionings of itself intricated in its public cohabitation.

An affective pull of this kind places the body in a mode where activity and passivity interfuse. Being lured is not a fully intentional act on the part of a subject. But neither is it a passive surrender. The body lends itself to its being led. It actively surrenders to it, in the form of following. The body takes the lead of its own attraction, following the lure. What ensues is a collaboration between the body's appetition and the figure's beckoning. Activity and passivity fall into a zone of indistinction. There is only one word for that zone: animatedness. Animate architecture

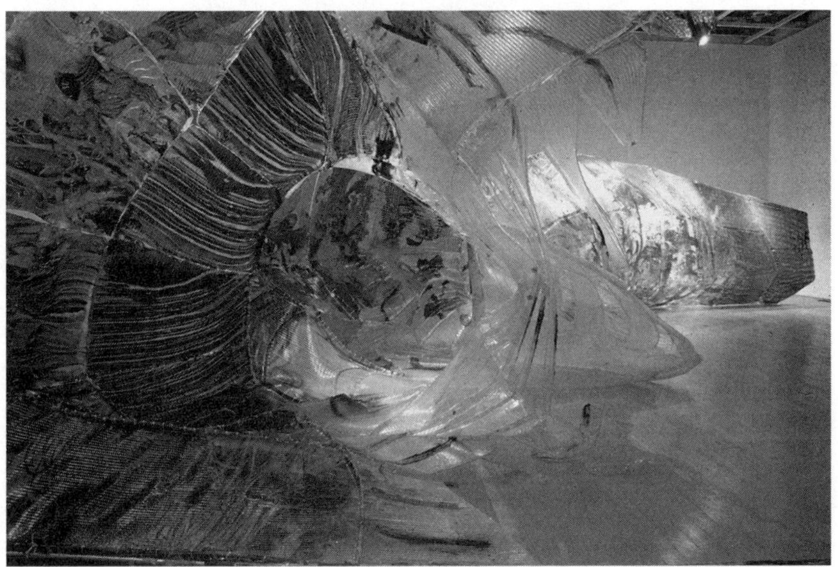

Predator. Greg Lynn and Fabian Marcaccio, 1999–2000.

doesn't have to make its constructions literally move, because even without them moving it can animate the body. The way this occurs requires, once again, rethinking what a body can be.

BODY-CURSOR

In the event, the body is acting as a flesh-and-blood cursor, incrementally refreshing the figure's integral appearing, adding a flickering variation to its expression. The body's movement coincides with the recomposition of the figure, in a live iteration. The moving body becomes one with the composition of the figure. The interfusion of activity and passivity conditions a transfusion between the body and the figure, as they operatively overlap in the zone of indistinction. The life of the body extends, through the medium of the affective atmosphere swaddling the figure, toward the concrete surface of the construction. The concrete surface describes the limit of the event: the point beyond which the body's extension does not penetrate, deflected instead into lateral movement following the topological spread of the figure's undulations. The figure, for its part, is reanimated—brought back to compositional life in a further iteration continuing its formation. This two-way movement of mutual extension is a transductive relation. The figure folds out into the life of the body, as the body's movement is infolded into the composition of the figure, becoming a formative force for its animate form.

Another way of putting this is that it amounts to the same thing to say that the concrete surface of the installation perceptually extends into the surrounding space to in-form an atmosphere of inhabitation, and that the body's movements come to indwell the abstract surface of the figure. The body is operating, *in the figure's furthered formation*, as a cursor refreshing its appearing. The body is figuring as a vector of the figure's actualization in a new variation. The figure's taking-off into its own integral appearance and the body's coming to it in perception are one. The body, its perception, its appetites, the movements they actuate, becomes intricated with the figure, operatively fused with it. In the final analysis, *there is but one abstract surface*, formed of the interfusion and transfusion occurring in the relational in-between described by the polar limits of the concrete surface of the construction and the film of the body. Perception is not in the body. It is not in a subject inhabiting the body. It is on the abstract surface, indwelling its reactualization. Perception is nothing more or less than a generative movement on an abstract surface that is one with its own appearing. *Perception is a surface effect*.[84] Even—perhaps even most intensively—when it extends itself into a surround.

As we learned with the stadium wave, the dynamic form of the transfusional surface effect can be considered with no exaggeration to *be* a body. *The abstract architectural surface itself is a nonhuman body*—an exemplar of what in his earlier work Lynn would have called an "inorganic body."[85] The concrete surface of the construction provides an enduring takeoff site for the iterative taking-form of ephemeral architectural-body effects. It becomes a storage site for the varying repetition of ephemeral body-events. The notion of dynamic form as involving the perceptual perfusion of the abstract surface in a transductive zone of interfusion was already implicit in the example of the stadium wave, through which the concept of the architectural body-event was developed earlier, as well as in the statement that blobs carrying on on-screen, in the unseemly manner to which they are accustomed, qualify as bodies. Manner is a key word. There are all manner of bodies, concrete or physical (bounded, volumetric, corpuscular) and noncorpuscular or abstract (superficial, energetic). There is an asymmetry in the "and." Physical bodies, as Simondon said, live at their limit:[86] where they peak onto an abstract surface whose matter is affect. In this sense, abstract-surface bodies can be said to envelop physical bodies, in affective wrapping.

Understanding perception as a function of the architectural surface provides the non-phenomenological approach to the body that Lynn's architectural design process requires. It allows the physical body and its perceptions to be reintegrated into the design process. But at the same time, it enables that reintegration to occur in what might seem an oddly peripheral manner, as a function of surface concerns. In Lynn's project descriptions, perceptual effects are mentioned with a nonchalance that seems to belie their integral contribution to the design process. Mention is made of their infolding into the topological variations populating the process, in the guise of virtual forces programmed into the generative field; as is their outfolding into a superficial taking-effect of that formative influence, defining the way in which the process continues into the built form (as described in relation to the Korean Presbyterian Church).

In Lynn's practice, techniques proliferate for the emergence of proto-architectural elements providing the taking-off points for architectural body-events that include as one of their dimensions affordances for the physical body. These result in non-standard fusions between architectural elements and types on the one hand (the *Room Vehicle* [2012] being the epitome),[87] and architectural surface and perceptual surface on the other. For example, the technique of finning returns in the *X-Ray Wall* shelving system that was Lynn's contribution to the 2000 Venice Biennale of Architecture. Here, the fin assemblage combines "varying modules" in a way that "integrates structure, envelope, and domestic landscape into a single system" composing an architectural-surface overgesture. "A single surface is responsible for structure, lighting, aperture, and spatial inflection" as "the striations of the CNC tool path [become] modulations of light, reflection, and translucency."[88] Many new geometric techniques are added to the menagerie of proto-forms, already populated by particle clouds, splines, and blobs, to multiply the potentials. "Blebs," for example, are curvilinear surfaces composed of networks of curves which sometimes whorl around one another to form pockets constituting proto-interiors.[89]

Even while the body and its movements continually resurface in the mention of things like lighting, aperture, and spatial inflection,[90] the concept of body is never again appealed to explicitly. And why should it be? Saying the word would just cause confusion. Inorganic, nonhuman bodies are difficult for organic, human bodies to wrap their heads around. Body talk would just bring phenomenological misunderstandings back in force. This is not a loss of the body, because surface talk implicitly includes both kinds of bodies: the inorganic nonhuman body that is the dynamic form of the architectural body-event, and the organic human body that serves as one of the conditioning limits, in transductive relation to the concrete surface of the event's construction. Talking about surfacing is just a shorthand for talking about bodying. Techniques for one are techniques for the other. Which means that the converse is true: speaking about the body is speaking about surfacing. "Dynamic form" is a handy synonym for this mutual inclusion. The term "embodied" cognition as applied to this is something of a misnomer. The "surfacing of experience" *as* a bodying would be the more accurate way to say it. When Spuybroek or Arakawa and Gins speak of the perceptual body in ways that suggest embodied cognition, they are figuring the body as a co-generator of emergent dynamic forms rather than as a receiver of already-constituted static forms. This is a way of speaking about the integral abstract surface of architectural becomings-body in other words.

RECURSIVE FILIATION AND OUTSIDE ALLIANCE

As earlier noted, Lynn's project for a processual architecture of animate, or dynamic, form erases the notion of the origin. The process is iterative, returning serially to the same generative matrix (most broadly, that of topological transformation,

as underwritten by differential calculus).[91] For each serial unfolding, forces of the outside are folded into the matrix, as in-
stantiated in the generative field as it composes for the coming
iteration. The differentials composing the field are disposed in
such a way as to energize the matrix with a certain vectorial orientation (toward the issuing into actions within a performance
envelope, or to put it more directly, remaining within certain
operational parameters). The in-folded forces thus fold back out
in proto-architectural form, to meet their cousins in the wider
world and interfuse with them (for example, patterns of urban
circulation in the Port Authority Bus Terminal project; valencies
of the landscape in the Long Island House; spiritual forces in
the Korean Presbyterian Church; appetitions of attention and
lurings of movement in *Predator*). It is in view of this encounter
that Lynn defines his project in terms of adventitious *alliance*
rather than in terms of filiation, with its reverence for origins.[92]

Architecture, it was argued earlier, is less a discipline than
an open field of practice formatively infolding foreign practices
belonging to any number of domains. Understood in this way,
the processual "generosity" of what was characterized earlier as
"affirmative" architecture consists in creatively *allying* itself with
other processes, and loving it—geometry, engineering, interior
design, and urbanism being the obvious candidates, but also the
dreaded client preference. Lynn's practices of alliance are particularly promiscuous, and increasingly so, spanning Hollywood
animation (from which he imported the topological software
tools that launched his process on its deformational way), installation art, graphic design, aerodynamics, sail design, and high-
performance vehicle design.

At any moment, the process can turn back on itself, fold
back in, and start over again, reenergizing the generative field for
a renewed iteration. Every stop is a potential return and recon-
tinuation. The generative matrix *accompanies* the process. It is
present potentially at every step of every run—requiring only a
cut to continue again, a stop to rebegin. This does qualify the
matrix as a certain kind of origin, but one whose nature is in
displacement: a *vagrant origin* that follows the movements of its
offspring like a wandering spirit—without actually going anywhere, because it is more that their process returns to its always

accompanying virtual ubiquity. Simondon solemnifies this kind of origin with the official moniker of "absolute origin."[93]

In its own way, this leads back to the idea of filiation. The successive iterations that spring from a recursive return to a generative matrix are processual siblings. An absolute origin expresses itself in *recursive filiation*. Lynn adopted recursive filiation in his Embryological House Project (1998–99). As it settled into his practice as a favored technique, he began to speak in terms of *families* of forms.[94] The siblings composing families of form come in litters. Rather than concentrating on one form and continuing its variation, the matrix is made to self-iterate right off the bat, running out batches.[95] A profusion of forms exfoliates in one iterative stroke, exploring large swathes of potential permutations. For the Embryological House, large numbers of permutants were produced.[96] Once the permutations are born, individual littermates that seem particularly proto-architecturally convivial to a wedding with forces of the outside (such as site conditions), and in a way favorable to the program, may then be remanded to a continuing topological evolution. Alliance cannot exist without some form of filiation, for the simple reason that it needs populating. There needs to be a generation of elements of

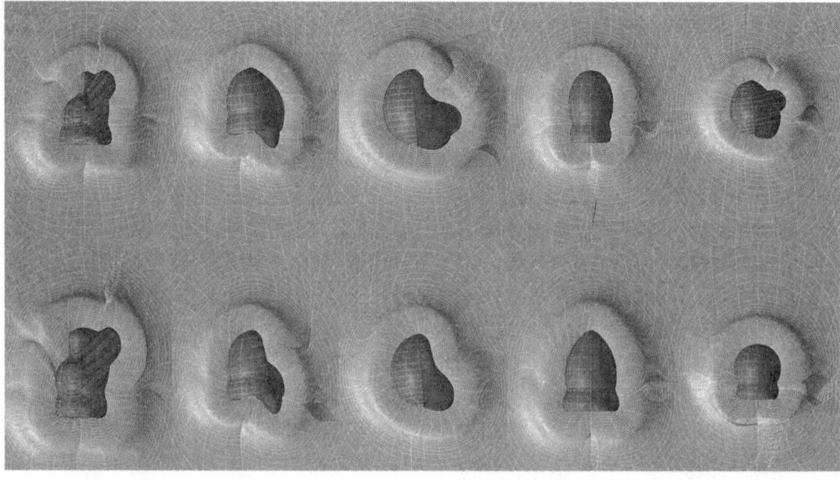

Recursive filiation: form by the batch. The Embryological House, 1998–99. Greg Lynn Form.

alliance. The absolute origin of recursive filiation is the form of filiation adequate to the generosity of outside alliance. It constitutes a movement of filiative *involution* conditioning the unfolding of the allianced evolution of forms.[97]

Proceeding in a family way brings with it a number of benefits for topological architecture. For one thing, it telescopes the concern with intricacy into the fundamental running of the process. "Details and components can be defined both individually and collectively at the same instance,"[98] such that there is "return of the whole and intensively defined part."[99] Here, the fusional flicker between part and whole that defined the experiential intensity of the *Predator* surface is fully integrated into the form-generating technique itself all along the line, rather than setting in at the end across the traces of the tooling. The unfolding of technique is less stratified here than in *Predator*, the cuts between its phases less sharp. Formation and perception, process and product, smooth together more, falling more into continuity with one another. In that sense, the expression of the process is more intense. Recursive filiation furthers intensive continuity.

A benefit is that this approach operationalizes *mass customization*. The streamlining of the technique overcomes the opposition between mass-production and custom-tailoring. This creates economies that take curvilinear design out of the architectural stratosphere and make it generally affordable. The direct feed-in to CNC milling is the great economizer. The end-forms can be sectioned, as was done with *Predator*, milled with CNC, and then assembled. This gives techniques predicated on topological continuity, not so long ago the province of the international architectural elite, the democratizing practical advantages of modularity. The CNC tool-paths may be used again, as in *Predator*, to crown the fusion of form-generation with atmospheric aesthetic effect. Because they share the same basic generational matrix, different projects can be promiscuous, coming together in a family way, across their differences.

All of this increases the robustness of topological architecture, and adapts it to contexts from which it was formerly excluded. Part of the motivation for the Embryological House was to provide the possibility of low-cost housing (including post-disaster emergency housing) that could be tailored to individual, cultural, or contextual variations without the cost premium usually associated with customization. In addition, the process can be scaled, applying these benefits across the spectrum of design, from small household objects to large buildings. Architecture fans out across the continuum of design.

BEYOND THE BLOB GUY: THE COMPOSITE PARADIGM

The result of this approach is a *streamlining* of architectural design, as the fusions and continuings-across discussed at many a turn in this account are telescoped into even greater processual solidarity. This streamlining accounts for the enormous range of Lynn's design activities, which have become so various that it is difficult to give them their due in an essay of this length. What might be mistaken for eclecticism is in fact a sign of increasing robustness, born of tighter cross-consistency among formative factors and techniques. The generalized focus on fusion is literalized as Lynn has moved toward the use of high-performance composite materials. These materials, used most notably in aeronautics and boat design, are *physically* produced through techniques of fusion. A whole new "composite paradigm" replaces the traditional tectonic paradigm.[100] The composite paradigm is characterized by "a shift from assemblage to fusion" in terms of the basic logic informing the process, down to the basic production of the materials in which the design will concretize itself.[101] With fusion, approached recursively, comes fissionability. Any element, form, or technique can become a reentry point into the form-generating process, providing a virtual infinity of angles of variational return to the accompanying origin, multiplying design flexibility manyfold.

The streamlining of the composite paradigm bifurcates in the opposite direction to the Embryological House, toward high-end products. High-performance design becomes another prong of Lynn's practice, integrated with the techniques enabling mass-customization but addressing a very different market. Fueled by fusion, Lynn's practice takes a turn toward the design of high-performance boats and a fascination with automobile and motorcycle design.[102] Never one for mutually exclusive variations, Lynn, the affirmative artisan of mutual inclusion, sees no contradiction in working both ends at the same time, as outgrowths of the same process—the high-end market of high-performance vehicles and the lower-cost end addressed by projects like the Embryological House.

Lynn explicitly marks the composite paradigm as a turning point, in self-critical terms that distance him from his "folding in architecture" persona of the 1990s. This is no doubt in large part to the enduring reputation as the blob guy that still dogs him in some quarters, despite the tremendous diversification of his design activities and techniques. It is not that he leaves behind any of his techniques, let alone topological architecture as a whole. He is a collector and cross-contaminator of techniques. The blobs melt into the crowd of proliferating techniques, but they don't necessarily disappear from use. Every technique is always in reserve, ready to recur. The concern for performance itself notably recurs to the boat hull discussed in *Animate Form*, whose form stores toggles between performance settings in its own form, as well as to the fins of the Korean Presbyterian Church.[103] The turn in Lynn's practice is not a renunciation of his curvy topological past. The self-critique concerns a specific processual strategy, rather than any set of techniques or the topological approach as such. That strategy is "form-finding."[104]

Form-finding is sometimes related to an adherence to a strong version of emergentism. It may involve the faith that the process, once virtual orienting forces are programmed in, will run all on its own, producing an end result that can just be cherry-picked by the designer. This is a bit of a caricature, but it expresses something about topological architecture: it can potentiate laziness. Lynn laments that it enabled "designers to pray, wait, invisibly guide, and/or filter the results hoping for a happy accident that might resemble a design decision."[105] This "unguided design" strategy gave topological architecture a bad name, leading to a stylistic monotony that many commentators have complained about. Designs can end up looking more like a curvaceous catalog of the special effects that a particular, recognizable software system can produce than a creative expression. High-performance design requires that the abstract virtual forces entering into the generative field be materialized in a concrete physical field, for example a wind tunnel in aeronautic design.

When Lynn criticizes the "unguided design" that he feels he himself fell for more than he should have, he is not advocating a return to the omniscient author, the architect as god of design. He is saying that the process must be tested by the outside physical forces to which its end result will have to answer: that it be guided more tightly by a recursive relation to outside force-fields, outfolding into them and integrating their guidance in return, as the form-generation narrows itself down to just the right performance envelope. In other words, he is advocating for a tighter integration between the design potentials of abstract and concrete forces, working in concert. Spuybroek, for his part, will make the strategic choice to embrace the form-finding approach, taking off from the work of Frei Otto. In Spuybroek's work, the exploration of intensive matter will ensure that his process does not fall into "unguided design." The back and forth between digital and analogue computing ensures the integration of abstract and concrete forces. Intensive matter is to Spuybroek what recursive filiation is to Lynn.

Lynn's love of high-performance vehicles—boats, cars, and motorcycles—is not a sideline. It is an integral expression of his architectural process, streamlining itself to the maximum. Looked at from another perspective, this can be seen as a taking of architecture to its limit. This is the point at which architecture has infolded its own outsides into its disciplinary "interior" so integrally that it can now easily stretch itself between a teapot and a BMW, in a self-stretching exercise in disciplinary yoga. The teapot, while not a traditional architectural object, can at least find a place inside an architecture. The high-performance vehicle takes to the road. Its curvaceous form hugs to the highway curves, wedding its movement to the topography. The high-performance bifurcation of Lynn's architectural practice sets architecture speeding into the landscape, careening toward parts unknown. It takes off on a *line of flight*, one integrally extruded by the architectural process's saturation with its own expressed potential. The line of flight is an ulterior limit to the process, immanent to its self-running. It expresses its furthest possible reach, like a pseudopod extruding a supple body into an exploratory tentacle, extending its performance envelope beyond its bounds.

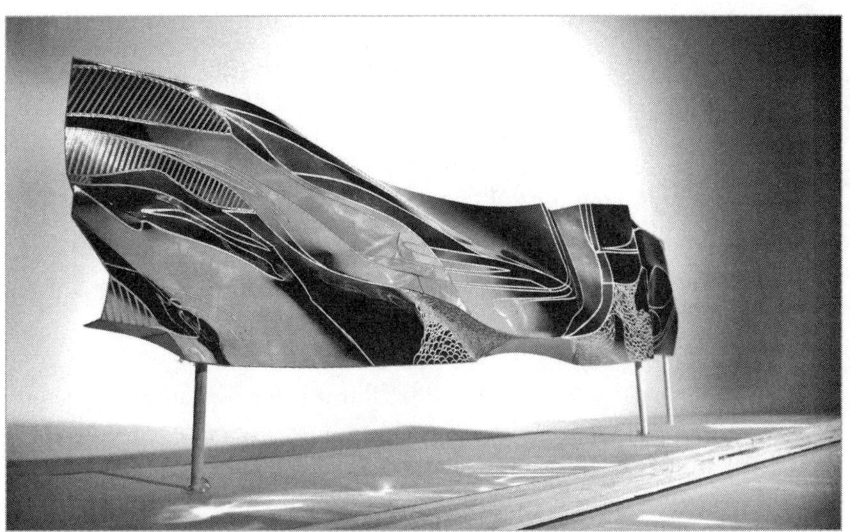

The architectural surface takes an automotive line of flight.
Façade study begun with vocabulary of automobile surfaces and pattern.
MW Design Headquarters Competition, 2007. Greg Lynn Form.

The limit can always be pushed further. The landscape is not the final frontier of architecture. It is only natural that affirmative architecture affirm the firmament beyond, launching itself toward the ultimate outside of outer space. Lynn's flirting with extraterrestrial design[106] and science-fiction writing[107] are no more sidelines than vehicle design, and are not mere flights of fancy. They are architecture performing its potential integrally out of bounds.

A FINAL QUESTION

A one-word question: politics? What I have termed the generosity of the openness of Lynn's process to outside formative forces, and its willingness to fold those forces in as processual collaborators, constitutes an ethics of design. But what of the politics of design? An ethics that mutually includes customizable low-cost housing and BMW design on an equal processual footing elides the question of politics. Must the politics come from outside, critically applied to design process and products? That would invalidate the entire premise of topological architecture, which is predicated on an integral becoming-immanent of any and all formative factors, co-composing toward the emergence of novel form. But where, in the process of topological architectural design, as conceptually shadowed in this philosophical retelling of it, does the political enter in as formative factor? Can the political not fold fusionally in, as the aesthetic did, so that it does not have to adjoin itself to the process extrinsically, as an external framing, imposed constraint, or outside judgment, and instead becomes active immanent to the process, as an orienting growth factor?

Lynn is silent on this question. But it is his own ideas of the body that might provide a starting point for an answer. Body-events are never neutral. They are never on an equal footing. Their manner of unfolding from the generative field continues across many an asperity. Their coming to expression straddles many an asymmetry. Most of all, the affective force of their taking integral effect distributes itself unevenly, in a tensional field riven by membranes and separatrixes. The open field of life into which the design process flows is, like the generative field of the design process itself, a differential field. In the field of life, the differentials between the design process's basins of attraction and repulsion recapitulate as differentials of economic and cultural access, and in different manners in which the follow-on effects can be further transduced: different degrees and kinds of capacitation or disenablement; different dispositions and tendencies. The affective force of the design effluviates into a complex landscape throughout which its effects are unequally distributed, and qualitatively vary. The transductive process cannot but continue on this, political, level. Iterate that. The topological design process owes it to itself to fold this dimension in to its foldings-out.

The reason why the foregoing account of Lynn's practice placed so much emphasis on the body, acknowledging that it explicitly falls out of the picture all the while charting the ways it continues silently to accompany the process, is that the body-event is the port of entry for the political. It is the threshold over which the always-already immanence of the political might be given a renewed processual welcome. Extending that welcome would amount to a significant transduction of Lynn's design process, adding a major twist to it that would deform its ethical performance envelope to extend its parameters.

Given the proto-formal level into which all the formative forces infold, the question then becomes: what constitutes a proto-political element of design process? How do our processual gardens grow political? The work of Rafael Lozano-Hemmer (chapter 2) has always explicitly integrated political factors. It has fashioned itself a "relational architecture" whose natural environment is the urban field, with due attention to its cultural and social gradients of power.

Relational Architecture

Rafael Lozano-Hemmer

STRETCHING THE BODY

TECHNO-SOLSTICE

Most times, my shadow hovers close, its tip a modest leap away. Not that I can reach it. It shies one step ahead. Although I can never catch up with it, I can easily reach where its end just was (where it now begins). It is perhaps for this that I have never lamented my shadow. I have never experienced it as a negative of my body, wraithlike symbol of a haunting absence to myself. It has always seemed to be just what it is: a projection. Not so much of my body's outline as its action. Its always beginning where my moving to catch up projects my action one step ahead of itself, in modest measure, on a scale with my body's everyday gestures. Rather than foreshadowing death, my shadow gives me a measure of my next human step. It casts my coming action in the world. It is the shape of my body in a future tense, penumbra of potential. My shadow comforts me. As long I fail to catch up with it, I know I am alive.

Today is winter solstice, and things are different. It is the day of the year when one's shadow is the longest. Standing in a meadow, my shadow stretches impossibly long, the full length of the field, far beyond my step. This gives me an uncanny sense of being drawn to the measure of a meadow, my coming action flattened and amplified to a stretch of grass. Now my shadow doesn't comfort me. It vegetates me. When I step and project a next stretch, I feel that it is the meadow that has grown in my motion. I take on the meadow's inhuman stretch, as the meadow takes on the future-cast of my animation. I am an ambulant spread of weed. I vegetate the world.

When Rafael Lozano-Hemmer projected amplified shadows of participant's bodies on the façade of a 350-year old arsenal in Graz (1997), he created a technological solstice stretching the measure of the human to the scale of what we can build.[1] When he programmed the shadows to disclose within their contours a live internet discussion on the concept of "Fear" involving participants from around the world, he solsticed us again, stretching our body-cast potential to the scale of what we can network at the scale of what we can build.

LOCAL–GLOBAL

Lozano-Hemmer titled this shadow work *Re:Positioning Fear* and named the interface *Tele-absence,* "defined as the technological acknowledgement of the impossibility of self transmission . . . the celebration of where and when the body is not."[2] If you think of the shadow in the way just suggested, as casting "absence" as a potential next action, the "where and when the body is not" becomes "where the body may relay," and "the impossibility of self transmission" becomes a reminder that every stretch of the body is not just a spatial displacement of it but a becoming. A body cannot transmit itself. But it can project its vitality. Its activity may take on new dimension. Seen in this way, "tele-absence" is perhaps not so different from "tele-embodiment," the term relayed into later work of Lozano-Hemmer.

In designating "tele-embodiment" as the desired effect of "relational architecture" Lozano-Hemmer is going against the grain of the commonsense idea of what a body is—as well as of the pronouncement of its loss which was the signature theme of the "cyberculture" of the 1980s and 1990s, which was the dominant context surrounding his work's beginning. In our everyday lives we tend to think of the body as an object. An object, we also tend to think, is all and only where it is. Just that. Our body, being all that it is where it is, locates our lives. Just there. It anchors us in the particularity of our life environment. Our own small, social world: it, too, takes on the inescapable weight of a heavy object. To the cyberpunk aesthetic, this weighing down in the body-local was tantamount to imprisonment. The fantasy of

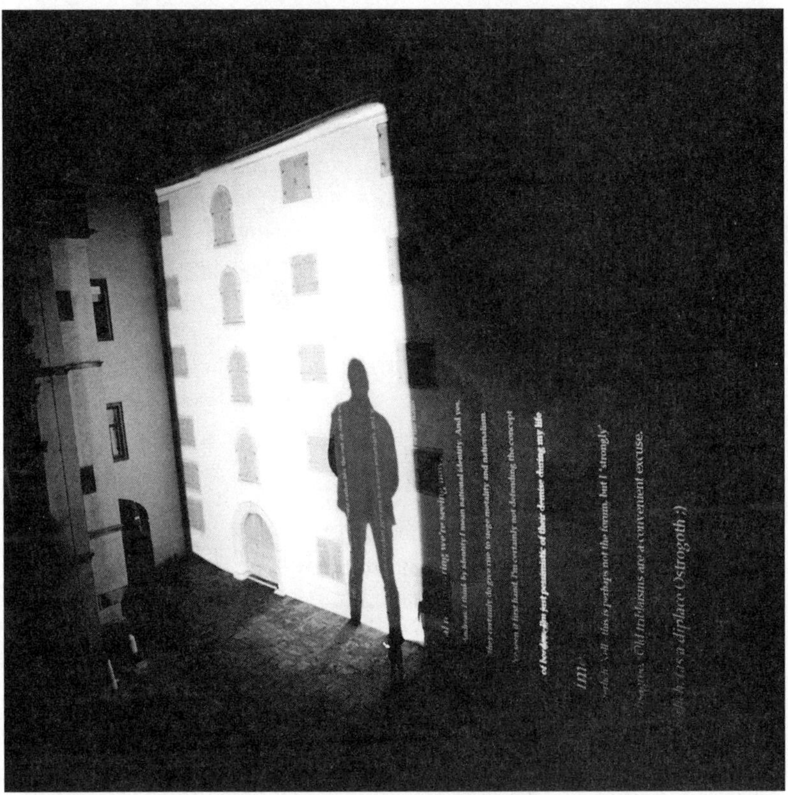

The body stretched to the scale of what we can build. Rafael Lozano-Hemmer, *Re:Positioning Fear. Relational Architecture No. 3*, 1997. Landeszeughaus, Architecture and Media Biennale, Graz, Austria. Photograph by Joerg Mohr.

jacking oneself into the computer offered a vision of liberation from the body and its weighty social contexts. Dematerialization. The "loss" was alternately celebrated and lamented.

Lozano-Hemmer is quite clear. The absenting of the body was never what was at stake in his work. It is not the body that is dematerialized but the "environment."[3] This changes the very meaning of "local." It also means something very close to another formula he is fond of: "the object becomes performance." Relational architecture takes the body to be what it performs. What it performs in this work is extending connection to out-of-scale activity, where the body and its object merge in extended vitality.

Not even the environment is "dematerialized" in the sense in which cyberpunk wished to dematerialize the body. It is not lost, or left behind. All of Lozano-Hemmer's work takes great pains to bring local historical and social determinations into the performance. But it does this in order to connect them to "alien memories" which concern the site but are uncontainable within its confines. The internet discussion appearing on the Graz Landeszeughaus used the building to connect the forgotten medieval fears of plague and threatened invasion to contemporary fears of a different order and magnitude. These are "decentered, distributed phenomena or syndromes" that are difficult to attribute to a single cause (God's wrath, the invading Turks), attaching instead to elusive risk factors that can only be grasped statistically. They operate at the extremes of scale: at microscopic levels below the threshold of the human (AIDS, genetic modification) or at a planetary level beyond the control of the State, the largest "local" level of human organization (global warming, transnational migration).[4] Risk is in a mode of futurity. It hangs over the moment without ever surrendering itself to it, ever-present alien. It is an impending you cannot forget: an alien "memory" of the future. In *Tele-absence,* contemporary modes of fear connect across the façade of the building with their historical counterparts: memories of the past, alien by forgetting. Forgetting, not being able to forget; the historical past of the present and the ever-present statistical future; the below and the above of the human scale; the medieval arsenal and the postmodern State . . . These connect with each other and with the everyday movements of the body acting in measure with itself, on the ground before the façade *and* amplified on it, projected into direct connection with the monumental scale of the built and the immeasurably proliferating worldwide network.

What is "dematerialized" are the limits of the local (its limitation to being all and only what it is). The local features in the performance from the angle of what passes through it: a sweep of times and a zoom of spaces for which the specificity of the site is a way station. The confines of the local open, without the locale disappearing. The status of the site changes. It features as a node in larger, global movements connecting through it with each other and the body.

It is for this reason that Lozano-Hemmer will say that he does not create site-specific installations but rather that he stages

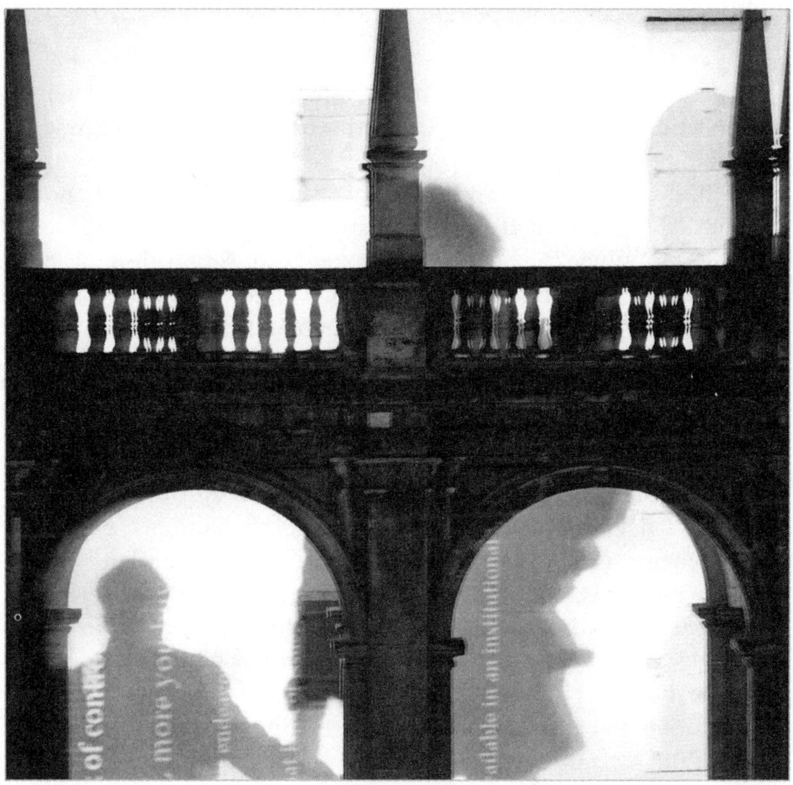

Rafael Lozano-Hemmer, *Re:Positioning Fear. Relational Architecture No. 3*, 1997. Landeszeughaus, Architecture and Media Biennale, Graz, Austria. Photograph by Joerg Mohr.

"relationship-specific" interventions. To say that the environment is dematerialized is to say that it is programmed to host an event of bringing-into-alien-relation.

DISTANCING THE BODY

"Tele-" means "distance." To "tele-embody" is not to distance oneself *from* the body—as if a residual self would remain, detached from the vitality of the body. To "tele-embody" is to *embody distances*, thereby augmenting the body's vitality. It is to impregnate the human body with dimensions of action and movement below and beyond what it takes to be its own proper limits.

This is not a metaphor. It is only the commonsense idea that the body is an object, with the accompanying, reductive belief that an object is single and "site-specific" (only what and where it is) rather than serial and relationship-specific (all the inter-connections it can go into) that prevents us from taking tele-embodiment literally.

The most cursory investigation reveals that a body is not where it is but *how it moves*. A still body is not one. Albert Michotte: "When the body is motionless . . . it simply disappears from the phenomenal world. . . . Movement appears to be essential to the phenomenal existence of the body."[5] The body is one only with its movements—which are on a continuum with its sensations and perceptions. The body is what it performs.

Henri Bergson pointed out that our perceptions are virtual actions. What we see, for example, is already a potential next touch or sight or step. "It is important to keep in mind that the *tendency* to respond determines the perception," a later researcher reminds us.[6] The body is more in the tending-toward than where it is. Vitally, the body exists more in the next step than the one it is now taking, and the step to come envelops the life's momentum of the countless past steps preparatory to it. The body, in movement, is always "more-than-one."[7] This means that the body's effective "shape" and "size" continually vary as its perceptions change in mode, scale, direction, and resolution. In its tendings, Michotte writes,

> the body appears as a somewhat shapeless mass or volume. There is very little by way of internal organization or connection between the parts. . . . Instead of any precise line of demarcation we find a number of regions with extensive connections between them gradually merging into one another. We can with some justification look on the body as a sort of *kinesthetic amoeba*, a perpetually changing mass with loose connections between the parts, and with the limbs constituting the pseudopodia. . . . The "volume" of which the body consists is not limited by a clearly defined surface, and there is no "contour." . . . It necessarily follows that the *whole* of the kinesthetic field of bodily sensations is filled by the body. . . . *There can be no question of any distinction between figure and ground.* . . . The limit of the body is like the limit of the visual field—an imprecise frontier with no line of demarcation.[8]

The theoretical implications of this account of the phenomenal reality of the body are enormous—not least, as we will
see, for the way it extends the body beyond its phenomenal
appearance. For present purposes, it is enough to remark that
work like Lozano-Hemmer's addresses itself to the "kinesthetic
amoeba." Projecting the shadow of a participant's movements
onto a façade creates an eerie kinesthetic feeling *on the wall*. If
the body's feeling fills the whole of the kinesthetic field, then the
body stretches *onto the wall*, where the eeriness is. "Not limited by a clearly defined surface," tendentially unconfined by the
"contour" of the skin, it is free to stretch its limits to the built
surface. There, its amoebically extended movements mix with
others' words. Through the words, local concerns of participants
in Graz and across the globe, along with alien memories past and
future, expressing a plethora of similarly telescoping tendings,
fall within the body's amplified field. On the wall, the body's
"volume" merges movingly, verbosely into other tendings. No
assignable boundary between figure and ground, just a surface of
tendential fusion. What is "performed," literally, is the creation
of a collective body, in pseudopod fusion, like microbe sex (with
words for genes).

I microbe the world (and the world microbes me).

What fun is a meadow anyway?

The pseudopod is a better model of the technological supple-
mentation of the human body than the old cybercultural model
of the "prosthesis." The active fusion of microbe sex is a better
model for the more-than-one of the technologically augmented
human than the representational confusion of "simulation"
(another ubiquitous theme of the 1980s and 1990s).[9]

THE AMOEBIC REALITY OF RELATION

The word "fusion" requires another vocabulary check. Digital media are commonly spoken of in terms of "connectivity."
Michotte says that the tending body is without specific organization and *without connection*. Without connection: for all the
more connectability. At each step a body reconnects differently
with the world. With each connection, it modifies its posture
toward the world, inflecting its tendings, adding memories and
impendings, modulating its capacities and desires, stretching
itself across a different range of dimensions, remixing in live

performance a varying selection of the available registers of life activity. Moment to moment, it reorganizes its living in the world. It becomes through its reorganizations. The reality of the body, at any given moment, is defined by the potential to make a next connection differently. This potential carries *across* the connections, in-forming each, in its incipiency, with the tendency a next step is coming to express. The body is without any specifiable order of connections, because at each one it is amoebically astraddle any number of them, extending-through into its own potential.

The body is thus more-than its connective organization at any given moment. It carries through its movements a surplus "charge" of organization to come. At any given moment, the body is more-than any particular connection it is in the process of making, and it is even more-than the sum total of the connections it has made. A body is also the surplus charge of coming connection it carries forward. To say that the phenomenal body has no particular organization and is without connection is to say that it exceeds its own phenomenal existence. In the about-to-come of each moment, in each gestating tendency, the body is its own dynamic *openness* to new connection and reorganization. It is its own *capacitation* for what's coming. In its dynamic openness and as its capacitation, the body's potential organizations and connections are all immediately present to *each other*, mutually included in the moment's gestation. They are integrally fused in the intensity of the tending just now taking individual shape as the determinate step it soon will have been. The fusional intensity is integrally felt. Since that feeling envelops, more or less vaguely, what is not present (present only in potential), it couches the body in abstract realms of its own extension, in a more-than of its phenomenal appearance. The kinesthetic amoeba is the phenomenal body integrally self-abstracting, ahead of itself, at a potential distance from where and what it is. Here, it surfaces across the architectural façade, become interface, in a becoming-body event of the kind discussed in chapter 1.

It would be a mistake to equate this fusional intensity with a "feeling" in any sense we might be tempted to qualify with the word "mere." It is not a mere feeling, as in mere subjective impression or a mere fantasy. These "meres" connote irreality. The charging of the moment with an integral life potential is not only real. It is the body's charge *of* reality: surplus reality. Not mere, more: a reality of the more-than of one's embodied self in movement and becoming. More wrapped up in feeling than can be merely felt.

Simondon calls this the body's charge of "preindividual reality."[10] "Infraindividual" is even better because Simondon's "pre-" is not a marker of chronological order. The surplus charge of becoming *accompanies* each step's performance, and feeds forward across the stepped series it helps compose. The preindividual is less a separate instant in a linear chronology than an accompanying dimension of reality's formation internal to each's moment's coming to be. The body continually folds fusionally back into the infraindividual dimension of its dynamic reality *at the same time* as its life's steps stretch out into the individuality of their occurring. This process doubles the phenomenal body with the dynamic form of its becoming.

As Simondon indicates, it is more precise to think of this topologically—in terms of stretching-folding for variation—than chronologically.[11] Think amoeba, stretching-folding, in ongoing variation. Think pseudopods formatively stretching forth then folding back to dissolve again toward the formation of a next step, the dynamic contours of a life's activity morphing from moment to moment, from step to changing step, recapacitating, reorganizing, reconnecting. *Re:Positioning.* Think telescopings between scales, surfaces, and registers of activity. Think the body shadow-stretching onto the surface of a building, really-not-merely feeling its potential kinesthetically fill with words and mate with their extending potential. Think Graz and plague. Think now, then, and again. Think memories of the past and alien memories of the future, immediately present to each other.

The kinesthetic amoeba is the reality of the body's performative, reformative folding into the stretch of its potential. The word *relation* is better for this than connection. The kinesthetic amoeba is the body's relation to its own potential's performative playing-out: dynamic self-relation, in it for the stretch. The specific connections the body enters into selectively *express* the ongoing of potential, enveloped in the determinate shape of a taken step. With each move, the body's self-relation extends itself down its path through the world. The dynamic self-relation

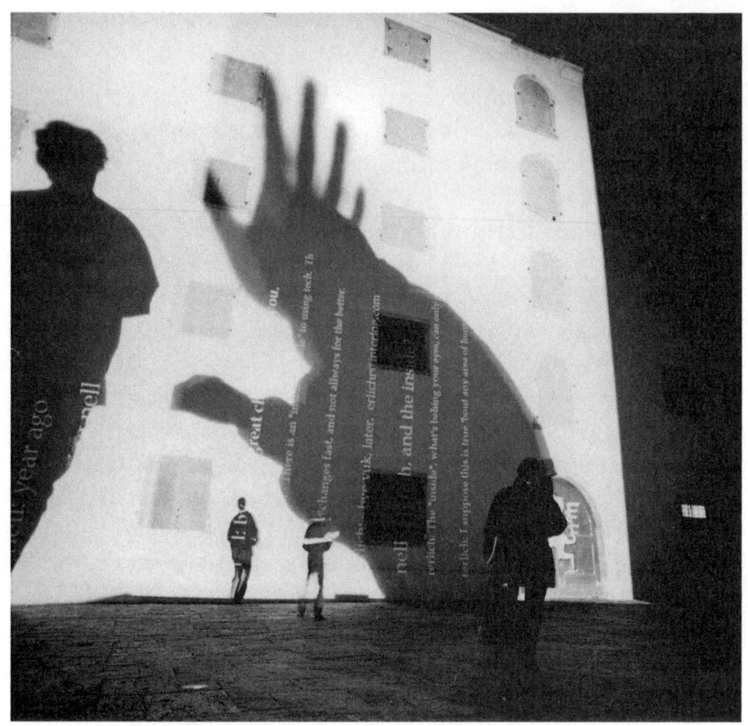

Rafael Lozano-Hemmer, *Re:Positioning Fear. Relational Architecture No. 3*, 1997. Landeszeughaus, Architecture and Media Biennale, Graz, Austria. Photograph by Joerg Mohr.

is, in addition, at same time and in the same act, a relation of the body's potential to its extensive expression, pseudopodically afoot in the world. No "mere" here. If anything, a doubly real: relation of relation. Integral self-relation extending into relations between discrete steps in a performative, reformative world of proliferating paths.

CITY OF WORDS

M. M. Bakhtin: "The components of the aesthetic object of the given work are 'the city's wide and silent streets,' 'the shadow of night,' 'the scroll of memory,' etc., but not the visual representations, not the psychic experiences in general, and *not the words*."[12]

There is a misunderstanding of words similar to the misunderstanding of the body as an object. It is the belief that words are inert, general reflections of "psychic experiences," cognitions or cogitations, which they would represent in the way a visual image is said (equally erroneously) to represent an object or a body. Bakhtin, however, is clear: it is not the "linguistic form" or its reflective content that "enters the aesthetic object" (which in Bakhtin's account is in point of fact always a *performance*). Rather, what enters the artistic work is the singular "*emotional–volitional moment* corresponding to that form": the eventful reality of the embodiable tendencies, with their attendant affect-abilities, that the words present (integrally reactivate and selectively trigger).

Performatively speaking, words do not represent visual perceptions or reflect general ideas associated with them. Words *are* perceptions, of a very special kind. A most striking demonstration of this is provided by the phenomenon of blindsight. People with blindsight have been shown to see unconsciously. For example, patients will not be able to see a cup on the table in front of them, but if asked to pick it up will do so without missing a beat. They retain the ability of vision to relay into a next step. They have the "nextness" dimension of visual perception without the visual perception. This is particularly telling when patients are shown words on flash cards. The follow-up step reveals that they not only see the words without seeing them— they *read* them without seeing them.[13] Patients are often only blindsighted in one area of their visual field. If their field of sight is shown a word with more than one meaning, like "bank," and their blindsight spot is shown another word reducing the ambiguity, like "money" or "river," their direct understanding of the perceived word will be *modulated* by the blindseen card. Their next response is *oriented* one way or the other. This suggests that there is a dimension of word use that imparts orientation or tendency-to in *immediate* perception—so immediate it needn't even register in feeling otherwise than in its effects.

This "priming," or subthreshold modulation, is very much a part of "normal" perception as well. Blindsight only provides a dramatic illustration of a process native to perception. There is a temporal blindsight at the heart of vision. The "attentional gap" is a hiatus of a fraction of a second after the cresting of a conscious awareness and the rising of the next to replace it. Micro-events occurring in the gap do not register consciously, but as in blindsight they orient what comes. For example, a written word shown so quickly that it falls into the attentional gap will not be remembered. But its affective tenor will register (whether its valence was "positive" or "negative").[14] This orienting effect also occurs with events on the periphery of attention, which might have registered consciously had the focus been there. The modulation even co-occurs with conscious awareness, without the effect itself being perceived. In these cases, the orienting is like a spin affecting an otherwise conscious activity unawares. Laboratory subjects exposed to a sentence containing the words "Florida" and "bingo," for example, experienced word-induced premature aging: they walked away from the laboratory building at a rate 15 percent slower than control subjects.[15] Affective toning/action inflection: "emotional–volitional." The emotional–volitional moment of language occurs in immediate, fusional proximity with extra-linguistic dimensions of experience that "blindly," bodily, inhabit its performance, and to which it owes an effective orientation. It is these dimensions which give language its immediate *force* for existence: a direct life-altering power.

Out of the laboratory, in a less controlled, more richly multi-sensory situation, language's force for existence—the immediate word-borne coloring of nextness—is multiplied, complexified, and varied. The range of what may spin forth expands indefinitely. The tendency imparted by words heard or seen, or even unheard and unseen, may be as readily a kinesthetic event of altered pace as a lexical association. It can be a predisposition to touch, as easily as an inflection of affective valence. And— why not?—the triggered tendency might be toward the dawning of a new idea, spun of a suggestive complexity of inter-register experience, rather than the tired acting out of a time-wrinkled stereotype. Bingo!

Words inhabit perception (as perception is inhabited by action).

MATERIAL QUALITY OF THOUGHT

The direct inhabitation of action-perception by words has enormous consequences. For interactive art, it means that text can be an immediate ingredient of the *performance as such*. The presence of text does not necessarily "mediate" experience. This significantly expands the parameters of performance and the field of relation—to the limits of language (and its inter-register gregariousness). In a very real sense, words activate their "content" as an ingredient in the interaction. Just without the actual content (tendentially).

In Whitehead's words, the direct hit, or "presentational immediacy," of a word "precipitates feelings" which "enhance"—add a modulation to—the event taking place.[16] Peirce calls these precipitate feelings the "material quality" of the experience: feeling in motion, at the "first beginning of a cognition."[17] "Corresponding to every feeling within us," Peirce observes, "some motion takes place in our bodies."[18] The inaugural feeling-motion is pluripotent. In its qualitative aspect, it is the *suchness* of the experience: its affective tonality ("how it feels").[19] The quality is "material" in an energetic sense: a suchness stirring toward an issue in action and perception. Just now, in this very "first beginning" of the experience coming, it has yet to go anywhere or do anything definite. The material suchness of the feeling-motion is the "substance," or "immediate object," of the nascent experience.[20] Its substantive stirring-*toward* makes it the *sign* of the coming action-perception. Whose occurrence it helps effect. Affect. Inflect. Strange emotional-volitional "substance," this. It would be better to call it an "element," with something of the sense we give the word when we use the phrase "the elements" to refer to weather: a sense of qualitatively changing conditions that are unmistakably material but lack the separate thingness we associate with substance. Like the weather, there is an elusiveness to the material quality of nascent experience, even in the insistence of its stirring-toward. The sign's passing into action-perception unawares, in the just-before of the coming experience, gives its inaugural effectiveness the abstractness of a thought. The material quality of the dawning event is indissociably a thought and a sign: a *thought-sign*.[21] The thought-sign as material quality: the body in its element.

The strangest thing: "it is not essentially necessary" that the inaugural feeling-motion of the material quality of experience's coming be "felt in order for there to be a thought-sign."[22]

Felt without actually being felt, thoughtfully passing unawares; directly lived but registering only on the level of its effect; just-beginning what is going on, as yet undone; blinked forward into life's nextness; materially operative, unappearing . . .

What it all adds up to is a *real but abstract bodily experience.* Material quality is where thought and body really come together, at the just-stirring again of the "animal body" tending as yet abstractly toward a next-inflected amoebic stretch.[23]

A further major consequence: this *forbids any distinction between "raw" experience and encultured experience*—as it does any empirical distinction between the physical or physiological on the one side and the cognitive on the other. Cultural factors associated with "higher" cognitive operations are already materially entering into effect in the attentional gap, in whose inaugural stir they are as already-abstract as they are still-bodily. The feeling-motions of the material quality of coming experience agitate in a zone of indistinction between body and thought.

Bergson calls these not-quite-yet felt feelings-motions "nascent actions."[24] Bergson's term emphasizes the next bodily step, and its kinesthetic relay out of the zone of indistinction into spun-out movement perceptibly registering. Another term, borrowed from William James, is "bare activity."[25] This term emphasizes that experience, in the first flush of its activating as a material quality or thought-sign, is only now barely there. Whitehead, for his part, emphasizes the inaugural abstractness of the barely-there of experience—"it is gone, and yet it is here"—with the term "nonsensuous perceptions."[26] Nonsensuous perceptions are what "energize" the immediate past for the immediate future.[27] It is this unfelt engine of experience kick-starting itself into continued operation that contemporary experimental psychology talks about in terms of priming.[28] Plain old "tendency" has the advantage of holding together in a single familiar term the feeling just-beginning with the already-in-motion of the action coming performatively to express it.

Whatever we call these "thought-signs," Lozano-Hemmer's work cues them into action-perception. His work *operationalizes the material quality of words.* It works to activate language *in enactive relation with nonlinguistic registers* of experience. First and foremost, comes the kinesthetic: stirring. Agitating: already tending toward a next step, and a touch it may potentiate. Through touch, proceeding stepwise toward a renewal through movement of the field of vision. Operationalizing the material quality of words not only activates language in enactive relation to nonlinguistic registers—it anticipatorily activates those modalities' relation to each other, in a stirring no-distinction between "raw" experience and enculturated experience. This bare-active "no distinction" is not the opposite of a determination. Remember: it is the tendency that *determines*. What is at issue is determination's pluripotent dawning across registers. Astretch a façade.

INFRAPHENOMENAL

Yet another terminological option would be to call thought-signs the "virtual reality" of the life of the body. It wouldn't be the best option. The term still suffers from the legacy of 1980s/1990s cyberculture vocabulary, for which "virtual" was a synonym for "artificial" and "illusory," in the sense of standing at a mediated remove from reality, in simulation of it. Material qualities pertain to immediately real yet abstract body events. They are fully and directly real.

Simondon, it was mentioned, dubbed the reality of this dimension of experience self-renewing "preindividual." The term "infraindividual" was suggested as a substitute to emphasize that the strange time signature of its elusively effective reality sidesteps the psychological time of the individual whose life's unfolding it tendentially determines. The emotional–volitional reality of the material qualities which are the thought-signs priming life now, for-next, is *not psychological*. More radically, it is *not phenomenal*. So immediate it is that it does not appear: here yet gone.

Material qualities fast-forward themselves into what comes. As operative thought-signs, they inhabit the phenomenal gaps, in precipitate nextness. The life of what Michotte calls the "phenomenal body" is the issue of nonphenomenal gap events: *virtual events* occurring in the attentional off-beat of experience, appearing only in and as the modulatory effects they precipitate. These gap-events are no less real, no less bodily, no less operative, no less tendentially determining, for passing actually unfelt. The scalar plasticity of the proteiform "kinesthetic amoeba" Michotte describes marks the phenomenal *limit* of the life of the body. The thought-signs, the material qualities, from which the kinesthetic amoeba's next stretch pluripotently emerges belong to a nonconscious dimension of *already-not-quite* experience stirring. Experience never quite goes there. It is always already issuing *from* there, into itself, across a constitutive gap. The virtual events occurring in the gap are not only infraindividual, they are *infraphenomenal*: effectively unappearing; appearing only in effect. The infraphenomenal is the constitutive limit of life where *body is event*: where the life of the body is integrally absorbed in the already virtually occurring of what is coming to pass.

It is this infraphenomenal reality, where language in immediate relation with its outside, that gives words the immediate power to "enhance" the life of the body.

"The city's wide and silent streets." Consider yourself urbanly enhanced.

"The shadow of the night." Consider yourself infraphenomenally solsticed.

A PROMISCUITY OF LEVELS

Levels of action and perception don't just connect. They mate. The stoking of nascent action-perceptions by words is not an external connection, mediated by an interface, between distinct levels of organization and registers of experience. It is an immediate fusion of them, in infra-relation: the activation of a zone of indistinction between them. They merge into one another, share and exchange tendential properties in a kind of cultural meiosis, then reemerge, each to its own level, at a next unfolding. The levels accordion into one another, then telescope back out at the next beat. Their distinction is rhythmically reborn, step after step, next after last. Like every birth process, this rhythm of reappearance carries the potential for mutation.

Lozano-Hemmer's early work is designed to supercharge the zone of indistinction. It often primes with words, as in *Re:Positioning Fear*. But it also sets mechanisms in place to ensure that the orientation is not only from the words into action (for example, from the words of the online discussion into the action of shadow-scanning a next phrase, or turning to a fellow participant to continue conversation on the ground). The shadow interface in *Re:Positioning Fear* fuses a perception of actual bodily movement with the presentation of words in a multidirectional mating of levels. When a text is read with shadow,

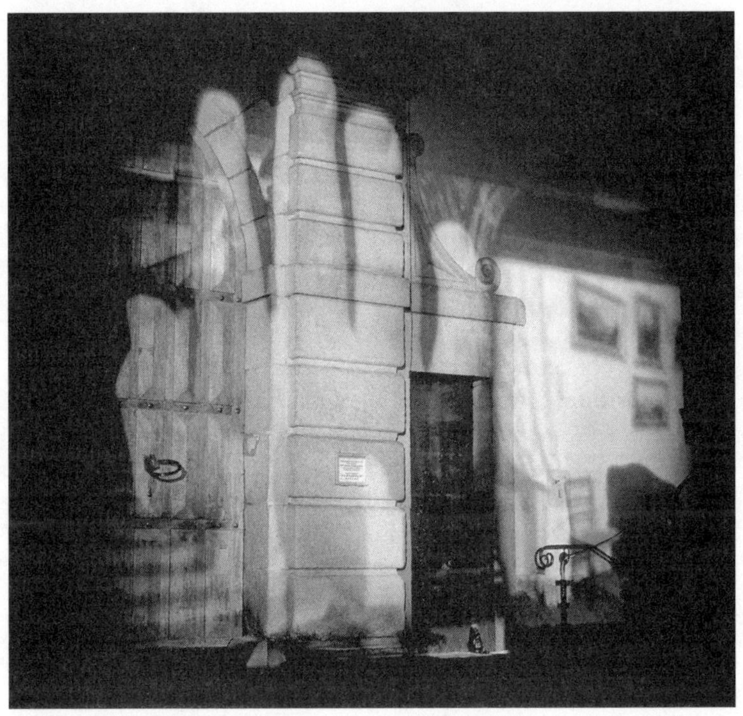

Rafael Lozano-Hemmer, *Displaced Emperors, Relational Architecture No. 2*, 1997. Habsburg Castle, Ars Electronica Festival, Linz, Austria. Photograph by Antimodular Research.

as the body stretches to touch a façade with a kinesthesia of word-scanning movement, the registers of experience dance a virtual event, activating each other with pluripotent excess. The experience doesn't just go from the nonsensuous feeling-motion of the virtual event to an actualization in sensuous perception. Even as the stretch to a next is under way, experience is already retracting into its zone of germinal indistinction. The last step orients the material quality's orienting of the next on the fly, telescoping the accordioning-out back-infra, in a lasting of next-ness. The mating runs as fluently relationally from actual action-perception, experienced in any dominant modality, back into the virtual-event zone of incipient action, as from that zone into determinate action and the accompanying sensuous perceptions. The multimedia format allows an intensification of the mutual meiotic inhabitation of levels of existence by one another, as they fold eventfully into and out of one another.

CHANGEABILITY

Potential for mutation: that's the point. Lozano-Hemmer's work plays on this multidirectional, pluripotent meiotic fusing of levels of reality to make felt the potential for change. There is no particular political program advanced. The work is not "political" in the sense of sending a specific message or militating for a particular ideology. At the same time, political issues and problems of urbanism are insistently brought into play, becoming part of the concept design of each event.

Re:Positioning Fear: Relational Architecture No. 3, as well as *Displaced Emperors: Relational Architecture No. 2* (Linz, 1997) and *Vectorial Elevation: Relational Architecture No. 4* (Mexico City, 1999), stage aspects of colonialism. The choice of prominent architectural monuments as intervention sites reflects a desire to reinject a breath of collective life back into what Emilio López-Galiacho calls "vampire buildings," buildings shielded from change by "necrophiliac" heritage protection measures that treat society and culture as collectibles.[29] Nowhere, however, is a solution suggested. The work is only incipiently political: proto-political. It doesn't propagandize, instruct, or consciousness-raise. More elusively, it concerns only the *potential* for change. It makes the potential for change palpable by programming a surface of multidirectional meiotic fusion. It expresses the potential for change, without actually determining what change. It reactivates nextness, without defining which next must be.

This might be considered a cop-out. Or it might be considered a principled practice of a different artistic politics: one that does not see its role as inculcating a particular awareness or analysis so as to make certain predefined follow-up actions seem necessary or inevitable. More modestly, this is a practice of programming conditions of incipiency. What might follow is pointedly vague, left tendentially open. It is up to the participants to stoke their own follow-up (or not). The role of relational architecture is not rigidly inculcative, nor even mildly instructional. It is modestly expressive, despite its flirting with the monumental. It expresses change*ability*—change felt but as yet undefined—through modulatory fusion occurring across the collective surface of a building. The expression is *exemplary*, as opposed to prescriptive.

To exemplify is to invoke an indefinite set of instances, each of which is different but which are in a kinship and belong together, in a way that does not need to be spelled out. One example invites another, and that other another, in a series potentially without end. Each example in the potentially continuing series includes all the others in itself, in that it implicitly presents itself as a variation on them—as they, should they eventuate, will include themselves as variations on the series. To exemplify is to populate the moment with virtual events of repeat-exemplification which immediately belong to one another, in mutual envelopment, even though each is absolutely singular. No two will share all their defining characteristics in a way that would allow them to be subsumed unequivocally or without remainder under the same general idea. The example, contrary to the common assumption, does not instantiate a type. It performs an immediately lived belonging to a lineage of typal variation. To exemplify is to populate a present event of expression with a lineage of virtual events of expression that belong together as kin, with all their differences—*as* differencings. The example displays in language the same recursive filiation we saw in Greg Lynn's batched "families" of topological visual figures.

THE MEDIUM IS THE MEIOSIS

It is often asked whether digitally assisted art combining a number of media is itself a medium. Is the medium of Lozano-Hemmer's work architecture? Writing? The phenomenal body? "The digital"? "The electronic?" Light? Movement? Silicon? The work involves all of these, but is not couched intimately or exclusively enough in any of them to qualify one as "the" medium. Does this mean that this kind of work is a simple hybrid, a messy catchall of media? The all-over-the-place eclecticism this implies is not at all in evidence in Lozano-Hemmer's projects, which manage to produce a highly unified aesthetic effect by very mixed means.

Another possibility is that the mixing of media transposes the medium from the status of material support to that of immaterial result. Perhaps the unified effect, heterogeneously achieved, must itself be considered the medium of the creative process that produces it. In other words, the medium of relational architecture is just what it names, just what it dematerializingly "builds": the event of fusion. Relation. The sweeping together of times; the zooming into each other of scales; the mating of levels; the pseudopod stretching of amoebic bodies; the arcing of tendencies across sense modalities; the reciprocal inflections of action, perception, and language; the potentially, collectively mutational meeting of all of these across a shared surface, or "interface," in a state of mutual incipiency; the expressed *-ability* of this meeting.

Perhaps performative arts, arts of the event, have as their medium the manner of event they stage—in this case events of relation. If so, they are in the odd, and oddly powerful, position of creating the medium of their expression in and as the very act of expression. The medium happens. It is summoned by its own unfolding event. The medium itself is ephemeral and emergent. This is the mark of "occurrent arts."[30]

This is taking "medium" in a different sense than usual. Understood in this way, a medium is not a technological or material support for the transmission of a content. The technological and material supports for relational architecture are architecture, writing, the body, the digital, the electronic, light, movement, silicon. In Lozano-Hemmer's work, by conscious design, they do not self-transmit or transmit something else that might come across as a specific message. What they do is come together. Not only dynamically, but materially *qualitatively*. When they come together, something happens: a tendential fusion relationally giving next-*ability*. This effect is not the sovereign province of any of its contributing levels taken singly. It is intricate. It happens *between* levels and elements, differentially, in and as their gap-active coming-together. A taking-place in media res.

That event is always a stretch. The act in which the event culminates, such as the reading of words with one's shadow on a façade, stretches its incipiency out across a fusional field of many a level and of indeterminate expanse. Its occurrence contracts that field of emergence into the punctuality of the act's performing, vaguely drawing its entirety into the region of clarity of its determinate taking-place. Folding out, folding in, in a single two-way movement of integral coming-to-expression in the discreteness of an act. The integral presence of the field of emergence is expressed in the *manner* of the discrete act: its unique inflection; the just-thus of its performance; its such-as-it-isness; its style. The manner of an act is the dynamic trace of its in-forming by its field of emergence. Its gestural sweep composes the dynamic unity of the event, in expressive effect. Thus it is a stretch to say that the medium of an act is the manner of the event it stages: the medium manneristically stretches all along the continuum, from the field of emergence at its most unfolded and more or less loosely encompassing, to the relational tightness of the field's fusional contraction into the punctuality of the act of expression.

CULTURAL DOMAIN

There is only one word for the kind of acts staged in the works of Lozano-Hemmer under discussion here: *cultural acts*. The specific way in which the stage is set for the act and the manner in which it is performed activates a spectrum of relation into which any number of things factor together. Alien historical memories as close as a plague pillar and as far-reaching as colonialism rub shoulders with memories of the urban future. The vampirism of the established urban power regime hits up against proto-political stirrings of resistance to it. To name a few. This mutual factoring into the act of that which constitutively exceeds it forms its historically inflected relational neighborhood: the *cultural domain* it inhabits. The vicinity of the artwork is not simply the city neighborhood in which the art is installed. Processually speaking, the art act's vicinity is the region of relation it contracts into itself and brings to expression.

The cultural domain does not preexist fully formed, and does not have any stable configuration. The wooden concept of cultural–historical "context" is just a stagnant still-image of it. The cultural domain is performatively drawn by the cultural act, for its own coming to pass in that vicinity. The cultural domain is co-emergent with the act. With each act it reemerges in a new variation. Companion acts co-occupy it, each with distinctive difference. The cultural domain is an event dimension of the acts' coming to pass in serial variation and processual neighborhood.

Given the amoebic tendings of the body in its material quality, it is not possible to draw a sharp distinction between the figure and ground of its actions. Nevertheless, it is undeniable that certain alien memories, certain historical effects of the playing-out of regimes of power, certain proto-political memories of the future, are more palpable than others in the vicinity of the cultural act, as a function of the how of the act's staging and the manner of its performance. Some things factor into the act at less of a stretch, pressing in around it. This relational neighborhood does not constitute a static background for the discrete figure of the act to stand out from. It constitutes an occurrent background for the act's kinesthetic figuring to amoebate through. The act, as fusional expression, is not reducible to its visible contours. It is seen to extend into the nonvisible, even nonsensuous, more-than of vision. Its dynamic form is the visible envelopment of a more-than what appears. However punctual and clearly occurrent as a gesture, it retains a degree of indiscernibility. The domain of culture *is* the zone of indistinction of the integral fusional field, as it homes in on the act.[31] Bakhtin's description of the cultural domain is instructive:

> A domain of *culture* should not be thought of as some
> kind of spatial whole, possessing not only boundaries
> but an inner territory. It is located entirely upon bound-
> aries, boundaries intersect it everywhere . . . Every
> cultural act lives essentially on the boundaries . . . we
> can speak about [the cultural act in] its autonomous
> participation or participative autonomy . . . that is,
> in its unmediated . . . orientation.[32]

There is an "autonomous participation" or "participative autonomy" occurring at an intersection of levels: of thought and feeling, of words and actions, of actions and perceptions, of mutations and organizations. This intersection of levels composes the domain of culture. Except that it is not a domain, in any sense of the term as a spatial whole. The domain of culture has no inner territory. It is composed entirely of the boundary lines of the levels intersecting. At the intersection, the levels edge over and into each other, forming a saddle. The lines composing the domain of culture are not outlines separating off an interior space. They are saddles, thresholds, over which relays may occur, following diverse orientations specific to each act populating the domain. Lines that intersect and overlap compose a plane. A surface. Oriented lines in movement are vectors. A domain of culture is a vectorial surface drawn of different levels and registers of life saddling each other, delineating potential relays, from thought to feeling and back again, or between words and actions, actions and perceptions, mutations and organizations, all overlapping in the immediate material quality of bare activity. A domain of culture is an embodied topological figure.

Given the infraphenomenal, nonsensuous nature of the what bestirs bare activity, the domain of culture must be seen as an *abstract surface* populated by virtual events.[33] Each potential relay is just that, a virtual event. If the abstract surface of virtual events is a domain of culture, then a domain of culture is more time-like than it is spatial. It is stamped with the attentional time-signature of the gap-acted life of the body. Coextensive with the event of its expression, a domain of culture is energetically co-"substantial" with the emotional–volitional *moment* of the body's infraindividual enhancement, run through with expressive *momentum*. The moment: life primed here, now, for more and again, telescoping/accordioning, lasting/nexting. The momentum: potential relaying among a multiplicity of co-agitating tendencies, in a vectorial pluripotence of parturient relation pressing for expressive outlet. In the gap-act, a whole population of variations on what the present act exemplifies are already stirring, vying for expression: companion acts to come. *Vectorial Elevation* (discussed below) makes light of this.

Each cultural act exemplifies the change-ability of the domain of culture. It makes felt the cultural domain's lived reality as a collective event-"space" for companion acts of variation to gather. Each cultural act virtually populates the present of performance with cultural differencings in potential relay. The pluripotence of the act makes "the" body performing it already several: in reality, a virtual group. A gregarity. The kinesthetic amoeba, gone culturing, extends itself to its own company. Lozano-Hemmer's works set the stage for tele-embodiment of this relational culturing.

CULTURAL ACT

Each embodied excmplification of the cultural domain is a cultural act: culture in the act. The cultural act selectively expresses the cultural domain in the shape of a determinate move. The cultural domain, as virtual group or potential peopling, is singularly multiple. The act exemplifying it for the moment can be more or less singled out as a separate figure. It is determinate, a clearly (if not wholly) perceptible figuring of the cultural domain's continuing variety. It can be more or less singled out in its *cultural* particularity *because* of the exemplary way its taking place is inhabited by the virtual group. The individual cultural act is a singleton, pregnant with peopling.

In *Re:Positioning Fear,* the stage is set for the cultural act through light projection on a concrete surface. The façade of the building serves as a sensuous surface for word-shadow projection. The projection is technically enabled by a digital apparatus. The abstract surface that is the cultural domain of each act arising through the projection cannot be separated from this actual, concrete, sensuous surface. Neither, however, can the cultural domain be reduced to that sensuous surface, or to the content of what is seen on it. The cultural domain is a bare-active fusion between kinesthesia, vision, and words, among many other levels and registers, occurring *through* the surface of projection; co-occurring *with* it in another, nonsensuous, event-dimension. The actual surface—the interface—and the abstract surface of the cultural domain double each other. The one a penumbra to the other's shadow play. The domain of culture composing the abstract surface "enhances" the cultural act that brings it to determinate expression on the concrete surface. The abstract surface doubles the concrete surface only in order to double over into it. It folds itself into the act's unfolding, in-forming it with more than its determinate figure can hold. It virtually infects it. It fusionally infra-effects it. It populates it with neighboring others, almost-present in processual proximity.

Since the lines that compose the cultural domain are not outlines separating off an interior space, there is no definite line of demarcation between companion others and aliens. Everything is on a continuum. The almost-presence of companionable others virtually co-populating the neighborhood shades into the potential intrusion of the alien. Other/alien: the nondividing line is fine. If you go from neighbor to neighbor, at what point do your neighbors fade off into strangers? The alien is at the threshold. Maybe not yours, maybe not next door's, but who knows for the next after that?

It is the nature of the alien to be always at the threshold, potentially. The cultural act can never purify itself of the alien memories discussed earlier. They are in the paradoxical condition of being in processual proximity at whatever distance, lurking in the folds of the event. Spied from the familiar vicinity of the cultural domain, they are the once and future feared. They are the already-feared unfamiliars, and as-yet unknown future intruders. They are faceless. They extend, plague-like, above and beyond the scale of the human. At the limit of their alienness lies not only the unknown, but the as-yet unknowable: unknown unknowns.

Are these necessarily to be feared? Really? Do we have to give the likes of Donald Rumsfeld the last word on potential? Doesn't work like Lozano-Hemmer's, in making potential palpable, and by deploying it in an open field of ultimately indeterminate expanse, invite a hospitality toward the unknown of potential, beyond the fold of the cultural domain? Does it not evoke the potential for a culturing beyond cultural community? Can it not put the alien on the spectrum, rather than fear it as a specter?

A summary formula: the cultural act is *the embodied taking-place of companionable expression on a continuum with alien memory (of the future)*.

CULTURABILITY

The cultural domain is an unmediated "participation" of heterogeneous levels of organization and registers of activity in *each other*, collectively mutually including, in a proximately neighborly way. It is a region of relation. The relation in-forming the domain is autonomous in the sense that the edgy in-each-other of the heterogeneities composing it abstractly doubles the singularity of the coming event with its own self-inflecting potential—with its as-yet unfully determined -ability extending, fold upon fold after fold, across the spectrum orienting to the alien unknown.

Once again, given the splay of levels and registers that fuse into continuity with each other in the dynamic unity of the cultural act with which the cultural domain is co-emergent—plagues now and then, invasions, memories of the past, memories of a future, past suffering, future fears, the strangeness of unknown potential, the comfort of community, the constructed local environment, the global network, the online chat, language and gesture—only one adjective can embrace the -ability of all of this to come effectively together: cultural. Culture -ability. *Culturability*: an *autonomous participation* of levels and registers in each other, toward the taking-place of a coming cultural act, already almost-there on the abstract event-plane of its own incipiency.

Culturability stretches from the region of clear expression that is the cultural act to the farthest reaches of the kinesthetic amoeba's multiplex potentiation. It stretches the plane of the cultural domain into a field—an open field, composed of intersectings of boundaries, while being itself unbounded. If the cultural domain is like the indiscernible background against which the cultural act nevertheless figures, the field of culturability is the ground of the ground: the ground's shading off in all directions into the background's unappearing. The cultural domain is what Whitehead would call the *real potential* of the act, in-forming its occurrence. The field of culturability is the shading off of the cultural domain's real potential into *pure potential* (Deleuze's virtual at its most really abstract). The real potential is the pattern of potentials that enter into close enough processual proximity to the act's occurrence as to palpably propose themselves for its expression, so that the act could be said to have infra-felt them—to have virtually "chosen" from among them to produce itself as their singular fusion, and thus in some sense to have known them, in the dynamic form of its own coming to pass. Pure potential is real potential shading off into the unknown: unknowable for this act, but perhaps not for the next, or another somewhere down the line. Pure potential is the reservoir of real potential, running out to the abstractest reaches of the real. It is the far-real. The aliennest memory of the real. The cultural domain in-forms the act with its real potential. The field of culturability out-runs it with maximally other potential, pure alien potential.

The cultural act is "participative," partaking. It partakes of the potential of the cultural domain in-forming it. The act's accomplishment is triggered by a bodily response on the part of a participant to what actually appears on the concrete surface of the interface. That response is interactive. The cultural act, in its surface manner, is interactive as opposed to relational (which is what its formative domain and its domain's open field of potential are). The cultural domain potentiates the cultural act. It primes and modulates it. But it does so vaguely, in "dim" nonconscious "apprehension," shadow of an act, forerun. The priming, or forerunning of the event, does not predefine the coming act in its particulars. That actual bringing to clear expression of the potential, in the form of a specific move, would not occur were its actual appearance not doubled by its forerunning (which simultaneously in-forms the act with real potential and out-runs it to the limit of pure potential, in a simultaneous rising of the ground into the figuring of the act and its receding into far-real, ground of the ground). Cultural act, cultural domain, and field of culturability are coordinate degrees of one another. They are not substantially different, but differ by the degree of effective contraction of potential into the actual event's expression.[34]

The cultural act is primed by its forerunning, but not predetermined by it. As it actually happens, the act occurs on its own enactive terms. It occurs selectively, fusing a certain bandwidth of mutual inclusion, to consciously perceived effect. The cultural act surfaces in the mode of interaction as a *participative autonomy*, partaking of potential. As it comes to actual fruition in its own terms, it figures itself interactively. Yet it still "essentially lives"—lives more far-reachingly than its sensuous surface appearance—in the potential domain of its relational infra -ability. Its taking-place is more extensively "relationship-specific" than it is interactively site-specific. The appearing form in which the cultural act surfaces is an interactive response to a sensuous display. But the cultural act is not reducible to the form of its appearance. It has nonsensuous stretch in it, shading off into the unappearing. The cultural act is the tip of the iceberg of its own infra-active potentiation and tendential modulation. It is able to select potential *because* it participates also in its more-than. It can appear in interaction because it relates. It can have its expressed domain because it also fields what recedes from that expression.

Culturability: the fielding of relation underwriting interaction at its most incipiently abstract. This is the element of relational architecture in this period of Lozano-Hemmer's work. Culturability is what folds into the cultural act's coming to its own expression as the manner of event it stages: in other words, as medium of expression. It is the ever almost-there of the cultural act, in-forming. Culturability is the forerunner of the cultural act: its -ability to come (again). Thought-sign of culture re-coming to figure in relation.

We are speaking of art. But is aesthetics relevant here? What would be the aesthetic form of the work of relational art? It could only be the dynamic form of the act of culture's coming, in an instantaneous sweep across dimensions of event: act, domain, field; response, fusion, far-reaching unbound. The act's aesthetic is the way in which the occurrent domain's autonomous participation feeds immediately forward into the participative autonomy of its accomplishment. The work's aesthetic effect is the live feeling of the sweep, replete with real and pure potential: the vitality affect marking its manner of coming to pass.

The relation of the aesthetic effect to the interpretable content of the interaction appearing in words on the wall is the same as the relation of the event as a whole to the apparatus of its interface: neither separable from it nor reducible to it. Meaningful content, reemergently modulated into a cultural domain and coming out in its expressive acts, is what is commonly called an *ideological* effect. Ideological effects may well arise as part of the cultural acts of expression enabled by relational architecture. But ideology is not where its politics "essentially lives." Relational architecture has no inner ideological territory. It roves the boundaries, feeling the impetus for its acts in the forerunning of the abstract surface they compose. It eventfully stretches far afield.

BEYOND INTERACTIVITY

It cannot be said enough: interactivity is not where relational architecture essentially lives. Relational architecture is *not an interactive art*. It is precisely what it says it is: a relational art.

It should be taken at its word. The sensuous, actually appearing interactive response of the physiological body, is just the tip of the occurrent iceberg. It is the figuring of the event through which the open relational field in which relational architecture lives comes to a surface clarity of expression. The event, as a cultural act, comes *through* the interaction, in which it peaks. The event is not the interactive response per se, but rather the manner in which the field of culturability has been relationally folded into it, to effect a selective recomposition of a cultural domain.

Interactivity pertains to function: patterned circuits of response; a cycle of actual stimulus and actual response. Relation pertains to the material quality of the becoming body-event: a nascency of feelings-motions, edging each other, just barely felt, if actually at all, on the plane of their mutual inclusion, participating in each other as thought-signs of an event of the culturable kind, virtually stirring toward a coming to pass. On the interactive level, the technological apparatus is mediating: it interposes its stimulus between one response and the next. Relation, on the other hand, is immediate: so fully, that it fails actually to register in its full stretch. Relation is and remains infra-. Interactivity is the manner in which the infra- actually peaks. Interactivity remains on the level of possible *reaction*. Relation is the dimension of potentiating *activation*. Interactivity is connective: to the apparatus, and of participants, across their mediated reactions to the apparatus. Relation is fusional: it mates a heterogeneity levels (including that of interaction itself). Bodies interact as what they are: from the angle of their acquired competencies and habits. Bodies relate from the angle of their life -ability to modulate what they will be: to continue to become, in an act of culture in the remaking. Only a theory of *immediation* can give this culturing its due.[35]

EXPRESSING RELATION

Vectorial Elevation: Relational Architecture No. 4 homed in on the expressive operation of relational architecture. Participants were offered the opportunity to design a light pattern on their home computers, and then remotely activate a searchlight array that actualized the pattern in the night sky above the Zócalo, Mexico City's main square. Every six seconds the pattern

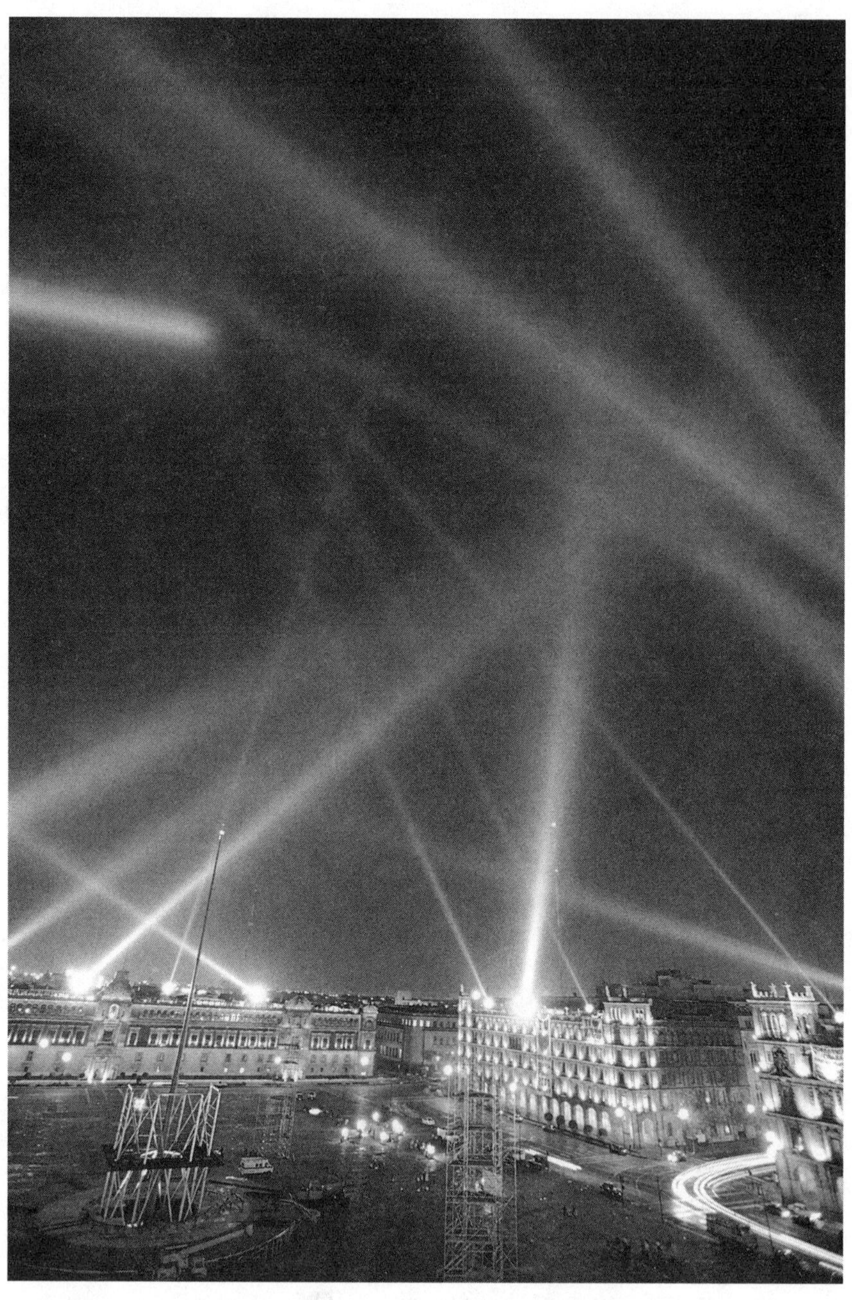

Rafael Lozano-Hemmer, *Vectorial Elevation, Relational Architecture No. 4*, 1999.
Zócalo Square, Mexico City, Mexico. Photograph by Martin Vargas.

changed. When it did, the searchlight beams would move in unison, crisscrossing in a choreography of light, until they abruptly set into a next position. A kinesthetic ballet in vision.

Tens of thousands of people watched, at home or in the square. What they saw was culturally and politically loaded. The Zócalo is ringed by central Mexican government buildings, and because of that has a long history not only as a seat of government but also as a major site of demonstration and contestation against it. The spectators interacted with the apparatus. They could attach messages to their designs on the website archiving them. They interfaced. They gave the event personal and ideological content. But they did not only interact. The interaction accordioned them into relation, from which their accomplished acts of expression telescoped back out.

"The transitions between positions [of the light arrays] were as important as the positions themselves," Lozano-Hemmer said.[36] It is in the transitions—accordioned into the gaps between stimulus and response—that relation is really, nonconsciously felt. What the project presented overall was less a series of discrete patterns than "a coordinated state of mutation." Collective mutation, minus the actual weight of collectivity: that practiced gravity of being functionally and interpretably limited to a particular cultural group. Between positions, lightness. Beam and motion. Tending-to planely rendered in intersecting vectors of light saddling each other, rays re-arraying. Relation reduced to its visible minimum of luminous appearing. The shadow of a shadow of culturability illumined. Penumbra of relational light. The human environment beamingly dematerialized through the relay from computers around the globe to searchlight on-site to spectators on-site and around the globe, accordioning into the gaps between positions. The distributed immediacy of that event could not fail to spark thought-signed feelings-motions in the individual bodies factoring into the collective becoming event-body on the continuum of community and alien memory. Felt movements that were certainly an incipiency, no doubt a tending, or many. Together. Locally–globally unified in the aesthetic effect of a shared transitioning of positions.

"Life lurks in the interstices."[37]

The point? Just "the essential pleasure of coming together."

FLOATING THE SOCIAL

THREE'S A CROWD

"A message for you is floating in the sky of Yamaguchi." On November 1, 2003, thousands of people around the world started receiving this alert by cell phone or email. The messages waited and flashed, like the seductive signals used by fireflies to find mates for coupling. At first sight, the light signals that *Amodal Suspension: Relational Architecture No. 8* sends pulsing into the sky are as illegible as the insect variety, although they are many orders of magnitude more visible. Standing in for the insect's abdomen is an array of the world's most powerful robotic searchlights.

In *Amodal Suspension* people send short text messages to each other using a cell phone or web browser. But rather than being sent directly to their intended recipients the messages are encoded as unique sequences of flashes and "deposited" in the sky, awaiting collection. A searchlight designated by the sender beams the message and rotates. Then a random second searchlight picks up the code, and the two beams intersect, flashing in unison. No sooner do they connect, however, than the first beam extinguishes. A third random searchlight then takes up the message, intersecting with the second. The messages are relayed in this fashion from one pair of searchlights to another, in a dance of lights. This touch-and-go mating of asexual rays is the only coupling that effectively takes place.

A number of processes have been designed into the installation to come between the sender and the receiver of the message. The bipolar transmission usually considered to lie at the heart of human communication is complicated to such a degree that one is forced to say either that what is being made visible here is not human communication (or not only that) or that human communication is not definable by the dual subjective structure—between sender and receiver—that is almost universally assumed to characterize it.

The first complication is that the message appears in an entirely different mode than the code that enables it. It is present in a purely visible way. It is seen before it can be read, and it cannot be read as it is seen.

This is because the flashing in the sky is a translation of the digital input into an analog signal that preserves only selected characteristics of the digitally encoded linguistic meaning. To each letter in the message corresponds a change in the intensity of the beam. Letter by letter, different light intensities daisy-chain without interruption, in a continuity of variation.

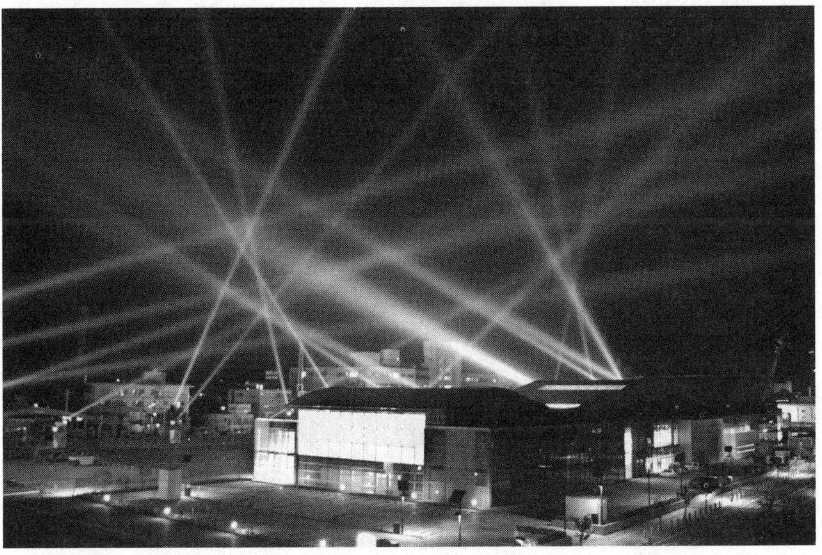

Rafael Lozano-Hemmer, *Amodal Suspension. Relational Architecture No. 8*, 2003. Yamaguchi Center for Art and Media, Yamaguchi, Japan. Photograph by ArchiBiMing.

There is a moment of near darkness between words, but this interval is in no way comparable to the off-state of the digital code. It is more a punctuation between the continuities of variation on either side than merely one half of the on–off binary. The off-state of the interval makes a threesome: the two series of intensities, with the punctuation between.

This "thirdness" (to speak like C. S. Peirce) is the basic articulation of the signal. But three's a crowd. Each of the variations punctuated by the almost off-state is multiple, consisting of a population of intensities. This complexity translates as a pulsation. The result is very different from the strobe effect ordinarily used to transmit code visually. Most if not all of the messages will consist of more than two words. Coming irregularly in the midst of a series of changes in intensity, the moment of near darkness will meld into the continuing pulsing, its threeness into the multiplicity it parses. Rather than an off-state that is the opposite of an on-state, it will come across as the low note on the same scale (brightness). In other words, the compositional principle of the signal, as experienced, is more a continuous modulation of a dimension of perception than an encoding of separate bits of data or a sequencing of units of meaning. Modulation is the very definition of the analog signal—a continuous variation in amplitude and time (that is, a smoothly varying value).

SOMETHING LIKE LANGUAGE

So what value is being analogically varied here? The changes in intensity are based on the frequency with which the corresponding letter occurs in the language of the message. The higher the frequency, the brighter the pulse. Letter frequency is a sociohistorical variable. It materializes in statistical form the particularities of a specific linguistic evolution. In *Amodal Suspension,* this sociohistorical frequency variable pulses into view as a visual rhythm. The encoding of letter frequency into the beam attaches it genetically to socially specific rhythms of speech. But the encoding is not visually decodable by the viewer, any more than the meaning of the message can be seen in the pulse and flutter. What comes across is, simply, the rhythm. A language-like rhythm—without the actual language.

Rhythm is the most perceptually salient dimension of language. Phonemes disappear into their meaning. You don't hear them to the exact degree to which you understand them. But their rhythm asserts itself, an experienced something-extra that conveys an emphasis, accent, tone, or mood. The rhythm carries the force of the phrase, above and beyond its structure and meaning. *Amodal Suspension* uses encoding to make visible this extralinguistic effectiveness: the force of language. This is the variable that is being analogically presented. The display conveys the feel of a statement's impact without its meaning. We get the same feel from the firefly's inhuman light show of exoskeletal love. It is impossible to watch them and not get the uncanny feeling that they are "talking" to each other.

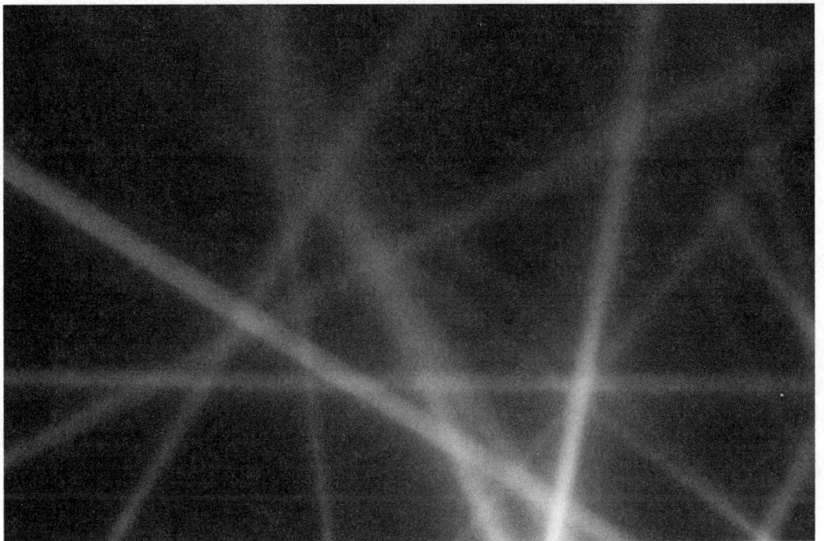

Rafael Lozano-Hemmer, *Amodal Suspension. Relational Architecture No. 8*, 2003. Yamaguchi Center for Art and Media, Yamaguchi, Japan. Photograph by ArchiBiMing.

The installation makes human language visible at a rhythmic limit where it shades into a dimension of experience that is necessary to its workings but is not of its mode, since it is also the province of the bug. The work creates a visual analogue of human language, something "like" it, that reattaches it not only to a particular sociohistorical evolution but also to the biosemiotic background from which it emerged.

The meaning and structure of language are "suspended" in the beam, against the forceful background of their own emergence. What is positively experienced here is a transitional zone where language in its human mode rhythmically returns to the animal fold from which it came, at the same time as its sound mode translates into a visual mode akin to gesture (which beckons to speech, heralding its possibility, in the human as in the animal). What lies transitionally between modes is "amodal." Hence the title of the piece.

The force of a statement never fails to make itself felt. But it also always fades, making way for the next utterance. The beams slowly rise into the sky and decrease in intensity while preserving the original rhythm. In the meantime, other messages are received and displayed. With twenty towers, up to ten messages

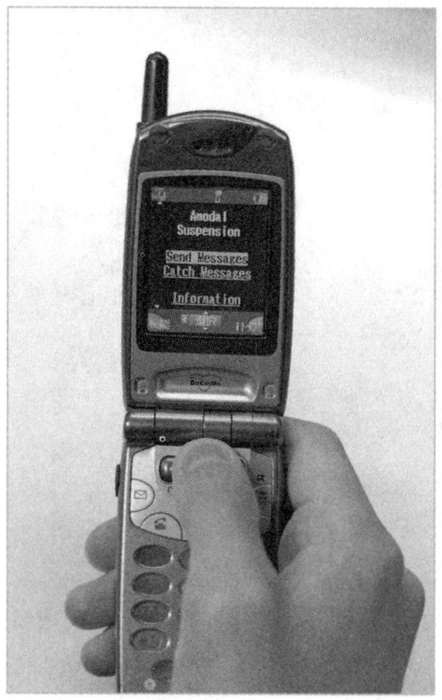

Rafael Lozano-Hemmer, *Amodal Suspension. Relational Architecture No. 8*, 2003. Yamaguchi Center for Art and Media, Yamaguchi, Japan. Photograph by ArchiBiMing.

can beckon at once, each with a signature pulse. The air crowds with the sight of language rising. The properly linguistic dimension is not lost. It is still there, latent as a definite possibility in the code that is never shown, though it enables the display.

To see the latent content, the addressee must "grab" the message from the beaming crowd as she would a pluck a point of light from a summer cloud of fireflies. This is done by clicking on the beam on the real-time website simulation of the event, or on-site by cell phone by entering the number of the tower currently carrying the message. To access the coded content, the participant must perform a digital analogue of gesture, beckoning delivery of the meaning content. And it has to be done fast. As the soon as the message is grabbed, the beam abruptly disappears. If someone beats you to it, you receive a message informing you of the name and location of the poacher. The message can still be accessed from the public log archived on the server.

LANGUAGE TO THE THIRD POWER

The base definition of linguistic communication is often considered to be the transmission of a syntactically coded content from a sender to a receiver. The problem with that bipolar transmission model is that it is incapable of distinguishing between insect communication and human language—and not because the model has complexly returned to their transitional zone, but merely because it has oversimplified. There may or may not be a syntax to firefly flashes, but there certainly is to the dance of the bees. The reason commonly given to explain what differentiates the language of the bees from human language is that even though it is capable of communicating syntactically coded message content, the message cannot be retransmitted to a third party.

The communicational system found in nature best able to do that is human language. Human communication is defined by this linguistic "thirdness," by its capacity not for linear transmission but for indirection. This complicates things: with the third party in waiting down the line comes the possibility of that party jumping the line and intercepting the message. Indirect relay and message poaching, or hacking, is of the very nature of human communication. With indirect relay comes the inevitability of noise and the accompanying distortion of message content. A fuller model than sender and receiver, with a coded message passing between them, would be a combination of the games of telephone and musical chairs.

"Third" parties never come in ones. Where there's one third, there's bound to be another down the noisy line. Three's a crowd again. But this time the triadic multiplicity separates human language back out, returning it to its proper mode. Lozano-Hemmer's installation also makes visible the rearising or reemergence of specifically human communication, in its first flush, or flash, seen for what it is: a nonlinear crowd phenomenon. The rising community of poachable beams is Lozano-Hemmer's visual analogue of what he calls the chaotic "social soup" of many-party thirdness: a literal flash mob.

Earlier it was said that a number of mechanisms interjected themselves between the sender and receiver in a way that complicated the linear model of message transmission. Also mentioned was the possibility of message poaching, which interjects between the sender and receiver the potential presence of a third party on the line. There was also the necessity of catching the message with a flick of the thumb or finger. This alloys the verbal dimension of language with the bodily dimension of gesture, bringing into the experience of the installation an experiencing of the limit between the linguistic and the extralinguistic, thought and the body, the human and the nonhuman. It brings what we normally tend to think of as mutually exclusive domains into a proximity, a convergence that is not stated or displayed but rather performed. To participate in the installation, one has to perform this limit of language. Speech and bodily action brush up against and relay into one another, in a way that redirects attention at least momentarily away from the message content, to the speech act as performance and as event. Embodied social performance becomes more noticeably, in fact unmissably, a part of the speech act in a way that brings to the fore the accompaniment of the linguistic by the extralinguistic—in convergence, but not necessarily entirely at peace with one another. The need to interrupt the understanding of the message content with the effort of the catch produces interference patterns between content and performance context.

There is a third mechanism of meaning interference built into the installation: translation. Messages could be entered in English or Japanese. If for example a message entered in Japanese is poached by a third party using English, the message is automatically translated using an off-the-shelf translating software system widely used on the web at the time (Systran's Sherlock). As anyone who has used an internet translating feature knows, automatic translation even today is not a very advanced art. Errors inevitably slip in, often to comic effect. Using automatic translation in this context brings interference into the very heart of the message, again frustrating the possibility of transparent communication. The linear transmission of message content is scrambled, in a technologically assisted version of the telephone game.

All of these mechanisms for interrupting transmission and creating interference make noise as much a part of the installation's content as the meaning of the messages conveyed.

SEA OF NOISE, CREST OF WORDS

There are different ways of thinking about noise. The most widespread is native to information theory and corresponds to our everyday understanding of the term. Noise according to this definition is the opposite of signal. It comes at the signal from outside its structure and disrupts it. On this view, the structure of the signal is clear and self-sufficient. Its meaning is as unambiguous as it can be made by the code used to construct it, unless it is perturbed from without. The extralinguistic element of noise is cast as the simple opposite of linguistically formed message transmission. It is its negative: the unstructured and unstructuring.

But in *Amodal Suspension,* when we approach the extralinguistic, we aren't moving into the simple opposite, outside, or negative of the linguistic. We are moving into a *zone of indistinction* where language shades back into what it emerges from—gesture, body, animality, the multiplicity of the population whose collective life gives rise to the need for communication, whose endless reserve of third parties ensures its continuation and plasticity, and whose history is sedimented in the structure of its language and the frequency of its elements.

This zone of indistinction is not the negation of language but rather the *field of its emergence*—not its unstructured opposite but the event of its coming into effect. The installation returns language to its generative field.

There is another way of understanding noise that dovetails with Lozano-Hemmer's employment of it in *Amodal Suspension.* It comes from certain philosophies concerned with ontogenesis and emergence, and has also been explored in some avant-garde art of the twentieth century, such as the work of John Cage.

In this alternate view, noise is as constitutive of the signal as its code. The following discussion of this conception of noise is based on Aden Evens's analysis in *Sound Ideas.* The book is primarily about music, but its discussion of sound and noise is written to apply as well to language—as it must. For the line between music and language is another of the zones of indistinction belonging to language's field of emergence. Language meets multiplicity in thirdness; it meets body and animality in gesture—and it meets music in sound and rhythm, and in the fact that it shares sound's own emergent relation to noise.

"It is noise," Evens writes, "that binds the signal" and that serves as "a baseline, a plane of relief against which signal stands out."[38] He describes noise as a background to signal, but not in the visual sense, where the static background is in contrast with the discreteness of the form that stands out against it. His use of the word "relief" suggests a geological image. Noise is like the underlayer from which signal, with its message content, rises in relief, upfolding under pressure from tectonic forces. Signal stands in relation to noise as a mountain rises from the continually shifting ground. A mountain is testimony to the past action of forces of emergence of the earth, and to the certainty that future tectonic shifts will continue to reshape the landscape. Like a peak, signal stands out against the generative, and regenerative, forces of its own tectonic formation.

The idea that *Amodal Suspension* makes perceptible the force of language can be articulated with this concept of noise. Central to that concept is the fact that a sound never entirely disappears. It dissipates. It relaxes, spreads out, becoming less and less contracted, but it remains, hanging in the air, a breath away from silence, fused with the relaxation of every other sound that ever rang out. This noise of near-silence is an imperceptible background buzz, a vibratory limit *of* sound at which *a* sound rejoins *all* sound, in an open field.[39] Evens calls it a "cosmic echo": a universal history of sound (the ground of the ground, infinitely more encompassing than the proximate ground against which a sound figure stands in tectonic relief).

When a new sound rings out, it ripples the surface of this cosmic echo. From the rippling, it peaks. Its own vibration resonates with the silence-nearing background buzz, or forms interference patterns with it. The resonance and interference of the background noise is a condition of the new sound's emergence, but also becomes an ingredient in it, contributing to its timbre or giving it an undertone. The emerging signal peaks from the background of noise. Given the energetic, vibratory nature of its "ground," it is perhaps less like a mountain peak than a wave, cresting on the sea. A wave can be thought of as contracting the calm of the sea into a new swell. The cresting of the wave gives new focus to the imperceptible stirrings of the deep, whose potential energy is brought once again to forceful expression. The emergent wave gives focus and expression to the forces of the sea, as the sea gives direction to the wave: toward the shore.

Similarly, a sound signal can be thought of as selectively contracting noise, the near-silent universal history of sound, into the clarity of a newly emerged meaning. It gives focus and expression to the reservoir of all sound, whose spreading depth reciprocates by giving the signal direction: toward sense.

A signal, to become meaningful, to become a linguistic sign, must be contracted a second time. It must ripple another reservoir, and bring it to a crest of focus and expression. This second reservoir is that of our perceptions and memories, our habits of attention and learned responses, our innate animal tropisms and acquired tendencies, our skills, hopes, and desires, as socially instilled, and as embodying a variation on the long and continuing history of nature and culture, and nature in culture: a nature–culture continuum coming into language. Each emergent meaning contracts this universal history into the clarity of its individual meaning, bringing its potential energy once again to forceful expression, and in return, receiving direction from it. Quoting Evens:

> Every string plucked, every throat cleared, vibrates a [background] vibration, modifies an existing difference [and is modified by it]. Sound is a modulation of difference, a difference of difference. . . . Noise is the uncontracted, the depth from which these contractions of perception are drawn, and, though sense-less and insensible [in itself], it makes sense or gives sense to sound, by providing sound with its direction and focusing it to a point of clarity. Noise is the reservoir of sense, the depth in which sounds connect to each other, the difference whose modulation is signal. . . . Sounds only have sense when what is heard includes not only what is heard clearly, but includes also the implicated in what is heard [the obscurity of the background, fading out into all directions to the ground of grounds, from which the clear and distinct stands out]. To hear meaningful sound—be it the articulate meaning of speech or the ineffable meaning of music—is to hear sound in motion, heading somewhere. . . . Noise draws along with it a residue of obscurity, lines of relaxation which anchor sound to the noise it modulates. Sound implicates these obscure tethers, which connect sound to noise . . . implicating worlds of forces not yet unleashed, but whose reservoir powers the music [or linguistic expression], driving it along. . . . Implication pushes [language] forward . . . and this motion is not created by the [words] but produces them as [the expression] of its force. . . . Implication is what connects isolated elements to each other, in a creative synergy.[40]

WORDS UPON WORDS

V. N. Vološinov echoes this in his formula that "expression organises experience."[41] The organizing center of any communication, he says, is not within the individual but in the open field of a collective outside.[42] This is not the kind of outside that stands opposite to or as the negative of the inner life attributed to the individual through which it expressively crests. It is the outside constituted by the whole of communication, its sea. In Vološinov, this whole of communication is defined, in language reminiscent of Bakhtin's definition of the cultural domain, not as bounded but as a boundary region:[43] a region of contact, a crossing point[44] between the linguistic structure of the message carried by the signal and the extralinguistic noise of gesture, body, animality, our perceptions and memories, our habits of attention and learned responses, our tropisms and acquired tendencies, our skills, hopes, and desires. The "whole" of communication is the ensemble of modulations of individual expression, in a churning zone of indistinction extending by degrees to the far reaches of the universal history of sound.

Like Evens, Vološinov describes this zone of indistinction as a current of self-regenerating expression. "Language," writes Vološinov, "cannot be said to be handed down—it endures, but it endures as a continuous process of becoming. Individuals do not receive a ready-made language at all, rather, they enter upon the stream of communication."[45] Our individual communications crest like waves from the sea-streams of speech.

Vološinov goes on to say that there is a reservoir of past communications into which each message dissipates. A message never disappears, especially in this digital age where everything can be recorded and automatically archived. A speech act doesn't disappear; it relaxes into the archive. Every message ever produced subsides in the potential for reported speech—the potential to be taken up again and reactualized in a third party report of what was said. In its widest sense, the Archive is the pure potential for speech. It is the abstract surface of rhythm and sound relaxing to the far-real and contracting noisily toward speech. An actual digital archive doubles the abstract surface of the Archive in far-real sense, contracting selected crestings on the sea of reportable speech into its own element—in this case digitality, the dominant manner of archival appearing in our age.

If reportable speech is the sea of communication as it contracts toward language, then an archived message is a "crystallization"[46] of a wave-crest of communication that once broke on its shore. Although crystalized, it is not exactly inert. Its crystalline structure retains a potential energy: add a splash of new rhythm and pinch of noise, and it can be brought back out from the depths of history, to reexpress itself.

An archive of reportable speech is a resting place of communication. But it still harbors an organizing force. Reaccessed, an expression inflects. It takes on an undertone and a new orientation. No utterance, as Derrida argued, is ever entirely original. A speech act is always a "citation" that regathers the force of the already-said, but with a difference, repeating it with a variation—modulating it (in analog fashion).[47]

Reported speech, Vološinov reminds us, bears testimony to an "active relation of one message to another." That active relation is the condition of emergence or real potential of communication: "words reacting upon words,"[48] to new but analogous effect, in a continuity of variation. At rest in an archive, that active relation becalms itself. Words already-said relax back toward the collective sea of communication, subsiding into Lozano-Hemmer's social soup, rejoining what Maurice Blanchot called the anonymous "murmur" that is both the Archival ground of language and its outside limit.[49] Actually archived words are in communicational reserve, poised for reactivation. Upon reactivation, they leave their backwater of repose to reenter the active stream of language. They come back in citation, undertoning and inflecting the cresting of a new event of language. Words regained, reacting again upon words. Language ebbing and flowing, relaxing into stagnant eddies and contracting again into the wave-crest.

The extra-effect or force of language—the experienced something-extra that conveys an emphasis, accent, tone, or mood—that is staged in *Amodal Suspension* is the power of language to rhythmically regather its active relation to itself and the open field of its murmurous outside, in a pulsed continuation of the always-crossed lines of communication. To assist in the regathering, the project includes its own automatically compiled digital archive.

The *Amodal Suspension* archive is many ways the beating heart of the installation. It will be very rare that the person to whom a message is addressed manages to catch it out of the air. The mass of messages will settle into the online archive.[50] The addressee will have to extract it from the archive. Once again, the process is designed to have a strong element of tactility. The messages populate a 3D virtual space that recedes in all directions. The farther away they are, the more blurred the words. To bring the words into focus, the participant has to navigate through the space with the mouse. The navigation has the feel of swimming. Using the mouse is like paddling with your hands in a liquid. You agitate the cursor to create eddies in the liquid archive of communication. The eddies will catch a message on their swell and flush it toward the front of the screen. When one washes forward, it crests into focus and can be read. The tactility of this eddy-fishing for the message gives the digital archive a turbulently analog experiential dimension.

The archive also works to return communication to the zone of indisinction between gesture and language in exemplary fashion. Just beginning to access what the archive holds already reactivates the words at the regenerative border zone between the extralinguistic and the linguistic, before their linguistic meaning reappears. It brings the infra-inhabitation of language by gesture to the fore.

The *Amodal Suspension* archive also exemplifies the return of communication to its constitutive "thirdness," the power of relay that, processually speaking, is more fundamental to its operation than the explicit structure of linguistic forms, or the digital code of the archiving of words. The archive plays a central role in the insistent thirding of communication in *Amodal Suspension*. Messages directly transmitted from a sender to a receiver will almost inevitably reach the wrong party. They will be poached from the sky by an unintended recipient. They will then detour to the archive, where they will rest, in an ever-expanding reservoir of reported speech. The computer becomes the third party through which messages relay indirectly to the addressee. This detour of digitally reported speech gives new technological expression to the indirection that constitutes the force of human language.

CONSTITUTIVE LIMITS

In the first part of this chapter, relational architectural works such as *Displaced Emperors, Re:Positioning Fear,* and Vectorial Elevation were seen to operate in the element of "culturability," the field in which cultural acts gestate, and from which they emerge to single themselves out as determinate relational moves. The region of real, proximate potential in-forming that event—its processual neighborhood—was termed the "cultural domain" (with reservations as to the spatial connotations of the term). At the limit of the cultural domain, and implicate in its acts, churned the sea of "culturable" potential that is the field of culture. Does *Amodal Suspension* swim in the same element? Is its operative domain also cultural? Is the cultural act its event-medium as well? How could it not be if, as in the first three works discussed, *Amodal Suspension* also harnesses the emergent force of human language, in a zone of indistinction with gesture? Isn't language one with culture?

Amodal Suspension suggests that instead of language being one with culture, it is of-a-many with it: integrally imbricated with it, yet not equatable to it. More than one domain overlaps in the cresting of language. There must be a distinction, for example, between the cultural act and the social act, each peaking from its respective domains and -abilities. There must be a field of *sociability* that overlaps with that of culturability but is not reducible to it. If so, each expression in language contracts both fields. But the distinction between them is not erased by this mutual inclusion in the event. Sociability and culturability are like two co-composing tonal systems. They are both in on each act, but only one gives the act its dominant tonality. In *Displaced Emperors, Re:Positioning Fear,* and *Vectorial Elevation,* the emphasis was on contracting into the event political and historical references and codings, across many a level and in many a register, from the angle of their infra-stirring, astraddle the translocal movements that intersect in the event's taking place in such a way as to also stir alien memories of the far-realest kind into the meiotic soup. Culturability was the dominant tonality: its element. In *Amodal Suspension,* by contrast, the emphasis is on contracting reported speech and the anonymous murmur into the event and its archive. Here, sociability is the dominant tonality: the element. Political and historical references and codings are suspended, in the hijacking of communication. Culture hangs in the air, unrequited. Sociability, however, persists. In fact, it comes out for itself. It flashes forth to express its native force.

Culturabilty and sociability are overlapping fields. Both are ultimately open fields, meaning that they are unbounded. It is nonsensical to try to demarcate a boundary between them. How then can they be distinguished, in their indefinite overlap? The distinction cannot be one of content type, because what defines them as -abilities afield is precisely their self-abstraction from content, which takes place in the very same movement by which their acts performatively peak into a clearly appearing dynamic unity of expression. The dynamic form of that expression fusionally folds the fields of emergence into the sensuous form of the content's cresting. In and of themselves, these fields are the potential for content. In and of themselves, they have only virtual content. The only way to adequately distinguish them is, rather than by trying to establish boundaries between them, to define their effective limits.

By effective limits is meant *processual limits*: the poles between which the process of their coming to expression passes, and whose polarity must be seen as activating that passage. Processual limits must be counted as formative event-factors. They are not enclosing, like set boundaries. They are constitutive, akin to what in chapter 1 was called the performance envelope of an emergence. The creative tension of their polarized differential describes the shape of an open field of emergence as it passes into domainal proximity. A careful recap is necessary to distill the constitutive limits of culturability and sociability as co-operating open generative fields.

The cultural act was described as a two-way movement. In one direction, it rejoined its potential for change, at an infra-individual level. Following this movement, cultural specificities—place, memories of the past and toward the future, generally shared affective orientations, language-borne behavioral and ideational tendencies of an effectively ideological nature, acquired competencies and habits—are placed in expressive suspense. This is an active suspense in which they are poised to return, under variation. In the tensed suspense of the infra-moment, their determinations "fuse" together, and their fusing together mates with levels and scales beyond the measured human pale. That is to say, they enter a domain of immediate proximity across their differences in an expanded field: they resonate. In resonant intensity, they modulate one another's potential next expression. When the next act comes, its course will have been infected, inflected, in-formed by the cross-mating of levels enveloped in words, in a region of language coming to clear expression. "Priming" was given as an example of this mutational-relational co-effecting of a coming act, immanent to its eventful emergence.

The eventuating of a next step is the other half of the two-way movement. The move that comes is determined in the course of its occurrence to have been just as it was. It has specifically taken place. It will become a specific difference. Its having specifically, differently taken place has given grist for memory. It has expressed a memorable affective orientation all its own. It has renewed behavioral or ideational tendencies, in a new variation, or it has run counter to them. It has furthered or confounded habit. It has rescaled its potential reach. It has achieved particularity. What it has been, has been determined. It has individuated. Its taking place has taken its place. In its individuality, it is positioned vis-à-vis other similarly determinate acts, occupying reciprocal positions in a cultural landscape. It has become a coordinate in a territory, or a domain. The movement of the cultural act toward its individuality is a *territorialization*. The inverse movement whereby it rejoins its relational potential in expectant suspense of what it will come to be, in and as the incipiency of that becoming, is a *deterritorialization*. The two movements, though inverse, are coincident: two facets of the same event.[51] When Lozano-Hemmer spoke of "dematerializing" the environment, he could have said "deterritorializing" the act.

Where territorialization and deterritorialization come together is in "bare activity." Bare activity was defined as the material quality of the event: its bodily dimension. It is in bare activity that the particular body shades back into the kinesthetic amoeba it always is, at the incipient level of its every moving act. The body's bare activity occurs in a zone of indistinction between thinking and feeling. The various modalities of sensuous experience fuse with each other, and together enter into "amodal" resonance with the "higher forms" of determination characterizing the cultural act, as they feed back to and through the emergent level. The cultural act is infused with the material quality of its event. Its event, therefore, is integrally bodily. In the event, the body may "stretch" beyond its scale. It may expand to the length of meadow, touch a façade on its own monumental scale, factor in a technological apparatus of immense complexity and heterogeneous composition, and take in or take on the planetary dimensions of the worldwide web. In bare activity, as the life of the body accordions into its expanded field of emergence, it telescopes out-of-scale, becoming in-formed by levels well beyond its own. This is the material quality of experience becoming cosmic. At this extreme point of expansive deterritorialization, the human body is in a zone of indistinction with nonhuman levels—extending through the biological into the inorganic, from meadow to metal, in wire and across concrete—with which its life is formatively imbricated, and are implicate in it. The out-of-scaleness of the nonhuman levels with which it enters, regerminally, into fusion gives the act a cosmic dimension.[52]

The cultural act hangs between two limits, with respect to which it moves following two inverse but coincident movements. Following one, it achieves human particularity, positioned on the cultural map vis-à-vis other acts similarly cresting into their specificity. At this proximate limit of peaking into position, the cultural act is interactive in the sense defined above. It participates in a back-and-forth of call-and-response, the aim of which is to transmit messages between positions on the map with minimum noise and maximum security against third-party poaching and collective drift. To the extent that separate human agency is attributed to the individual senders, this communicational interaction is intersubjective. Intersubjective communication is the *human limit* of the cultural act: its human extremity, the extremity of the cultural becoming of the human. The coordinates of communicational activity are now intersubjectively inscribed and recognized. The flip side of this recognizability is the imperative to own up to one's actions. The owning-up holds a body to position on the intersubjective grid. The cultural territory is now striated with two-party lines of person-to-person message emission and reception. The noise of culturability's folding in and out, accordioning a cosmic continuum, is mediated and muffled. The noise-laden latitude of emergent variation is restricted to set intersubjective channels of communication. At its human limit, the cultural domain snaps to grid.

The contrasting limit has precisely to do with the cosmic dimension of the event. The *cosmic limit* of the human (as of everything that moves and expresses, potentially informing the human) is the pole with respect to which the cultural act in the bare-active incipiency of its becoming enters into resonance with nonhuman, out-of-scale levels and formations, on a continuum, potentially, with all of nature as well as the utmost infectious spread of technology. The cosmic limit is a limit in a different sense of the word.

The human limit is an *internal limit*. An internal limit is one that can be reached. It is internal to a domain. When the movement reaches such a limit it passes a threshold, whereupon it expires. It is then taken back up, after what may be an imperceptible hiatus, and makes a movement of return. In other words, an internal limit is a threshold between exercises of the same kind of passage. For example, a message is sent and reaches its addressee. It has completed its communicational trajectory for all intersubjective intents and purposes. It has exhausted itself. Upon reception, all it is, is said and done. Said and done and owned. The sender has no choice but to own up to it, as the addressee takes it back up, to return a response, which she in turn must own. In crossing the threshold, the message's communicational movement has passed from first-person communicational call to second-party communicational response. The sent message, received, perishes into its interactive follow-on effect on the two-party line of intersubjective communication. Internal limits are interactive in that they concern dual relations of action–reaction. They govern cyclic movements remaining internal to the same domain and exemplifying the same manner of event—the kinds of events that are functionally intolerant of the amoebic mating of dimensions of experience and the nonlinear rhythms of third-party noise, and endeavor to filter it out to the extent possible in order to safeguard a regularized back-and-forth. Such is the cultural act at its most communicationally human.

The cosmic limit, by contrast, is an *immanent limit*. There is no going beyond an immanent limit.[53] However far the present stretch, there is a still a potential further reach. The immanent limit is always ever-more approachable. It infinitely recedes from reach. The closer a movement comes to it, the more intensely it recedes, into its own potential. At each approach to this limit, the cultural act is amoebically reborn. It rebounds, renewed by a reinfusion with potential. It relationally rearises, in sea-tossed variation. Rather that backing-and-forthing in call-and-response, it rises and subsides in an abandon of mutational heaving. Rather than responsibly safeguarding, it rhythmically mates its eventful fate.

The two limits co-operate. They coincide, crosswise, co-generative of culturing. They are inverse and simultaneous. Every cultural act of communication, however intersubjectively functionalized, returns to some degree to the immanent limit, if only by default (by the impossibility of entirely filtering out amoebism and thirdness). The cultural act is strung between a cosmic limit of repotentializing run and return, and the achieved human limit of its determinately taking place; between cosmic deterritorialization, and making a recognizable mark on the human map; between relational emergence, and owned interactive exchange; between a relational nature–culture continuum of indeterminate self-refreshing expanse, and coordinate intersubjective positioning; between the regenerative whole of its potential variation and the perishing particularity of its having been said and done, to functional effect. Such is its scope. Such is its field.

Given its scope, the field of culturability from which the cultural act emerges *cannot be equated with culture in the normal sense, as opposed to nature*. The possibility of that opposition sets in on the level of cultural domain comprising the proximate neighborhood of the cultural act. It is a feature of the content coded into that domain. Culturability, for its part, cannot be opposed to nature. It is on a continuum with it. The process running through it is the continual enculturation *of* nature: the furthest cosmic stretch of elemental potential expressively folding into the tightness of the particular cultural act, in-forming its taking-determinate-form of the essential unboundedness of its open grounding, groundless ground.

LANGUAGE: CAUGHT IN THE ACT

In *Amodal Suspension,* there is a two-way movement of this kind between co-operating limits. But the limits are offset from the ones just described as marking the poles of the cultural domain, constituting an overlapping but not fully coincident field.

Amodal Suspension organizes a crosswise co-generative movement that intersects, once again, in bare activity. There is once again a playing out of the material quality of an event, involving an amodal fusion of registers of experience, gesture with vision with tactility. But *Amodal Suspension* suspends the said-and-doneness of the cultural act, which is admitted in the other works. In *Amodal Suspension,* the movement of communication is not allowed to complete itself in a particularizable, individually ownable message making a functional difference in effective call-and-response. The messages sent are bounced back and forth between machine-translation smudged Japanese and English, thus preventing them from settling into a specific coordinate of a particular cultural map. Insistently detoured into a thirdness of poached and reported speech, the messages are prevented from channeling into a two-party exchange. All of this creates interference, noise on the line, by design. The messages subside forthwith into the eddies of the archive/Archive. Mission doubly incompleted. Even if a message reaches an intended recipient, it does not do so without being simultaneously refracted into indefinitely prolongable third-party transmission and the indeterminate afterlife of citation. The language act is unmoored from the shores of finalized human communication. The internal limit of human communication is disenabled. This remits communication to the open field. Messages are deprived of the luxury of snapping to grid in a cultural domain. *Amodal Suspension* disenables the achievement of noise-reduced intersubjective communication. It contrives for the language acts it does enable to fall short of ownable human individuation. Its flashes flush the internal limit away. This jogs it toward the immanent limit, by default.

However, unlike the earlier works, *Amodal Suspension* contrives *not* to stretch itself amoebically out-of-scale to the maximum extent. Its falls shy of full-force becoming-other, setting its approach to the immanent limit at the point where the force of language enters a zone of indistinction with the animal. This is the zone where language shades into gesture and the coded linguistic sign into the firefly flash of the signal. Gesture remains intimately tied to the emergent force of human language (the better to be in a position to disenable the internal limit of the human) even as it enters a zone of indistinction with the animal. However large the installation, however long the beams, however sprawling and complex the technological apparatus, the participant act remains a grab at *words*. The material quality of this act remains in the orbit of language. The kinesthetic amoeba is bodily suspended in its reach for language. That reach is performed independently of the content of the words, which may never be known to any given reacher, and is in every case detoured, thirded, and set a-sea in the sky.

Vološinov famously distinguishes the "theme" of language from semantic content. The difference is that theme is singularly marked by the noisy "whole" to which the speech act emergently belongs.[54] The particular "evaluative accent," or affective tonality, with which a speech act crests qualitatively marks its constitutive belonging to that ever-changing, open whole.[55] The evaluative accent is performed, not just signified. It is always performed extrasyntactically (in tone or rhythm), and often extraverbally (in gesture or facial expression).[56] The whole to which a language act emergently belongs is infra: infra-present, infra-individual, infra-cognitive, infra-determinate meaning. In *Amodal Suspension* the event of language is incipiently enacted at a more expansively formative level than it is individually understood. It amoebates somewhat, without reaching so close to the cosmic limit as to fall beyond the zone of indistinction between the human and the animal, toward, for example, a becoming vegetable or mineral. These dimensions cannot but be in-forming of the act, but the predominance of grasping at words keeps them distantly backgrounded.

Priming was given earlier as an example of how semantic content is enacted at a more formative level than it is understood. In priming, the content of the word gets directly into the act at its bare-active incipiency. It is as active a factor in the individuation of the cultural act as any muscular effort that may also figure, even if its action is absent by nature to the present of understanding, acting as it does in the gap. In the gap-action of priming, the contrasts, levels, and scales distinguished by semantic content and its present cognitive understanding are telescoped into action across their specific differences and grid-positionings. Old is in immediate proximity with young. Florida is as effectively here as there. This fusional wholeness or holding-together of disparate potential is always already tending toward a specific playing out. There is already an orientation on the way. In the example given earlier, slowness of step was the extraverbally performed evaluative accent of gap-acting "bingo." Vološinov's concept of theme asserts that this enactive on-the-oriented-way from indistinct potential whole to particular evaluative accent is the "meaning" of the speech act in its fullest sense—more than formally semantic; including the act's informal, even deforming, performative implication with the extraverbal. Theme is what effectively makes the speech act an act. It is the *force of language* as it comes more-than-meaningfully to pertain to content.

What *Amodal Suspension* suspends is the semantic finality of the "as pertains to content." The understanding of the semantic content of the messages is refracted and interfered with. The cresting of the evaluative accent is deferred, if not lost in the ebb and flow. Priming is largely disabled, or gets scrambled. The speech act's particularity, its taking on of determinate content, is suspended.

The taking on of determinate content is suspended in gesture: in the reaching-toward staged through the flashes. The speech act is *suspended in the very act of reaching toward language*. Language is caught in the incipience of its own act.

What is left is the "theme" of *language itself*. What participants are primed for is *language as such*, aside from any particular enaction of its content. Its force is felt, in gesture, just out of reach of achieved content. The formative implication of language with the extraverbal is gestured to, in a grabbing at words hanging out of reach at the tip of the thumb and the sweep of a beam. The element of *Amodal Suspension* is no longer culturability. Instead, it is reaching-toward-language, finality of meaning deferred. The event of language is compellingly incompleted. This event is performatively one with its content, which is now nothing but the force of language as such. This is what shows between the flashes.

SOCIABILITY

If the earlier works were in the element of culturability, the element of *Amodal Suspension* is *sociability*: *the reaching-toward language of relation*, freed from the finalities of interaction. Sociability is to language-as-such as culturability is to the body. It is the material quality of the thought-sign as it attaches to language, as if assuming a different focal length. The difference is great enough that sociability must be treated as a different element to culturability. Here, "element" is taken in the sense of a kind of lensing by which the integrality of the relational field is refracted through material quality, giving the processual span of the coming act a focal length setting constitutive limits proper to that act. The element is the refractive angle by which the relational field folds into the act's coming to its own expression as the manner of event it stages (as its own medium of expression).[57] The element might be said to be the *manner of the event's potential*, as opposed to the event-medium, or *the manner of the act's performance* of that potential. In *Amodal Suspension*, human–animal language -ability is socially refracted, becoming of that element.

A *social act* is open to the sayings of others. It doesn't have to be rebegun, for the simple reason that it never ends. It undulates across a continuous rhythm of words reacting upon reservoired words, in rippling waves. A social act doesn't perish. Its rising already subsides into the background noise of the sea of sociality. Culturability culminates in a placeable determination. Sociability ebbs and flows with the vagueness of a continuous background murmur. Sociability and culturability overlap. A cosmic culturing current runs through sociability, overspilling it at both limits. Culturability incipiently outstretches the social at the immanent cosmic limit, to rejoin the full bodily stretch of the nature–culture continuum. At the opposite pole, it oversteps sociability to enact its own internal human limit in a taking determinate communicational form as a specifically cultural act. The two domains are overlapping, interfused, but asymmetrical, hanging between offset limits and angling their enaction through different elemental lenses.

THE SOCIAL DEATH OF THE PERSONAL

Vološinov calls the in-forming of an act of expression by the open field of culturability and sociability, in their overlap and interfusion, "*impletion*."[58] The concept of impletion is akin to that of implication, as understood by Evens. It is the packing into the speech act of its backgrounded field of emergence, making it into a groundswell. Impletion is not a constant or a universal. It undergoes adventures of becoming. Vološinov is centrally concerned with a certain adventure of impletion that he sees beginning in the nineteenth century and culminating in a bifurcation of the relational field characteristic of the greater part of the twentieth century. In the terminology of this essay, this partition increases the offset between culturability and sociability, paradoxically through the strictest of cultural means. It is the story of the genealogy of the presumed interiority of the bourgeois subject of language—and its withering. It revolves around the question of what constitutes personal expression.

"Personality, from the standpoint of its inner, subjective content," Vološinov writes, "is a theme of language." *Personality is a theme of language*. The consequences are enormous. It makes it nonsensical to speak of speech as being in any fundamental way subjectively owned, as if there were an isolatable private person lurking "behind" the act. Etymologically, impletion means infolding. There is no behind, only infolding and folding out again, in a to-and-fro of the open field torsioning on itself. What we call our personal thinking is the thinking *of* the open field, as it passes language-ward through a given bodily locus in a simultaneous two-way movement. Our thinking is integrally in-formed by the thinking-feeling of the open field. It rides astraddle scales and dimensions of experience, telescoped into processual proximity in the material quality of thought-signs. It is not effectively separable from this bare activity. Thinking is not effectively ownable. It ultimately belongs not to me, but to the process expressing itself in and through my acts. My personality is the unique way the open field of thinking-feeling is immanent to my acts of expression, the way it is implicated in them and impletes them: the way the field inflects and modulates itself through the following one upon the other of the ongoing series of acts I claim as my own and experience as manifesting what it's like to be me. "The inner personality is generated along with language."[59] Personality is the way the open field of relations channels through the ambulent locus for the production of acts of expression whose proximate neighborhood is my individual body. My personality is my theme. Processually speaking, "*a word is not an expression of an inner personality; rather, inner personality is an expressed or inwardly impelled word.*"[60]

This gives personality a cosmic coloration. The bourgeois subject, on the other hand, is characterized by its colorlessness and predilection for pettiness. Cosmic is not the first word that comes to mind to describe it. The emergence of the bourgeois subject coincides with a shift in the meaning of "inner" from the *immanence* of the relational continuum of the field of becoming to the speaking body, to *interiority* in a purportedly self-enclosed being of the subject of speech. Now words will indeed come across as the expression of an inner personality, rather than inner personality coming across as an expression of the world. This inversion occurs when "stable constructions of language" grow around an embodied locus of expression that "abstractly segregates" the series of acts channeling through that locus from others.[61] The eddy of bare activity that marks the turning point where the open field's infolding unfolds is abstractly segregated, as if it did not belong to the field but only to its locus in the field. The potential that issues forth turns back on itself, more like water swirling around a drain than waves cresting in the sea. Thought-signs carrying expressive potentials are forced down the drain before they are allowed to issue forth. The personality, thus interiorized, is the catchment basin for these inwardly impelled thought-signs. It holds in place a surplus reservoir of thought-signs carrying drained potentials, turning over on one another in their piped confinement. Some will gurgle back up into the issuing of an expressive act. The expression will appear to have been locally originated, piped back up from the restricted confines of the catchment. It will be heard as issuing from a segregated locus, from a separate coordinate position on the cultural map. Cultural acts will no longer be experienced as fusing relationally. They will only appear to interact: to connect extrinsically, at a segregative distance, through stable constructions that mediate expression by channeling it through regulated routines of call-and-response. Every interactive exchange will now be doubled, not by the fusional-relational abstract surface of transindividual becoming-body, but by a private subject, an inner personality "sharing" thoughts drawn from a private reservoir. The kinesthetic amoeba is muffled. It gurgles away in the drain trap, gagging on its own potential. Culturability is maximally channeled toward its internal limit of intersubjective human communication. When the expressive act is communicationally segregated in this way, thinking-feeling disaggregates. The thinking pulls away from the feeling. No more lascivious amoeba thinking-feeling with pseudopod reach extending in all directions. In its place, moral, upright me. It is only "I," the stable, regulated moral person, owner of my own expressions; it is only "I" who thinks. My body and its movements are now little more than the outwardly visible positioning of my inward private thinking, mediated for public consumption by the stable constructions of the prevailing norms of expression. Culturability is captured by the all-too-human. The eddy has declared its independence from the stream. Speech is individualized. The "sovereign" bourgeois individual raises its flag. Theme in Vološinov's sense, with its immanently formative connection to extraverbal levels, has been abstractly separated off on the side of the isolatable individual, in a way that effectively confines it to a segregated personality. A stable partitioning has been instituted between the "private" sphere, dedicated to the subjective manifestation of the "inner personality," and a "public" sphere of intersubjective communication where statements are answerable to norms of expression and subject to public judgment as to their "correctness" and "objectivity." This carries out another abstract segregation: of judgeable semantic content from theme. Theme may continue, personalized, inwardly impelled, eddying on in a barely discernible gurgle "behind" the intersubjective exchange, but it is only the semantic meaning of language, properly mediated by the formal structure of its stable constructions, that counts publicly.

According to Vološinov, it was in the nineteenth century that specific mechanisms began to be invented to abstractly segregate cultural acts from their impletion.[62] A partition is instituted between the "private" sphere, dedicated to the subjective manifestation of the "inner personality," and the "public" sphere of intersubjective communication subject to rules of propriety and purported objectivity. The public sphere is the collective correlate to the segregation of expression in the individual person. It comes to be synonymous with the social, appearing in the externalized figure of "society" over and against the individual: *the social domain.* In well-regulated social interaction, the cultural differences persons may carry as a trace of their belonging to a field of life larger than themselves, in unplaceable continuity with the alien, and extending the cosmic threshold of expression beyond the vicinity of known potential, must be checked at the domainal door of the public sphere—lest personal sensitivities be insulted. Banish outsized intensities of thinking-feeling; cage the animal. The same mechanisms that individualize expression segregate "culture" from "society." Impletion fractures. Human society fractions itself off from the human–animal continuum, taking refuge from it in inner personality. The offset between culturability, in its cosmic stretch, and sociability widens.

Publicly, acts of language do not intensely express; they judiciously "represent." What they represent is the socially recognized position occupied by the private person vis-à-vis socially acceptable others after its own segregated kind. Rules of decorum place the public expression at a polite remove, maintaining a safe distance between "inner personalities." A slightly expanded circle draws itself around the individual, allowing for intersubjective communication that remains restricted enough still to be considered "private" from the regulatory point of view of the public sphere: the circle of the family, or the circle of friends. Such social circles are segregated spheres for the representation of the inner personality to more or less intimate others. What remnants remain of the formative, bare-active intensity of expression is allowed a restricted expression within the concentric circles of the private. There, it manifests as "moods," quirks of personality, and private pathologies—subjective inflections of expression whose public broadcast would be improper. The pseudopods of expression retract and pathologically wither. The virtual immensity of expression contracts to the size of an "I" whose uprightness is now haunted and shadowed by what will be figured as the personal unconscious: stagnant repository of inwardly impelled thought-signs of indecorous tendency.

There is only one word for language segregated from theme and reduced to its semantic content and formal structure: "dead."[63] Society, understood as a public sphere at a decorous remove from the full open range of the "inner personality," is the death of culturability as it is understood here: as a relationally mutational regenerative movement running the length of the nature–culture continuum to the cosmic limit. It is ironic that *the death of culturability is a historic cultural achievement*. It is a product of a certain genealogy of enculturation taking itself to the public–private extreme (corresponding, not uncoincidentally, to the policing of the internal limit of the human). The public as social domain of the sovereign individual is the self-overcoming of cultural expression; cultural expression separated from what it can do. Or: it is a culmination of a particular (European) culture's turning against the amoebic sweep of its own immanent potential. Cultural expression becomes vestigial: museumified, folklorized, packageable, and saleable, reduced from its cosmic dimensions to the size of a shrink-wrapped commodity.

The externalization of the social in the figure of a public sphere populated by private individuals is a historical achievement that actually militates against sociability. Society, in the sense of a social order policing the internal limit of the human, is also the death of sociability. The murmur of the thirdness of expression—the transindividuality of the inhabitation of every expression by others—dies on the now-disconnected party line. There are no circumstances that are recognized as in any way important where sociability is allowed to manifest the theme of language itself, as *Amodal Suspension* was able to do under the cover of art (itself too often commodified). "Language as such" wanes moribund. Sociability has been euthanized by the social. The deed, paradoxically, was done by culturability coming to a certain conclusion. It was perpetrated by culturability extruding a pale, social copy of itself that ends up mothballing its own cresting in the cultural act in the checkroom of the public sphere.

It did not take long, however, for this self-stultifying achievement of culturability against itself to come to be felt as the deadening that it is. It was not long before Debord and Baudrillard, to name the most prominent examples, proclaimed this achievement of a de-nature-cultured society as actually marking the "end of the social."[64] All it took was for the mass media to bring "transparency" to public communication for "society" to audio-visibly implode into its emptiness of "theme"—its voiding of that "extra something that converts the word into a whole utterance"[65] expansively implete with cultural-difference-regenerating potential running all the way to the cosmic limit of nature. That "extra something" rides the waves of the murmurous sea-swell of third-party noise in the lines of communication. *Amodal Suspension* brings it to a flash point, from a certain processual angle that counters the segregation of culture from society in its own paradoxical way: by bringing sociability as such to expression, offset from culturability by different constitutive limits. Not segregating it, but refracting it, in the element of the reaching for language.

We are no longer living in the mass media age. Debord and Baudrillard are so twentieth century. The pronouncement of the end of the social was embarrassingly timed. It came at the threshold to the passage to a new regime. Sociability surreptitiously survived all along, waiting to make a comeback. Deadened, but not dead-ended. One of the places it survived, in local backwaters, was in gossip: hearsay. Its comeback took the name "internet": the technological reinvention of gossip, no longer as a slightly shameful local perversion of the public sphere troubled by unregulated personal expression leaking from private circles, but as the universal of communication. With the internet, hearsay becomes the "formal structure" of expression. In the youthful heyday of the mass media age, we had reporting, reliably attributed to identifiable sources (at least in theory). Now, rising phoenix-like from the ashes of the mass media implosion of the social, we have Facebook. With social media, sociability makes a comeback, beyond both well-regulated society and the end of the social.

THE RISE OF THE QUASI-PUBLIC

"Life," Vološinov remarks, "begins only at the point where utterance crosses utterance."[66] The life of the social is where words co-generatively react upon words. The mutual reaction of words upon each other survived in shriveled trace form even in the public sphere, in the way in which every expression "constitutes a germ of a response."[67] If the present act of expression constitutes the germ of a response that may come next, then it stands to reason that it was itself a response which a preceding expression likewise contained in germ. But might not that preceding expression very well have germinated into more than one response? There is, after all, a whole population of individuals co-habiting the public sphere. Could not that ancestor expression have contained two germs? Or three? Or four? Or $n \ldots$? Each expression is an infectious forking of the paths of sociality away from well-regulated call-and-response into a potential infinity of lines of transmission. In all that complexity, how could the lines not get tangled? How could each act of expression not resonate with any number of others? Is it not undeniable that every romantic pop song lyric is filled with the echoes of any number of other love songs, as if it were citing them en masse in its specific difference, as an individual variation on their never-ending, ever-branching collective theme? Is it possible to hear an individual political position-taking without a ring of the déjà-heard? The regulation of the public sphere is designed to background this endemic third-party noise on the line as much as possible, holding it to a residual minimum in order to safeguard the private/public split, its accompanying forms of individual recognition, responsibility and ownership, and their historic deadening of expression. But neither the deadening of the social nor the implosion at the end of the social were ever total.

Gossip is the genre of speech that from time immemorial has stealthily re-insinuated the tangled web of third-party lines into whatever sphere or technology of communication was available. Every piece of gossip purports to be a direct report of something specific said by a particular other. Its citational practice, however, is sloppy, to say the least (and so much more). You never quite know if the "he said x" is in fact a "she said he said x." Or even a "he said she said he said x." You never know how far down the line the utterance has actually come. The "owner" of the speech reported is essentially vague. Because of this, what is ostensibly a "private" exchange between two parties is on a party line. Not only is there is a cited third speaker necessarily involved, because the statement presents itself as a report of another's utterance, there is the distinct possibility of a fourth person in line, behind what the reported-upon third person is reported to have said. Gossip is actually in the *fourth-person singular*.[68]

And there is more. The receiver of the tidbit of reported speech is not involved in the exchange with a clearly individual status. He or she is equally present as the representative of what "people will think." Where there is gossip, there is a teeming crowd of "he saids" and "he said she saids" and "what people thinks" and "theys." In gossip, two's a crowd. The crowding is such that the distinction between social type ("they": people of an interested ilk, however ill-defined) and self-representing individual "I" is expressively blurred. The vagueness of the subject of speech is compounded by the fact that the evaluative accent with which the speech is reported does not distinguish between the present speaker's individual accent and the implied evaluation of the third- and fourth-party speakers whose potential voices echo on the line, or between the present listener and the virtually overhearing "they" that overpopulates the exchange. The "theme" of the language act is collectively owned in its speaking. It is no sooner emitted than it is already recognized by a virtually listening multitude pregnant (in the sense that a significant pause is said to be "pregnant") with an oversupply of implied response.

Gossip is much maligned. It is commonly denounced both as threat to privacy and as a degradation of public discourse. But who are "they" who can convincingly say they viscerally prefer a well-sourced news report to the latest gossip? Despite the tendency to stereotyping inherent in gossip's collapse of type and individual into each other and in the normative, even hectoring accent that often accompanies the gossipy evaluations of the virtual "they," gossip is simply more socially alive than Walter Cronkite ever was. It brings us back to the sociable place where "utterance crosses utterance" and words gleefully react with irresponsible abandon on other words.

What is so threatening about gossip to defenders of privacy and regulatory watchdogs of public speech is that it is neither: neither private exactly, nor public. Its crossing of the lines between individual and type, its blurring of the lines between "I" as this speaker and third-person other of an ilk, its collectivizing of the individual ear and socializing of evaluative accent, all of these things enable it to slip into the space between the two. Gossip inhabits the zone of indistinction between the private and the public. It has special status. It is *quasi-public*. Which is much the same as saying "quasi-private."

Gossip is a machine for bringing expression a step back from the deadening internal limit of regulated all-too-human intersubjective interaction toward that zone of indistinctly potentiated fusion marking the fold where the social act overlaps with the open field of culturability. Gossip back-steps from the historic achievement of culture that is the speaking bourgeois subject toward an ever-rolling, sometimes rollicking, movement of unregulated sociability, in overlap with culturability but mundanely offset from its cosmic continuum. Gossip has been characterized as many things, but cosmic is not one of them.

A QUASI-DIRECTNESS OF EXPRESSION

Vološinov saw something similar happening in the nineteenth-century bourgeois novel, already chomping at the bit of the well-regulated bourgeois individual, under cover of art. A new mode of reported speech came into prominence. The conventional markers that formally separate the reported speech of a character from the author's reporting speech in traditional indirect discourse (he said *that*. . . ; she said, " . . . ") are eliminated. The character's speech is directly inserted into the author's expression. This creates a "paratactic" connection between the two utterances: a direct contiguity without any marked subordination, as if "both the author and the character were speaking at the same time."[69] "The boundaries of reported speech become extremely weak," as if the two activities of speech generation were "breaking into each other."[70] Each retains its own evaluative accents to some extent. These "collide and interfere."[71] "Two intonations, two points of view, two speech acts converge and clash."[72] The result is a single "varidirectional"[73] stream of language which envelops within itself a social "interorientation."[74]

This "merging of differently oriented speech acts is *quasi-direct discourse*": "speech *interference*."[75] Expressive social noise.

The literary use of quasi-direct discourse is one thing. What worries Vološinov is "the social tendency it expresses."[76] He saw quasi-direct discourse gaining ground outside literature, around the edges of respectable public discourse. It was clear to him that "quasi-direct discourse lies on the main road of development of modern European languages, that it signalizes some crucial turning point in the social vicissitudes of utterance."[77] Without giving specific examples, he laments that in the rising tide of quasi-direct discourse "typifying and individualizing coatings of the utterance" become "intensely" differentiated, hypertrophied to the point that they undermine the "responsible social position implemented in it."[78] In other words, the extreme of typicality and the extreme of individuality converge and clash. Not unlike in gossip. The two extremes combine, without mediation, in a single interorientation, a varidirectional stream of de-positioned—deterritorialized—language from which "serious ideational consideration" has been quasied out.[79] What is left is the "expression of an adventitious, subjective state" of indeterminate personhood, as intensely typical as it is hypertrophically individual. First person? Third? . . . Fourth it is. Folding together. Topological personhood?

Vološinov is attached enough to traditional notions of authenticity and truth in speech to see this development as a "depression in the thematic value of the word."[80] He calls the tendency of quasi-direct discourse taken to this extreme the "contrived word."[81] It might have been more in keeping with his own philosophy to see it on the contrary as the beginning of a coming to performative expression of the theme of the sociability of language itself, in an exemplification of language's *essentially* contrived social nature: an incipient surfacing of sociability for itself, in all its noisy inauthentic glory.

SOCIABILITY GIGANTICUS

Today we live out the far side of the social tendency that made Vološinov cringe. From this vantage point it appears much less frightening: as mundane as Facebook. How more "contrived" could the word get than when it is digitized and refracted through a technological apparatus of immense complexity and tentacular reach. The same clash and convergence between extreme typicality and the hypertrophied assertion of individuality is to be found on the "personal" posts of social media. But the posts are not "personal" in anything approaching the nineteenth- and early twentieth-century sense, when there was a clearly contrasting "public" for individual speech to be set against. Social media is the reign of the quasi-public. Facebook friends exist to interlink. The "personal" connection is made to drift across the propagating links, rippling into expanding social circles, to the point that mutual "friends" will often not actually know who each other are. Facebook posts are designed to relay, propagating indefinitely across the rippling sea of digital sociality. The relay function is taken even further with Twitter. Citations proliferate in paratactic contiguity with each other, merging at the limit into a single varidirectional stream of social expression. Evaluative accents clash and converge in multitudinous inter-orientation. Already as of April 2011, barely five years in, it was estimated that one billion tweets were being emitted each week. *Sociability giganticus*. Peer-to-peer sharing, for its part, has weakened the ownership of expression, sparking often draconian rearguard actions in defense of "intellectual property." Hacking even more so. This, as "personal" expression on social media sites falls under the proprietary control of corporations. Content posted by individuals on Facebook belongs not to them but to Facebook Inc. The rules of ownership formerly in place have been scrambled by the predominance of a new operator: corporately patrolled "access" replaces individual ownership (a shift pre-diagnosed by Jeremy Rifkin in 2000).[82] To gain access, users are required to accept interminable contracts whose terms they never read: contractual "private" expression? In this oxymoronic brave new quasi-public social world, gossip—used here as a catchall term for speech falling under the sway of the fourth-person singular—has attained a new level of prominence.

The point about gossip is not that the gossipy content has increased. It was always high volume. It is that, with social media, the internet itself has brought to global expression and previously unheard-of prominence (at a level not even "they" would have suspected) the tendency of which gossip has been the most historically constant and reliable agent: the quasi-directification of social relation. The internet has taken quasi-direct relation to a global scale, and made it unmistakably the dominant mode of expression. Under the impulsion of social media, the internet has ushered in the reign of the quasi-public. It has massively back-stepped the cultural act into the domain of sociability—closer to "*pure sociality*" as the "field of immanence" of expressive variation, "the intrinsic nature of association" in its reaching for language.[83] This is what *Amodal Suspension,* a year before the founding of Facebook, had heralded artistically (in much the same way Jacques Attali says that music is capable of heralding social change).[84]

The internet-led back-stepping of the cultural act into pure sociality has been decried as the death of culture. The internet has also been lamented for undermining the objectivity of public-sphere expression. It has been demonized for undermining the implementation of responsible social positioning in speech and tainting the seriousness of the ideational content of expression. (Just a minute, haven't we heard that before? Isn't that Vološinov's version of intellectual property? Except . . . whom did *he* get it from?) The internet's malevolent effects on the "inner personality," particularly in its tender childhood shoots, have been voluminously fretted over (not least of all, on the internet).

This last worry comes to the heart of the central issue that Vološinov raised in relation to quasi-direct social relation: the replacement of the responsibly self-positioning and seriously ideating sociocultural subject by a quasi-direct "adventitious subjective" growth.

Adventitious (the definition bears repeating): "1: coming from another source and not inherent or innate 2: arising or occurring sporadically or in other than usual location."[85]

Ultimately, the question the internet poses for culture and society is what this adventitious subjectivity, now unleashed, can become. Whatever it becomes, its singular quasi-public/quasi-private status marked by ultimately disowned, de-positioned, irresponsiblized utterances, will ensure that its becoming will be a *collective individuation.*[86] Will it rejig the respective limits of the social and the cultural? Will it refigure their overlap and immanence? Will its monstrous complexity and tentacular stretch take sociability itself to the pseudopodic "cosmic" limit of culture? How will it redraw the map of the human territory, as it rests on the nature–culture continuum? Will it rejuggle the zones of indistinction between the human, the animal, the technological, and the generative forces for variation that crest from them? Or will the pseudopods instead retract, withdrawing back into a successor form of human containment?

There is no paucity of futuristic prognostications on these subjects. This essay will not add more. It will content itself to briefly mentioning what has *always* been the case for language and communication, according to Peirce: that, given the quasi-directness of discourse the "interpretant" of an expression is ultimately a "quasi-mind": a collective individuation of thought beyond the pale of the bourgeois subject, and at the contrasting limit to it, decidedly nonhuman (or naturally more-than-human). The full implications of this, and how it plays out from here, are yet to be seen. Now Peirce will have the (not and never) last word.

THE DETERMINATION OF A QUASI-MIND

It is undeniably conceivable that a beginningless series of successive utterers should all do their work in a brief interval of time, and that so should an endless series of interpreters. Still, it is not likely to be denied that, in some cases, neither the series of utterers nor that of interpreters forms an infinite collection. When this is the case, there must be a sign without an utterer and a sign without an interpreter. . . . Neither an utterer, nor even, perhaps, an interpreter is essential to a sign. . . . I am led to inquire whether there be not some ingredient of the utterer and some ingredient of the interpreter which not only are so essential, but are even more characteristic of signs than the utterer or interpreter themselves.[87]

Two separate minds are not requisite for the operation of a sign. Thus the premisses of an argument are a sign of the truth of the conclusion; yet it is essential to argument that the same mind that thinks the conclusion *as such* should also think the premisses. Indeed,

two minds in communication are, in so far, "at one,"
that is, are properly one mind in that part of them.
That being the understood, the answer to the question
will go to recognize every sign,—or, at any rate, nearly
every one,—is a determination of something of the
general nature of a mind, which we may call
a "quasi-mind."[88]

Admitting that connected Signs must have a Quasi-
mind, it may further be declared that there can be no
isolated sign. . . . Accordingly, it is not merely a fact of
human Psychology, but a necessity of Logic, that every
logical evolution of thought should be dialogic.[89]

CODA

"From this vantage point [the contemporary mutation of sociality]
appears much less frightening: as mundane as Facebook." How
quickly things can take a new twist! Between the first versioning
of those passages not so many years ago (circa 2011)—before
the Pollyannaish prognostications of online togetherness had
entirely faded out from their 1990s heyday—and this final revi-
sion (2018), "sociability giganticus" took a malignant turn.
Quasi-directness of discourse has grown a troll-like tumor the
size of the internet. Hearsay has hardened into "fake news."
The polyvocal stream of utterance indefinitely crossing utterance has rebecome disjunctive, pooling into mutually exclusive
social media bubbles. "They" has splintered into predatory
packs at each other's throats. The social dynamic for which gossip was the privileged figure in the foregoing analysis has grown
fangs. By all appearances, the quasi-mind has suffered a stroke.

It is tempting to psychologize these developments, attribut-
ing them to the personal faults or deficiencies of a scapegoat
category of human. The alternative is to construe it as another
more-than-human adventure in the social story of the inwardly
impelled word. There is no more an "inner personality" processually separate from the relational field than there ever was.
No less than before is there infra-relation contracted into speech
acts, to implete them with collective individuation. What there is
is the emergence of a new mode of impletion capable of reerect-
ing what are heard as hard boundaries in the sea of utterance:

hateful waves whose crests slam those of neighboring waves with a vengeance before receding back into the swell of noise. In other words, shouted-out social domains cresting in as mutually exclusive a way as possible, clashing as hard as they can given the general convergent conditions of quasi-direct discursive flux.

In a step back from pure sociality, this new mode foregrounds the element of moral judgment and hectoring implicit in gossip, intensifying the reactive element in its constitution, to the extreme where it loses all pretense of bourgeois propriety. It now shamelessly unleashes the severest of moralism, without a hint of the uprightness that the mediating gears of the old public sphere affirmed as an ideal. Is this the kind of "hypertrophy" of quasi-direct discourse that Vološinov was afraid of, wearing a new distorted face he could not have imagined in his grotesquest nightmares?

This unleashed bullying does not entirely eclipse the kind of operations afoot in the now quasi-public field that are benign enough to declare "mundane." But it cannot be ignored, and it cannot be understood using nineteenth-century categories of sovereign subjecthood and identity that were long ago washed away in the cacophonous tide. It cannot be counteracted by a return to the presumptive safety of the public sphere. It must be grappled with on its own twenty-first-century terms, in the name of autonomous participations and participative autonomies to come, of an expansively relational, joyfully fourth-person-singular kind.

Grappling with the contemporary becoming-reactive of sociality requires a specifically political analysis that is beyond the remit of this book. Such an analysis would confront another complex processual overlap that poses at least as thorny a problem as the one posed for this essay by the not-entirely coincident co-implication of the social and the cultural. Namely, the co-implication of the political and the economic. An analytic of capitalism, equal to the novelty and complexity of its present-day neoliberal avatar, is a necessary undertaking in this connection, closely coupled with a study of the power formations with which it is implicated. I have tried to make a start in this direction in other recent work.[90]

3

Making to Place

Simryn Gill

THIS PLACE?

A gash in emptiness. From a plane's eye view, it is hard not to see it that way even though one knows better. The land below, we know, is vibrating with history. It is one of the oldest geological formations on earth. It is also country to the world's oldest continuous culture. It is alive with traces of passage, as animated with care and rejuvenated with ritual as it is worn by the elements. This is not to say that it is without scars, that history does not also burden it. The gash in the emptiness that it is hard not to see as both the culmination of a conquest and a new iteration of it.

"Hardscrabble (ORIGIN early nineteenth century): place thought of as the epitome of barrenness." The hardscrabble labor of massive machinery has hollowed out the land. It has overlaid the history of the place with a hole, which now epitomizes it. It is as if the surrounding land were under obligation to mirror the emptiness of the excavation in its own expanse. What else is a mine, other than a taking of the earth for tabula rasa? "(ORIGIN Latin) 'scraped tablet,' denoting a tablet with the writing erased."

What else? An extracting. Here, iron is extracted. From here, iron is exported to build other places. The steel-girded cities of China rise from here. Also from here rare earth metals go into handheld devices, magnetizing the everywhere and nowhere-in-particular of the communication web that instantly links the

149

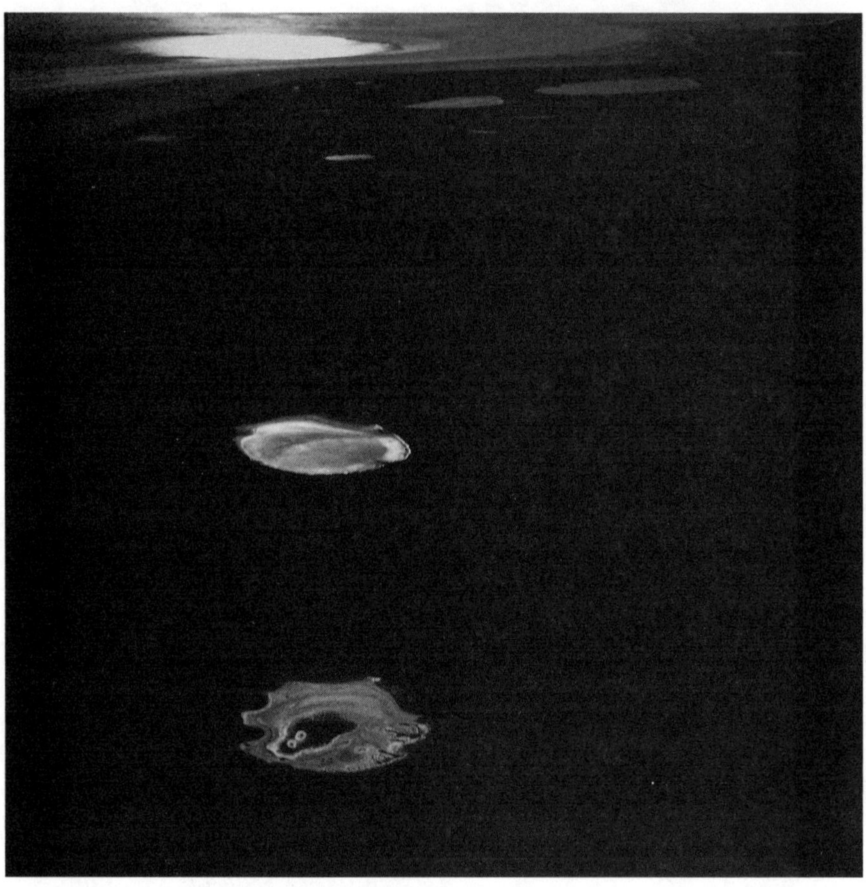

Mine. Simryn Gill, from *Eyes and Storms*, 2013.
Twenty-three Ilfochrome prints, 125 × 125 cm.

cities of China to their counterparts in Australia and across the globe. Gold goes, too, to give psychological ballast to the global financial markets whose own over-networked weightlessness cyclically whirligigs into free fall. From the point of view of the everywhere and nowhere-in-particular of what goes from here, the hole below the plane's eye view is the eye of a rising storm of global activity. This is not just a metaphor. Not far from here coal is also massively extracted, fueling unbridled industry and climate change. The bright economic outlook of the outback mine is a distant twinkle in the Sandy eye of our "once in a century storms," which of late come every five years.

How, the airborne artist asks, can she claim a connection to this land?

An immigrant from Asia, she is not of this land's history, nor of its erasing. She is neither indigenous nor a settler. She does not excavate with massive machinery, nor speculate using the abstract instruments of capital. She does, however, carry a cell phone.

What are the things that connect us?

PLACES OF STONE

In the artist's hometown of Port Dickson is found an oil refinery as well as the largest power station in peninsular Malaysia. There are also ancient cemeteries and shrines. Some of the shrines house rocks. Some rocks, we know, are deities. What makes a rock a deity, the artist asks? What gives power to a rock, and through it, to its place? What draws one in to the power of a place?

Whatever its nature, the draw in this case was not well disposed to respect the divisions of the official social order. The artist has an "alternate tour" of Port Dickson on which she likes to take visitors. One stop is a shrine next to the power station. It is dedicated to a paving stone. The stone is marked by a red spot, reminiscent of the bindi Hindus wear on the forehead. It also bears Chinese characters. Its power drawn in two traditions, wed together in this place. This syncretism is characteristic. Or was, in earlier times. Images of the Hindu god Ganesha are still to be found in the Chinese cemetery. A short journey away, near the border with the next state, there is a site where Chinese shrines, Hindu temples, and a keramat shrine of the local Sufi folk tradition honoring spirits of the land cohabit. Muslims no longer go there. The authorities, in the service of the State project of imposing a proper Islam more in line with the Saudi Salafist model, threatened to blow the site up if the worship continued. What was now deemed "proper" to this place swooped in from another place, half a world away. A power of a far-off place visited itself upon this place, to divisive effect, in the name of unity, of building a national identity to which it must belong. What is proper to an identity that divides?

What is proper to an identified place?

THE BAD CITIZEN

Put another way, what belongs?

Not I. I'm a bad citizen, the artist confesses (with a twinkle in her eye). She never knew her place, she explains. The traditional role reserved for her by family and community as a Sikh woman was not one, from the earliest age, that she would allow to contain her. She was the unruly one. As a result, her community itself could not contain her. She would marry a Chinese Malaysian, whose familiar postcolonial trajectory into overseas education, coupled with the ethnic tensions agitating the nation-building project of post-independence Malaysia, had left him a non-citizen in his own country, with only the passport of an adopted country to his name. With the resulting move to Australia the artist found herself the non-citizen, on top of the "bad" citizen she started out as. Her family had internalized the tension between citizenship and non-citizenship. It incarnated in its very structure the gap between being in a place and being of a place, between living there and belonging here.

Oddly, Australia itself seemed to echo this tension. "When I first lived here I used to imagine a vapour rising above the city, a confounded, teeth-gnashing, collective sigh of *what am I doing here?* and I added my angst to that imaginary cloud . . . In fact what I thought was my personal mantra—what am I doing here?—was something of a national chorus. I would say that this lament has a long lineage, probably going back to the time of white arrival and settlement."[1] A cloud of agitation rising up from the city: in the eye of a storm, of impossible belonging. As the mine is to the open land, I am to the city (and the city to this nation).

LITTLE NOTHINGS

One of the things she did here (there) was to begin collecting. Collecting things normally plays on a strong sense of origins. The thing collected is a token of attachment to the place and time of its origin, of which it stands as the enduring trace, carefully identified and labeled. The attachment to the collected thing is to an enduring out of its place after its time. The investment in the collected thing, in present time, care and attention, in anticipation and temporarily satisfied longing, draws one in to this. There is something inherently melancholic and nostalgic about collecting. It shares this characteristic with all endeavors playing on a sense of origin. Is not any original sense of identified-labeled belonging, whether to a nation or an ethnicity or even a city or a neighborhood, or again to a gender or an age or a stage of life, a melancholic-nostalgic attachment to enduring traces? Are these not ways in which we *collect ourselves*? Ways of regaining our composure in the essentially out-of-place? For an origin is by nature out of place—forever at a distance in the always-before of this after-time. Like birth.

Does identified belonging really answer the question, What am I doing here? Or does it simply apply a bittersweet balm to having been born?

For one whose here is the eye of a storm of impossible belonging, collecting things does not provide the same bittersweet balm. But there is a certain power in the present-time care and attention, the anticipation and temporarily satisfied longing, that comes with collecting. The artist will collect. But she will not collect things. She will collect nothings.

Soon after her arrival in Australia, she begins a practice that will continue throughout her artistic life. As she makes her way through the city, she keeps an eye out for "naughts": discarded little things in the shape of a zero, like the plastic ring from a soda bottle top. Little zeros: the shape of emptiness. They lie where they are found because they have come to naught, from where no one cares, discarded. They have been emptied from an anonymous passerby's quotidian cargo. Dumped, without so much as a passing thought. As litter, the place they occupy is tenuous. They have no claim to place other than the unadorned fact that this is where they happen to be, for no good reason. This is not the same as being out of place. It is being in a place without an alibi.

Hollowed out by their own shape, naughts have none of the charm or personality of the fully collectable. Having no meaningful origin, their happening to be in the particular place they are found betokens no attachment. They are traces, but of nothing of note. The artist does not collect them in the key of melancholy and nostalgia. They are kept, but not cherished. They are not for decoration. They are not an indulgence in a trash aesthetic. They are there, simply to be kept. And counted. Counting: the most minimal activity to which a collection lends itself.

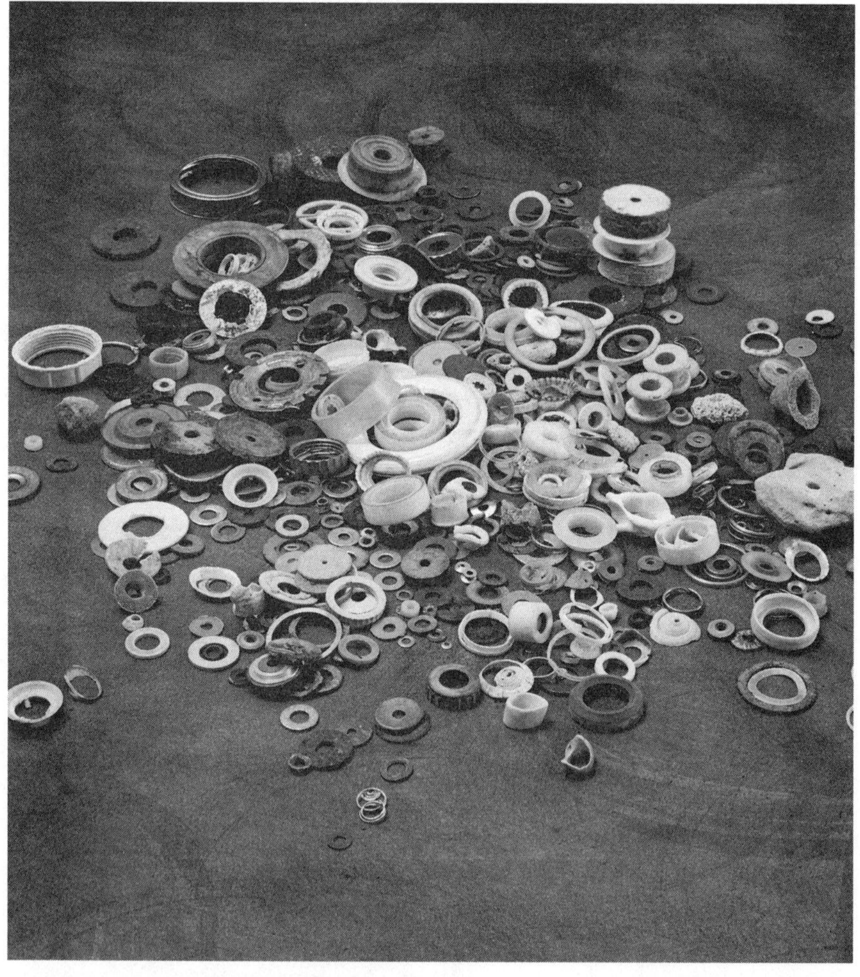

Simryn Gill, *Naught*, 2010. Method of display and dimensions variable. Photograph by Jenni Carter.

There is no meaning to counting. There is only procedure. The procedure involves going back over a collected-together plurality of things, in an abstract movement through the neutral space of number. All that counts is the bare fact of this many having come together. Counting registers little nothings in a belonging-together as tenuous as their individual claim to place.

JUST NOSING

The emptiness of the artist's little nothings clears a way for her. She, like them, is without alibi in the city into which she has landed. The knowledge that whenever she ventures out more collectable nothings will have fallen in whatever path she takes becomes a lure to go out and move through the city. Her movements are not purposeful, for example, in the way a worker's beelining to the office is. They are not exactly purposeless, either. The lure of the naughts yields a third way: a direction without a purpose. The direction is not toward any particular point. It is toward venturing out, and passing through. Just being out, in movement through the city, with a heightened attentiveness to what may present itself, but no agenda. "Just nosing," she calls it. Or in Malaysian pidgin, "looksee looksee."

She thought she was looking for her place in Australia. But what she has found through her nothings is a *way*. She now has a way of being where she lives, far from origins, unfixed in place, undivided by overlaid identity and the divisive historical weight of assigned meanings with which it bears down. She has an alternative to the impossibility of setting down roots: holding herself afloat in her moving through. She has a way of moving in place, looking, seeing, nosing along with a calmly expectant openness to what might fall into her path.

It could be anything, really. For when you are venturing out nosing for naught, with openness and attentiveness, something else is just as good. The expression of the passenger next to you on the train catches your eye. That's something. Where are they going? What ephemeral musing or mortal concern just flitted across their face? And why for heaven's sake are they dressed like that? There's something else. You get off the train and a motled sunshine falls across a façade, dappling it, fleetingly, with patches of light and shadowed reminders of the building stand-ing across the way. Strange, how what stands so stolidly in place takes account in itself for what stands away across from it. What more distant places might likewise, if less visibly, cross into this place? In what dappled connection at a distance does this place cross back to them? Could this crisscross, this mutual refraction, this reciprocal taking into account, be what place is really all about, more than any proper standing or being here by right?

SMALL EPIPHANIES

If it is, then the question "What am I doing here?" cannot be construed as asking if I am where I belong by right of origin or reason of identity. As asked by the artist, it is the open ques-tion of how, wherever I happen to chance, I am dappled by my elsewheres as I go, and how I might dapple them back in my passing. To answer questions like that, you don't look inward and you don't look back. You just venture out again, and con-tinue on your way. In search of little nothings. That way, you encounter "small epiphanies." That is what the artist calls being taken by surprise by an unsuspected connection. A little joy of happenstance.

Small epiphanies, unlike their Romantic or religious cousins, are mundane. They do not stand out from the everyday. They rise up into the everyday, from its refractive background. You wouldn't go so far as to call them sublime. They are not spec-tacular, but they do have a certain power. They have an allure, a drawing-in-ness, the artist will say.

What draws one in to the power of a place? Sometimes it's the little things, nothings really, more modest than even a minor deity. It is the this-worldly things with the unimperative allure of happenstance that softly, almost surreptitiously, draw one in.

AN ALIBI

The empty practice of collecting naught has given the artist something of inestimable valuable: an alibi. She now has an alibi for her being in a place without an alibi. It's not that she has found her place. She has found her way: through place.

Say, in addition to collecting little nothings, she also collects the small epiphanies she encounters en route. That would raise different questions, beyond "What am I doing here?" For example, can the happenstance of a place be transferred elsewhere? Can its quality be conveyed? Can you put it into words? Unlikely, because one wouldn't be liable to call it an even small epiphany if there were not something of the ineffable in it. Then can it be photographed? How do you go about photographing not an object or a place, but a happenstantial quality? What happens when happenstances from different places are combined together in an elsewhere stranger to them all? Through this displacement can one reconstitute the lived refractive background of place? How can that encountered connectability be conveyed so that it does not allow itself to be weighed down by the history of a place, or contained by its identity, or tethered to the official belongings attaching to these? Can one capture that elusive background, whose appearing comes precisely from emptying the place of just such ballast, in favor of a drift in the purposeless direction of a different kind of care and attentiveness open to an emergent sensibility to place?

These are artistic questions. Art will be the alibi for passingly inhabiting otherwise, in an encounterful crisscross of being-heres and elsewheres.

THE ART OF NO REASON

The art of this inhabiting otherwise is also strongly procedural. The collecting of little nothings provides the template for its procedure. Venturing out with open-ended attentiveness, coming back, and then going over the harvested traces with an abstract movement. Now the abstract movement will not be the minimal one of counting. It will be the more taxing one of reexpressing, through the traces, the lived quality of befalling that recommended them for harvesting in the first place. It will be a re-tracing of their happenstantial allure in an artistic movement of abstraction. The reexpression, although not minimalist, must retain something of the economy and neutrality of collecting's counting procedure.

This is not an art that starts with the adornment of a concept. The artist is acutely aware that she must beware of being led on by verbal propositions. It is necessary to be wary of words, because the weight of history and the authorized associations they carry predesignate a destination. For the surprise of connection to take—for being in place to take place—one must clear the way for it. Place must be emptied of the meanings already embedded in it. Otherwise, all paths will just lead back to designations that were already in place. To avoid this circular journey, the procedurality of the art process must take the lead. It must do so without the security of an alibi, without a framing concept or already elaborated analysis in place, with studied indifference to known categories.

A PROCEDURE FOR LIVING

There is a whimsical edginess to this. The whimsy lies in proceduralizing the unknown in so mundane a little-nothing way. There is a playfulness about tackling the unknown without all the self-important handwringing and pretentious second-guessing that often goes along with that. The whimsy is the humor of dedicating oneself to a minor practice of the unknown. The edginess comes because by this approach you are always in the middle of it, figuring it out as you go along. You never have it in hand. You're always reaching-for, moving forward, at the speed of life. What you're doing, as you're doing it, can't be described. It's like looking over a cliff, the artist muses. The ground of history and identity, one's rooting in already communicable meaning, has fallen out from under you. All you have left is a fickle background that makes its appearance in its own good time, taking you by surprise every time. There is no way of knowing en route, let alone in advance, if it will work. Until it does.

The edginess, the artist says, is somewhat addictive. From nothing has come an intensity of inhabiting otherwise. Art without alibi—or art as the alibi for having no alibi for being where you are—becomes a veritable lifestyle, a way of life. This art of no reason gives a reason for living, one that is no less effective for being empty. The no-reason is to keep on keeping on going, always on to somewhere else, in attentive openness to the surprise of relation. This is not a justification. It is a journey whose continuing is its own end.

The edginess comes from the same place the procedure's

power comes from. Art as a means without end for re-tracing life's happenstances in a minor key of joy and emergent sensibility has no predesignated style. The artist does not think of herself as having a medium, and says that she does not work from materials. She works from passing through. This makes her hard to place. It is not clear what category she belongs to as an artist. The impossibility of belonging threads through every stage of the journey. She is never cured of it.

But the art of no reason is nevertheless curative, in a way. For minor joys are oddly not incompatible with major horrors. Horrors like mines making a tabula rasa of someone else's history and meanings. You are fully aware of the horror, you understand its grounding, you have studied its history, you don't deny or neglect or paper over any of that. You don't empty other people's place, or take their place and speak your concepts and analysis on their behalf. You hold your tongue and empty your own relation to place: in order to retrace it, attentive to emergent connections. The horrors and injustices of a place are part of what creates the conditions for that encounter. They are not in any way neglected. They are refracted. In a sense, *the ground rises with the background.* It is a contributing factor in the artistic retracing. It is re-presented, horror and all, in some manner of trace, along with the small epiphany that emerged in contrast to it. Without it, the small epiphany would have nothing with which to contrast its little joy. Art, practiced as a procedure of living, is an affect-conversion apparatus. It extracts a modicum of affirmative intensity from all that weighs a place down. It's a bit like a mining operation itself: a telluric extraction and refinement of what is found on the ground. Unlike the mine, it does not simply mirror its own emptiness. It does not hollow out the land. It refracts its complexity in an emergent minor key. It empties, to otherwise refill. It applies no balm. In its own little way, it intensifies.

IT'S NOT "ABOUT"

Needless to say, the artist is highly skeptical of the concept of site-specific art. The clarity of her procedure requires clearing the site. "The clarity," she specifies, "comes from the action, and not the space cleared."[2]

To clear the sites of her art, she ventures out into them without alibi, not knowing what she will find, and without any preconceived notion of what form the forming artwork will eventually take. The journey is full of stories, styles, historical frameworks, and material textures. None of these, however, will be what the artwork is about. For the stories, styles, frameworks, and materials, she uses an action word rather than an indicator of linguistic reference: triggers. There is no "about" here. It's simply not about. It's round-about the place. It's all in the activity, in the moving through and back and forth, and what the action triggers into taking form.

Mindful not to be on about, the artist often proceeds by indirection. For example, she is going to Venice, so goes to the outback. She is drawn to the mines without yet knowing how they might possibly relate to what she will end up doing as the Malaysian Australian representative to the Biennale. She returns to Sydney, and her collections of small epiphanies, with more to add. She takes her curator on her alternative tour of Port Dickson. Still more additions. The count rises. The ground also rises. This latest reencounter with Malaysia, as always, triggers things from the past, including from the family and social histories she worked so hard to unrule herself of. She is drawn to a kind of Hindu bronze ritual vessel, and collects that drawing-in. She is drawn into a certain style of chair she associates with her grandfather, and collects a number of them together. She remembers the small epiphany from her childhood of realizing that after they fell the leaves of a certain local tree, called the sea jambu, dappled themselves with abstract patterns that she felt anticipated modern art. On an earlier trip, she ventured round the town nosing about, seeking, talking to people, and finally found a still-living specimen, halfway down a cliff to the sea. Talk about looking over a cliff.

Small epiphany: *Here Art Grows on Trees*. Nice title—but what does it mean? Wrong question again. It's not easy to keep the wrong questions from coming back. That's why procedure is so important. Think trigger. What does this trigger? That's the right question. But that question cannot be answered in isolation. What the jambu triggered in place, over the cliff, is one little thing. But what it might trigger displaced, its drawing-in

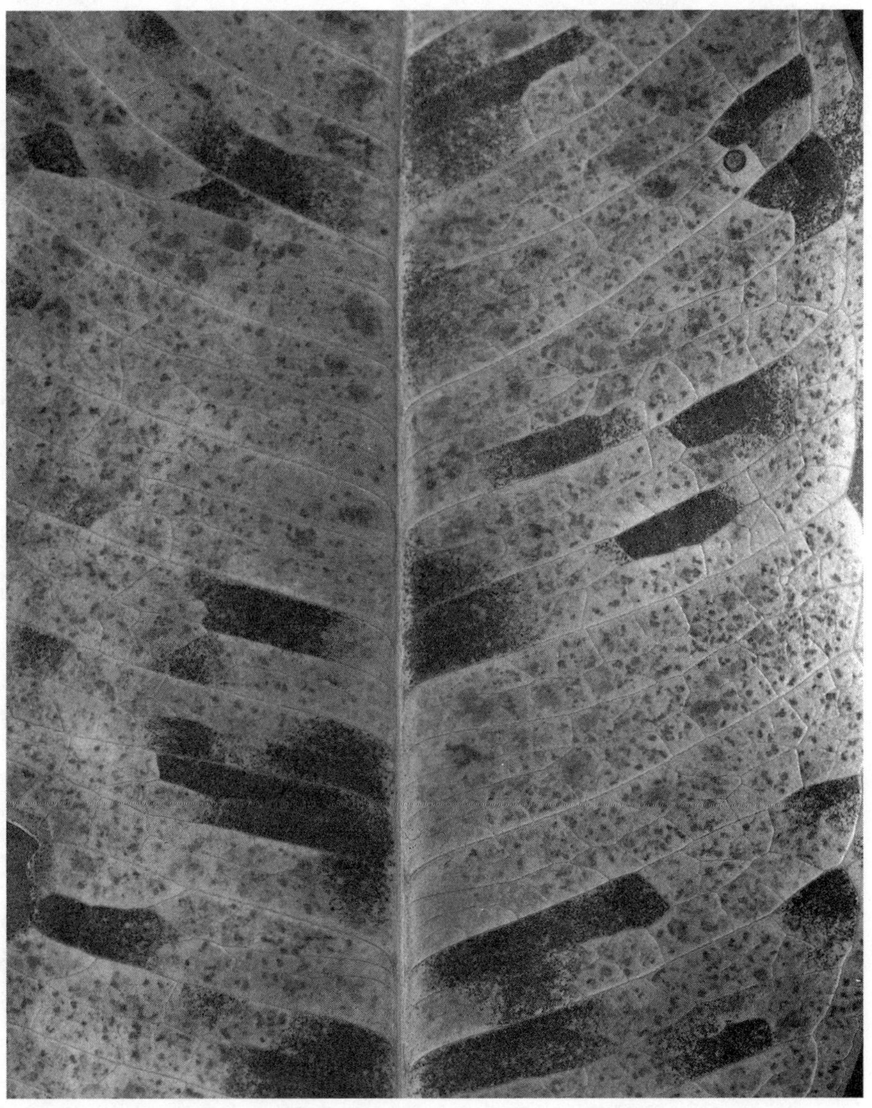

Detail of a jambu leaf. From Simryn Gill, *Jambu Sea, Jambu Air*, 2013.
Bound offset prints, Roygbiv Editions, Sydney.

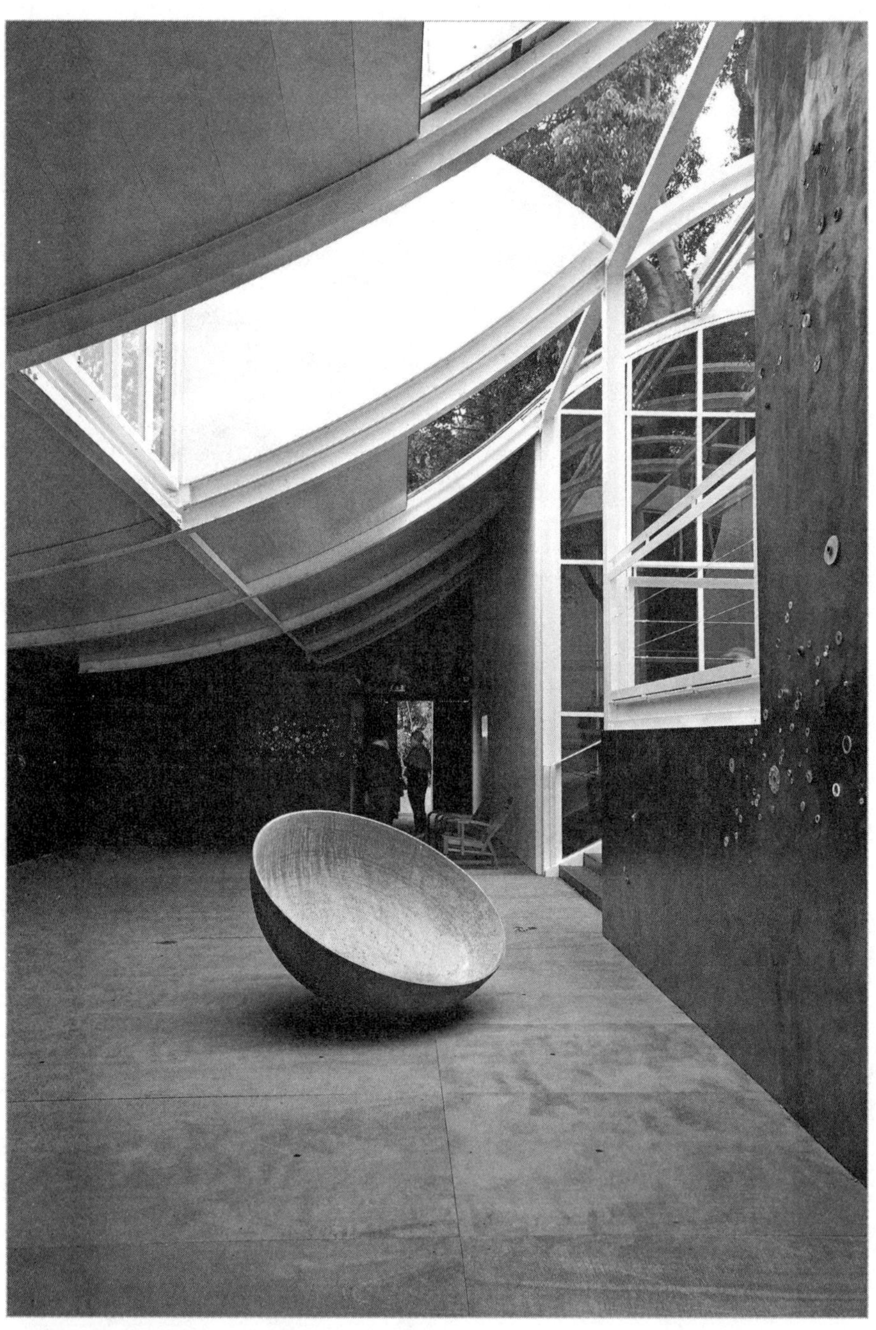

Bronze ritual vessel with naughts. Simryn Gill, *Here Art Grows on Trees*,
Australian Pavilion, 55th Venice Biennale, 2013. Photograph by Jenni Carter.

brought together with that of other collected elements of the artwork in formation, is another question entirely. When all of them come together in Venice to inhabit together their mutual displacement, it is certain that very different things will trigger. The drawings-in will mutually refract, as each other's elsewheres. Outback Australia, urban Australia, peninsular Malaysia, and Venice will cross to singular effect, all depending on the *way* in which they are reexpressively brought together. To retrace places with their elsewheres is not to squarely reproduce what happened on-site. It is to obliquely renew takings-account of each other, re-making their relation take place here.

Remaking a relation of mutual taking-account is very different from accounting-for. It is not done from the subject position of the artist. It is transpositional, triggering in-between, roundabout, and back and forth. It does not satisfy the criteria of any conventions of commentary-about, illustration, or analysis.

MAKING TO PLACE

The problem is finding a right way: one that does not bring back the wrong questions, that avoids triggering responses in others that return to conventions of commentary-about. The artist confesses that she struggles with the urge to just dump together the things she has gleaned from her art procedure for living, in the same way her little nothings were unceremoniously dumped. After all, her little nothings led her to her small epiphanies. Won't a second dumping do the same for the visitors to the artwork?

She realizes that it is not likely to work that way. The ground of the art space and the ground of the outback are not the same, nor are the sidewalks of Sydney, Port Dickson, and Venice. This means that the conditions for an effectively intensifying rising of a refractive background signaling its contrast to ground are different in every case. What happens in each case is less site-specific than relationship-specific. You have to start from prior relation to remake relation. There are conventionalized, identified, labeled relations already everywhere embedded in place. This is no less true—in some ways perhaps even more true—of art sites. These existing conditions of embedded relation fixed in place are what must be cleared away, to make way for triggering otherwise. Although the emergently triggered relation is not reducible to the ground of its triggering, and is not effectively contained in the definition of the site, every detail of the site, the smallest characteristic of the lay of the land, can become a contributing factor to the emergence that happens in the clearing. Or it can become a contributing factor to a swerve back into the "about," with all the identifying and categorizing and assumed overlay of meanings and officialized versionings of history that come with that. The lay of the land must be taken account of. To dump is not enough. The lay of that land must be grappled with.

In the continuing process, as in its punctual sojourn in an art site, it is necessary to make to place. That's an odd way that the artist has of putting it, but it makes immediate sense if you think of making to place on the model of singing to tune. Singing to a tune involves following a piece of music, attentive to its composition, just as making to place involves passing through, following the lay of the land, attentive to its features. When you sing to a tune, you don't have to slavishly follow it. You can vary it, adding your own embellishments. The same is true of making to place. You can vary place with your passing. The analogy starts to break down when the place is an art place where a number of makings to place are slated to come together. It's a bit like singing to more than one tune at the same time. How to keep it from degenerating into a cacophony? Where do you find the middle ground between site-nonspecific cacophony and being on "about"?

PEELING A ROOM

One answer: build into the art place its own creative undoing. That doesn't mean demolishing it. The idea is to empty it in a way that creates the conditions for an expressive retracing, a refractive remaking of relation, in key with the artist's practice of art as a procedure for living. The challenge is to clear the site in just the right way, without literally clearing it.

Although . . . a bit of tactical demolition can be revealing. So the roof comes off. The brought-together traces of places passed will now be exposed to the elements. The exhibition will be rained on. Leaves will fall and litter it, like so many little botanical nothings. The collected objects will undertake a journey of their own together, an adventure of weathering. Along the way, their qualities will change. They will lose some of their characteristics, and take on character. What will that trigger, in the various stages of this journey in place?

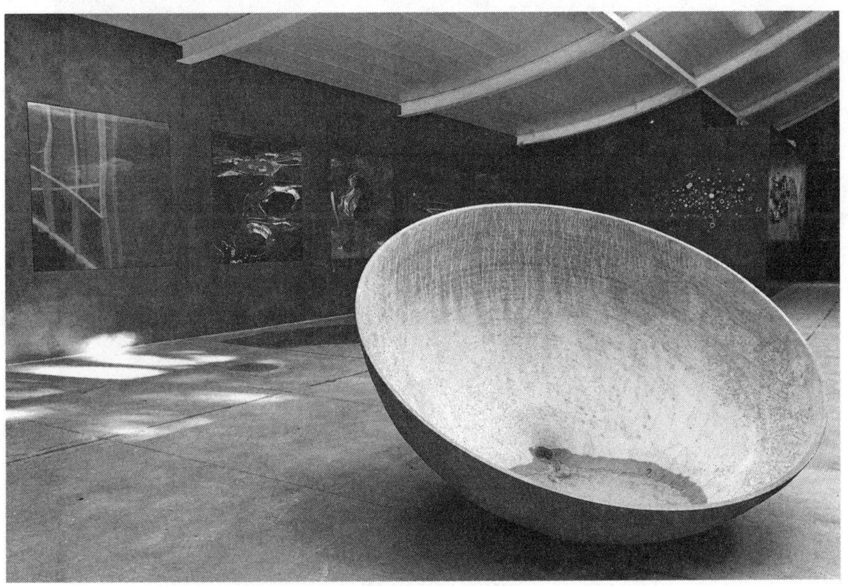

Weathering. Simryn Gill, *Here Art Grows on Trees*, Australian Pavilion, 55th Venice Biennale, 2013. Photograph by Jenni Carter.

The artist doesn't dwell on the idea of demolition, or think in terms of deconstruction. Demolition is just a procedure for conditioning the site for the arising of an emergent effect. She thinks of it in terms of peeling an orange to make the juices flow. She will peel the pavilion to extract its relational juices from the contributing places so that they flow together in a liquid refraction nonspecific to this place, but singularly taking place here. Making to place is making taking-place. It is making the exhibition of the art an event—even if little or nothing happens by the usual criteria of what an event is. The kind of event that is conditioned to take place is an emergent effect of the liquid

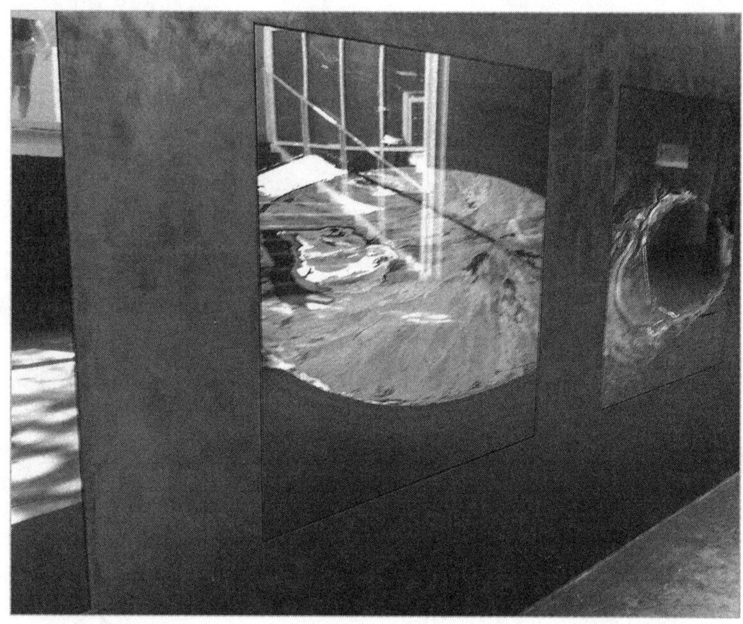

Refractions. Simryn Gill, *Here Art Grows on Trees*, Australian Pavilion,
55th Venice Biennale, 2013. Photograph by Brian Massumi.

refraction, like a rainbow forming between raindrops. That is
what the things that have been brought together in the exhibition are. Not sited objects: placedrops. Which makes the small
epiphanies that may form between them lifebows.

FLOATING-SPECIFIC ART

The artist has a vocabulary for talking about the enabling conditions for refracting places in this way. She refers to a certain
loosening of ties to the real, by which she says she means undoing the accepted sense of the "right" way to be in the world. This
loosening of accepted ties is a mode of extraction from place.
The extraction segues into a mode of abstraction. The non-site-
specificity of art-making to place is by nature an abstraction
from place. It necessitates a loosening of ties to the consensual
"reality" in place.

To keep the making to place sufficiently abstract, you have
to create an artificial space, one without the usual constraints.

But not without constraints of its own. There is no such thing as a place without constraints. Existing art spaces are highly artificial already. They are in a way pre-abstracted, full of embedded abstract constraints that are so familiar they are easy to overlook. The artificiality of the places of art is naturalized by over-familiarity, ingrained expectations, and many a tendentious overlay of meaning and identifying/labeling history. That is why it is necessary to peel them: to re-artificialize them. To make them live up to their artificiality and the living power of abstraction they are sometimes capable of housing, providing they don't have their top on too tight. Otherwise there is precious little chance for a lifebow to form. The emergent effect is more likely to be a knowing nod, or weary sigh.

"Housing": not the right word at all. It connotes a domestic space. The art place, arrived at from this direction, is not an analogue of the domestic place. What it is certainly not "about" is domesticating the horrible wild world out there. No balms allowed. Domestic place, as it is conventionally lived, is all about balming. It is just as necessary to peel the domestic away from itself as it is to lift the lid on site-specific consensual realities—the accepted public sense of the "right" way to live here. Don't take refuge from the public in the domestic. Float the difference. Refract them in each other. Lifebow between them.

The art of making to place is the art of knowing "how to empty one's world" of just this kind of division. Not just the division between the public and the domestic, but those having to do with national, ethnic, and gender identities, and age and stage-of-life labels.

It should be clear by now that this is not the kind of "empty" that is simply the opposite of full, or its contradiction. It is the liquid kind that "floats" an effect.

> Making something out of nothing. Order out of emptiness, through the labour of doing, redoing, and redoing again. Because. It's as if all of life is in that because, which stops just there and doesn't go any further. An unattached reason. A floating specificity: whimsical, empty and very full. I have been able to call the actions of this urge "art."[3]

Art of no reason: just because. Because I need to stay afloat. And I can only do that with my full potentials in place, undivided, with all of life in it.

LIVING BEYOND BIOGRAPHY

Art for the artist is a procedure for living, for staying afloat to the fullest of her potential. Yet she professes to be extremely uncomfortable with any biographical framing of her artistic journeying. Is there life beyond biography? Wrong question. Again. Ask instead, Is one's own biography livable? Not with the constraints that come with being so identified. A case in point is the artist's complicated relation to her own official name.

Malay Muslims' naming practice is based on the Arabic tradition. A person's given name is followed by a patronym composed of a vocable indicating heritage (similarly to the Arabic *bin*) plus the father's given name. The names of Malaysians of Tamil descent, who form the majority in the Malaysian Indian community, are similarly structured. Most Malaysian Indians of Punjabi descent, however, like Malaysian Chinese, have patrilineal surnames, or family names. After independence, efforts were made to rationalize names. In practice, this boiled down to ensuring that kinship with the father was registered in the names of individuals of all ethnicities, as a patronym or a surname depending on the case. This impulse, the artist feels, was primarily an inheritance of the British colonial obsession with labeling and categorizing. But it would not be unreasonable to speculate that the inherited colonial impulse was reinforced by Islamic cultural priorities regarding gender and family that were being reaffirmed as part of the postcolonial nation-building project. Oddly, the fact that Malaysian Indians of Punjabi descent already had surnames did not register. It is as if the difference between Punjabi and Tamil naming practice was not perceivable in its specificity, but only as a marker of minority lack. Malaysian Indians were lumped together, with differences within the community appearing as an irregularity in need of smoothing over. After all, an Indian is an Indian, for all intents and divisive national unification purposes. The relevant division for those purposes was Indian versus Chinese versus Malay. So the artist's name was rationalized. The authorities took her father's three names, first, middle, and last, and declared them a new composite family name. This name was then added to the three the artist already had. Simryn Kaur Gill Ajaib Singh Gill. That is what it sounds like to be taken for a lump. This is rationalization, fully Stated. Talk about overlay! State nationalism overlaid upon colonialism converging with patriarchal cultural values overlaid upon half-recognized ethnic identity. Overzealous labeling, taken to the point of redundancy. Simryn Gill Gill? Biographical overkill.

But is not every biography overkill, in one way or another? Even when one is free to self-label? It still loops into redundancy: I–me–mine. Even a biography rightfully inscribed in its community of identity is redundant: I–you–we. Who "we"? Who are you lumping in with that "I" of yours? Do I-and-I have to mirror you? Are we under obligation to mirror the emptiness of your excavation of your biography in our expanse? Are you to we as a "mine" is to the open land of community?

Take the biographical roof off. De-lump. Peel, abstract, refract, float, intensify. Now that's living.

Is there a contradiction in making a move beyond biography using a biographical detail, and in an essay that started on a biographical note, no less? Not at all. To see it as a contradiction would be to mistake biography for life, and the personal for the world. To live beyond biography is to relate to biographical detail as you would a sacred paving stone or the ring from a soda bottle top: as a trigger for a movement of expression, in the world and of the world.

WHAT IS WINNING IN ART?

The artist delicately suggests that success as an artist has its challenges. She has made it. She has made it to the pinnacle. She has won. She is in the Venice Biennale. Few art places are as identified and categorized and overlaid with meanings and versionings as the Venice Biennale. It's like an Olympics of arts. Can you imagine? Putting art in national pavilions. Overlaying national identities onto art practice, in this postcolonial day and age? Making the individual artist inhabit that overlay? Housing that individual inhabiting in a pavilion flying a home nation flag?

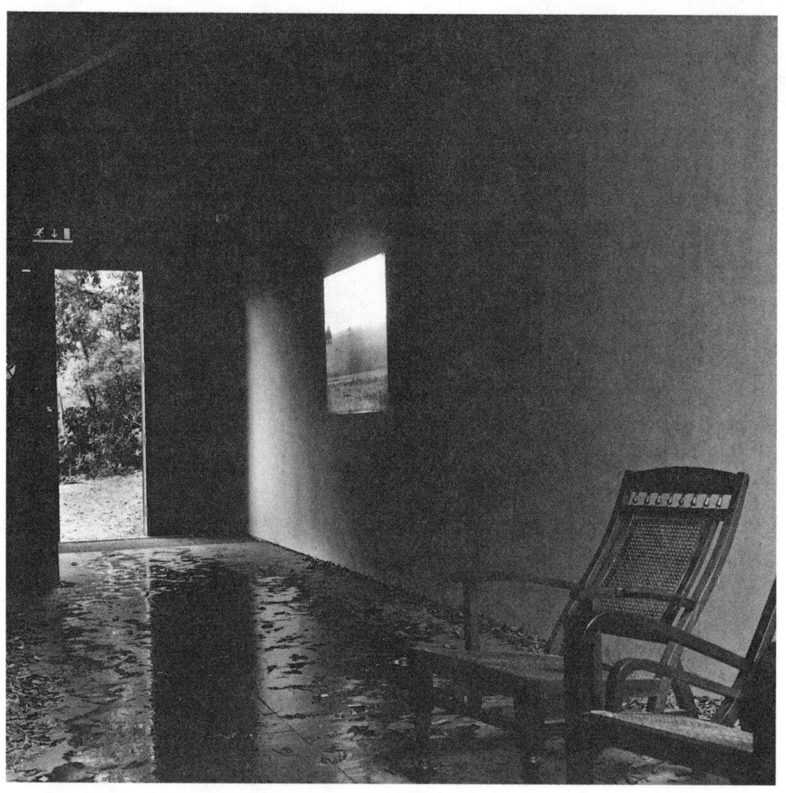

Weathering. Simryn Gill, *Here Art Grows on Trees*,
Australian Pavilion, 55th Venice Biennale. Photograph by Simryn Gill.

All very good for the artist's official biography, to be sure. Even though a good deal of lumping is afoot. For example: What is non-citizen Simryn Kaur Gill Ajaib Singh Gill's "home nation"? Still, good for the official biography, and good for the nation-building history of art of which this exhibition will enter the books as a recorded episode. But what about it is good for the living art—not to mention the art of living?

If it is true that this is the Olympics of art and Simryn Kaur Gill Ajaib Singh Gill is playing for "her" national team, it raises one last wrong question.

What is winning in art?

Concluding Remarks

Immanence (Many Lives)

A book exists only through the outside and on the outside.
—DELEUZE AND GUATTARI, *A THOUSAND PLATEAUS*

The outside has been a refrain the full length of this book's existing through it. *Architectures of the Unforeseen* introduced itself as a series of philosophical problematizations germinating from encounters with its nonphilosophical outside. Or rather, outsides. For "the" outside is not one. It is a topological figure par excellence: a singularly multiple generic. It reiterates to different effect in each coming-to-expression. It reexpresses itself in each determinate taking-form that cuts its own emergent fore-figure from the background continuity of variation of the great processual outside.

It was in topological terms that the abstract space of architecture's outside was analyzed in chapter 1. The process of expression's becoming-architectural was seen as an adventitious growth from formative factors self-sown in the non-architectural field. The architectural process came into itself by taking up these outside elements as proto-architectural potentials, and folding them into its own unfolding to shepherd them to a processual peaking in finished design and built form.

It will not have escaped the reader that this thinking of the outside threatens to fall into a mise en abyme. Architecture, for chapter 1, is the outside of philosophy, which philosophy folds into its process. But architecture has its own outside, which

171

it has folded into itself. The outside of architecture is then an outside twice removed that is wrapped up in architectural process and folds with it into philosophy. Fold upon fold. The infinite regress threatens when it is taken to heart that the architectural outside, too, is multiple. Factors such as characteristics of the site, forces such as gravity and resistance to it, client preference, and zoning were mentioned, and to this list many more could be added. Each of these in turn envelops its own outsides, and so on ad infinitum.

What prevents this from becoming a mise en abyme in which process disappears into the bottomless pit of its own infinite regress is the *act* of ingression that brings the outsides into its fold. Each such act has its own wholly specific take on the complex imbrication of outsides. For one thing, it is selective, infolding outside factors from a very particular angle. For another, it has a particular *manner* of angling their entry that colors their factoring-in and tints each with the others' activity. In other words, the act of ingression is inseparable from technique, and technique from artfulness.

In Greg Lynn's architectural practice, the ingressive act channeled outsides through digital design. Proto-architectural formative factors were rendered as virtual forces. Actual outside formations that have deposited themselves in the world as the already-given, with all of the constraints and obligations that come with that, were *revirtualized*: reopened to potential, for the re-forming. Taken into the same processual plane selectively together, they play out their differential tensions to integral emergent effect. This concerted effect's coming to pass culminates in a finite and fully determined taking-form that has contrived to lift off into itself from its outsider conditions of emergence. It is not a free variation: it carries its own constraints and obligations. Coming into itself, it affirms its own standing out, effectively astraddle the void of its own genesis. It floats itself, buoyed by its own appearing. Its being insistently such as it is expresses the infinity of its conditions in limited form, added as a supplemental given to the world. It cuts its figure from the infinite continuity of the world's process, and adds its finitude to it.

Revirtualization is a necessary component of any processual (that is to say, emergent or ontogenetic) practice of thought, art, design, or politics: any "occurrent art." Each practice creates its own techniques for it, in its own manner. In Rafael Lozano-Hemmer's "relational architecture" practice, the avenue of revirtualization was the urban interface, and the manner was stretchingly bodily in the case of some works discussed, and thirdly reaching for language in others. In Simryn Gill's mixed installation practice, the revirtualization technique was the composition of in situ local–global refraction, and the manner of the contributory factors' making effective ingress was "just nosing." For this book itself, the revirtualization device was ventriloquist encounter, and the manner of ingression was in the attempt in each chapter to maximize mutual relevance among the concepts emerging from a given encounter (so that, in words of the introduction, what is indefinable in one concept cannot be abstracted from its relevance to the others).

Construing creative practice as a creature of the outside is not just a conceit. It is itself a device, designed to enable a certain logic to set in, and unfold. The outside is a conceptual operator (others could have been selected) for activating an image of thought that differentiates process thinking and doing from other approaches (and from all method). It does this by troubling our ideas about *distinction*: what makes something graspably different from something else. Acquired habits of thought make it difficult to talk about distinction without appealing, implicitly or explicitly, to the opposition between inside and outside. When the inside/outside dichotomy is taken as a given, and treated as foundational to difference, the image of thought installed revolves around *extensive* distinction. This is a fundamentally spatialized notion of difference modeled on the mutually exclusive occupation of space that we see as obtaining between objects. This is a juxtapositional model figuring difference as external relation. What is proper to a thing, by this reckoning, is what lies within the external envelope of its boundaries. It carries its nature inside, and bumps up against things outside itself. These external relations are secondary to its nature, which inheres in its relation to itself: the identity it carries from one external relation to the next. This spins difference as extrinsic to a thing's nature, so that the reasoning is not basically about difference at all, but self-sameness. This model of extensive distinction and extrinsic difference can be transposed from the dimension of space onto that of time. All that is required to make the extrapolation is to string out juxtaposition as a line of succession. This enables the identity a thing intrinsically carries to have a history, still within the terms of extensive distinction (one instant being separated from the next on the timeline by an invisible boundary). At each successive step, the thing is still self-same. It carries its inside nature with it, even as it undergoes development or evolution through the external relations through which it passes. Add memory, and extensive distinction can be transposed yet again, this time into a psychic dimension: subjectivity (interiority with a cumulative history; self-relation with a story line).

While this image of thought hinging on extensive distinction enables a certain take on history and development, it excludes the kinds of formative acts and ontogenetic events highlighted in this book. These events occur through an interfusion of the respective activities of the contributory factors, across the boundaries and extensive distances separating them. The stadium wave described in chapter 1 was a case in point. The "shape" of the event was an integral appearance lifting off from the multiplicity of local gestures composing it. The integrality of the appearance was the way in which the gestures came *together* in the event. Their coming together in the precise manner in which they did supplemented their extensive distinction from one another— their differences of position and timing—with the added distinction of a global waveform cutting across these to come into its own. The global arc of the wave was a taking-form occupying its own event dimension, its effect drawn on the nonsensuous surface of affect. Existing only on that abstract surface, the wave had no interiority. It had only affective force, one with its surfacing. The local gestural elements were "intricated" in its passing taking-form. Their difference from one another was not erased but supplemented by a different differing: the *emergence* of just this wave, as the joint effect of their co-activity. In the emergence, local contributory gestures are effectively taken up *in each other's activity*. It is this in-each-otherness of local elements, actively resonating with one another, that constitutes the global. Each instant of the wave's global unfolding integrally rolls the distributed activity of the preceding moments into its already now rolling on. This mutual envelopment of succeeding moments takes up the spatiotemporal distance between the local elements into the immediacy of a nonlocal interfusion. The result is not a timeline, but a *becoming* across a continuous variation. Interfusion, intrication, envelopment: these are things for which the logic of extensive distinction has no words. Its loss for words writes integral emergence and nonlocal becoming out of the story. It botches process. The logic of extensive distinction is process aphasic.

Emergence, becoming, process: these are things that require a vocabulary of *modal* distinction. But at this point, it is difficult to continue speaking of "things." As David Lapoujade writes of Étienne Souriau's modal philosophy, "One must accept the consequences: there is no longer any being, there are only processes; or rather, the only entities are henceforth *acts*."[1] "Things" only figure in intrication, as actively fused into rolling events of processual emergence. The basic unit of the logic of modal distinction is not the thing (neither object nor subject) but the act of emergence, the event of being as becoming.

Factoring into each event of emergence is a plurality of modes. Modes of activity are intergiven. They are gregarious by nature. Every thing at every step finds itself at a crossroads of them. There exist only modal mixtures. This does not mean that everything is an undifferentiated mess—just the opposite. Generalizing from what Bakhtin was quoted as saying in chapter 2 about the cultural act, everything is located entirely upon boundaries; boundaries intersect it everywhere; everything lives essentially on the boundaries. If anything, there is an excess of differentiation, offering more opportunities to make more, and more nuanced, distinctions. Rather than a single extensive distinction between inside and outside and a stepwise linear advance through the succession of moments of time, there is instead a layering of boundary conditions. Bakhtin is very clear that he is not talking about spatial boundaries. If we think of them instead as modes of activity, each boundary is the edging into ingredience in the act of a mode of activity, in unison with others to whose own manner of activity it must adjust itself. Under obligation to co-compose, it is unlikely to be able to take its activity to the extremity of what it can do. It will insist on itself only up to a certain point, with an agreeable (or perhaps just bearable, maybe even dissonant) accent. In other words, it will act in its mode according to its abilities up to a certain degree, which cannot be reduced to a quantity, because the accentuation it carries gives it an irreducibly qualitative aspect: more manner than magnitude. The mode of activity's contributing itself to a graduated qualitative degree leaves unactualized, lying in reserve, any number of other qualitative degrees of itself that it may well yet express under other circumstances. These other degrees of the mode of activity remain in reserve for acts to come. They constitute a domain of potential. The entirety of the domain is implicated in the act, in potentia.

The nonspatial domain of the mode of activity in potential is infinite, but limited. It has operative limits: a maximal limit where it does as it does when it is carried to highest power, and a pessimal limit where it is too weak to register in any act. In between are an infinity of qualitative degrees of power, forming a continuum. Think of the continuum as an abstract rubber sheet stretched between these limits, patchworked with a variety of accents, or qualitative variations on that manner of activity. Then imagine the act seizing the domain somewhere in between the limits, bunching it into itself while wringing it around other co-ingredient modes of activity, similarly pulled in. The domain can then be visualized as edging into the act *by the middle*. It contributes itself somewhere in the middle of its continuum (or at least not at its limits, which are actually unreachable) as a boundary condition for the event. It is a boundary condition in the sense that this particular act was able to go this far into its domain and no further. It was able to color itself with its accent only so; avail itself of the variety of its potential just in this manner. This is a way of dynamically envisioning a qualitative boundary condition pertaining to a nonspatial domain, and exceeding linear time.

The domain of activity exceeds linear time if it is considered that as it is being selectively pulled into edging into the co-composition of the act, it is exerting on the act an attractive pull toward its own domain. All of the potential variations on its mode of activity effectively proposed themselves for ingredience in the act, as it incipiently grasped at their domain's edging in, as part of the act's coming into itself. The might-have-been-included-instead of varying qualitative degrees of that mode of activity positively itches at the event. It is bequeathed, full-spectrum, its full continuum in some way felt, as a vague but alluring proposition for a next act's grasping. That is what the degrees on the continuum of a mode of activity are: propositions. They are attractors, forces of attraction describing *tendencies* pulling at each event finding itself at the boundary of their domain.

The tensile character of the act is the product of this two-way pull: on the one hand, toward a finite expression in the determinate, occurrent composition of an emergence that takes place and has its time; and on the other, toward a whole-cloth infinite spectrum of potential, in all its provocative variety and qualitative attractiveness, that bides time, in that it belongs no less to one moment than the next, so that it is so dynamically full of itself that neither does it fit in any given place. That tension—that *intensity*—is heightened by the multiplicity of domains contributing boundary conditions to the event, and the differential between their tendential pulls. Every act is located at the bundled edgings-in of many tendencies; tendencies intersect it everywhere; everything lives essentially in tendential complexity. The act's mixed-modal constitution itself constitutes a mode of its own.

The overfullness of the domain of activity as field of tendential potential is the intensive dimension of the event. Thinking in terms of modal distinction is the only way to account for the felt intensity of acts of expression: their *impletion*, as Vološinov would say, with a spectrum of potential; their making felt an overfullness; their expressing more than they manifest; their "in-forming" (as it was often put in this book). Intensity must be attended to, with as much conceptual precision as possible, if the *singularity* of the act of expression is to be accounted for. It is precisely an act's overfullness with quality, its coloring by the spectrum of potential, that gives it the inimitable accent of its own unique character. It is the impletion of its taking-form with all it could have pulled into itself, which we sense held in reserve for a next iteration, that insists as its singular style, or aesthetic effect. The differential potential of the multiple modes of activity or domains of potential that itch at the event constitutes an *implicate order* enveloped in its taking-form. The implicate order has a different logic than the extrinsic order to whose arrangement it emergently contributes through the addition to it of its own finally determined form. The implicate order is a field of immanent relation holding potential for taking-form: an envelopment in the event of formation of a multiplicity of domains of activity and their respective qualitative degrees, all coming together to propose themselves in unison, to in-form the incipience of the event's just-now moving toward the emergent expression of its own eventual form. That emergent form is a limited expression of the field, standing out in its own coming to pass, in contrast to other takings-form around it. Standing out in contrast to others around: in extensive distinction and extrinsic difference from them. Extensive distinction is the finite, end-expression of immanent relation, coming out of its overfullness with itself into a determinate taking-form that cuts its figure out of the continuum of potential. Extensity and intensity are processual reciprocals. They are oscillatory phases in the pulsing process of expression.

The arc of an integral emergence, like the stadium wave taking-form, is an extensive appearing of the field's intensity. The wave rolls its local contributory elements together into its own emergent duration, taking their distance in time and space from each other into its own formation. The differential in-each-otherness of the wave's local factors forms its arc, which is nothing other than an intricate, occurrent image of the field of immanence, rolling out into actual existence in a determinate way (what I have elsewhere called a "semblance").[2] The wave is the dynamic form in which the intensity of the field of immanence extensively expresses itself in this particular occasion. The field of immanence never expresses itself as such. And neither we as subjects, nor acts as self-grasping emergences, are ever "in" it. Acts of expression come into themselves, from its outside. It is the ever outside. The ever great outside is not something "in which" other things are (not even potentials). To put it that way reinsinuates extensive distinction into it, mistaking it for a space. Rather than that kind of in-which, immanence is an in-each-otherness. It is the infinite in-each-otherness of modes of activity, "in" potential (which is uncontained). The intrication of actual elements in an emergent taking-form, the manner in which the activity of each is in each other, is the way the field of immanence effectively appears. Intrication is its surfacing through, and adding to, the world of extensive distinction. Surfacing through: taking up extensive contrasts (of spacing and timing) into its own unfolding. Adding to: contributing the added element of an emergent form, asserting its own unique characters standing out in contrast from others around it. Yet: the partitive surfacing through and adding to leaves no less integrally in reserve. The full spectrum of modes' activities and their qualitative degrees remains in infinite in-each-otherness of immanent potential. The field of immanence globally remainders itself with each added local expression, holding all potential contrast in reserve for reexpression. The great outside ever abides.

In chapter 2, this logic of modal distinction and intensive difference was used to differentiate the cultural act from the social act. This distinction is clearly nonsensical from the point of view of extrinsic difference and external relation. Social acts and cultural acts do not come separately. You cannot point to one act as belonging to the category of the social as opposed to that of the cultural. But modes of activity are not categories, and they come rolled up together in a joint event. They only express with regard for their mutual in-each-otherness. Their nonseparability in mutual inclusion does not, however, make the distinction meaningless. It makes it intense.

The social act and the cultural act are convivial in the sense that they always come together, to one degree or another. But they do not have a balanced relationship. Their domains always overlap, so that each act is a mixed result, but their pull is differential. The act is pulled into itself from different directions. The manner in which it expresses itself is a rendering of that tension, a resultant of the differential between tendential domains. The differential is the product of the domain's limits being offset from each other. The social act was defined in chapter 2 in terms of a reaching-for-language as such, which tenses it in the direction of quasi-direct discourse. When the reaching-for-language is taken to the maximal limit of what it can do, it dissolves into the quasi-mind's anonymous murmur of thirdness. That is its upper limit. When the social act moves toward that limit, it is orienting away from its pessimal limit, which was said to be that of animality. Animality is the "lower" limit of the social act, away from which it moves, because only human language has the power to carry thirdness to the extreme. That maximal limit is reached-for at the risk of becoming all-too-human, to gossip or perchance to troll. The social act's movement to the maximal limit moves it away from the domain of the cultural act, because it pulls it away from the act of expression's intense belonging to the animal body. That belonging does not connote the lack of language potential, but rather its modal melding into a cosmic continuum, in whose potential it participates from the precise angle of the manner in which it contrives, under just these conditions, occurring across this split of scales, splayed between such and such locations and semantic connotations, to overfill its own gesture with its own degree of intensity. Or, in Vološinovian terms: the manner in which it impletes its performance with a world of theme—and the theme of worlding.

The cultural act and the social act intersect in gesture. They pull in unison on gesture, bundling differentially into its occurrence two offset continua of potential co-ingredient to the event. But not just two. Gesture is itself a mode of activity, or domain of potential, and it intersects with a plethora of others. For example, gesture is pulled by and pulls on the kinesthetic amoeba that is the boundary condition of the domain of potential of embodied animal sensation and perception. The body's lived animal experience is in turn pulled by and pulls-in memory. Memory intersects with custom, and custom with neighborliness, and neighborliness with comfort of familiar context, and familiar context with habitual circulations: domains of potential, all. But they are all of the kind that tenses the cultural act away from what was characterized in chapter 2 as meiotic cosmic congress orienting to the maximal limit of the cultural domain, toward a truncating of the ambit of expression. Following these tendencies, the cultural act tends to rest on its laurels, accenting the specificity of its taking-place and touting its role as honored successor on a progressive timeline, to the detriment of its overfullness with a world's worth of theme, and the theme of worlding.

Cultural specificity describes the pessimal limit of the cultural act. It lies toward the lower end on the continuum of potential of the cultural domain because, by expressing the tendency to pin culturable potential in place and time, it underexpresses the fullness of the act of expression with immanent relation. It pins the act to its extensive coordinates, and attempts to contain it within them. This represents an intense limitation of the full latitude of the cultural act's potential, as it animally envelops the plenum of the nature–culture continuum. Paradoxically, the movement toward the pessimal limit of the cultural act creates the conditions for the social act to reach toward its maximal limit of unleashed thirdness. As we saw with Vološinov, the emergence of the bourgeois subject resets the coordinates of the cultural act as a function of a new master extensive distinction, that of the public and private spheres. The accompanying model of communication unleashes the power of circulation. This intensifies the word's external propulsion through the public sphere, at the same time as it intensifies its inward impulsion into the more and more communicationally overbloated—and as a consequence, increasingly leaky—interiority of the subject. The social act exploits the cross-pull of this two-way intensification of communication to push through into its own movement to the limit, bursting out the far side of the bourgeois interiorized subject and the external milieu of its complementary public sphere.

All of this is a necessarily complicated way of saying that history can be understood processually. Understanding history processually means reattaching the extensive distinctions that arise in its course to their conditions of emergence: to the field of immanence overfull with intensive relation between qualitatively different modes of activity constituting a translocal and transindividual reservoir of potential that integrally resurfaces in a determinate taking-form whose coming to final expression effects the transition between one moment of history to the next. It is only by reattaching the acts of expression that make history to their formative field of immanence that the world's power to ceaselessly generate new, emergent distinctions can be accounted for, and that the becoming *of* history can be glimpsed. This cannot be done unless the reflex to parse according to established disciplinary compartmentalizations is resisted. Contenting oneself with extensive distinction positing extrinsic differences between mutually external, contrasting periods of history, cultural traditions, media of expression, and artistic styles are so many ways of botching process. They are designed as if to miss the formative force of the in-each-otherness that potentializes these very contrasts' becoming. They forget that history is made by what surfaces *across* all such divisions, in their overlap and offset, in tension of potential. They forget that an act is located entirely upon boundaries, that boundaries intersect it everywhere, that everything lives essentially on the boundaries. They forget the intensity of mutual inclusion, whose tendential propositioning of the act's in-forming with potential energizes the movement of becoming. The intensity of becoming underwrites history, as it surfaces in the coming to expression of new distinction added to history. No sooner does this happen than that newly determined emergent form is overwritten by becoming's passing, as the process of history turns a page.

The aim of this book was to chart this movement of becoming as it courses through a limited number of creative practices. In the attempt to be true to becoming, it had to eschew the traditional methods of the discipline of art history, and the norms of aesthetic judgment in alliance with it. It had to skew the author's own discipline of philosophy toward a border region, and to make that move of mutual inclusion its aparalleled "method." This required a sustained, even technical, attention to the dynamics of emergent form; an eye for intrication; and of not only the reaching toward language but, just as compelling if not more so, the reaching with words for re-bodying: in short, an interested concern for the many manners of surfacing of potential. All of these things were enabled by a relational deployment of thought (the method of symbiotic encounter) and a strategic deployment of language's sometimes disturbing power of quasi-directness (the third voice of "ventriloquism" as a way of bringing the relational encounter to variant expression).

What was generated along the way was a set of extra-disciplinary, nonnormative criteria for the evaluation of a creative practice in its own processual terms. These are immanent criteria, implicate in the problems a practice poses for itself, and works through as the creative engine of its singular self-expression. Transposed into writing-with, they take the form of "how" questions, with not an "ought." The evaluative questions are thoroughly pragmatic, but with a speculative edge. They bear on how a practice speculates on what it can do, in the very form of its unfolding modal mix of activity, as it is borne witness to by the manner of effects it produces—and through which it is witnessed self-producing as event-medium, flush with the immediacy of the occurrent emergence that it composes and that composes it.

How do the acts of expression that a practice iterates animate form, impleting it with virtuality? To what effect? How does a practice stretch the body, to implete it with the nature–culture continuum? Again, to what effect? How, and to what effect, does a practice float the social, impleting it with a quasi-minded thirdness of relation? How does one make impletely to place, to effect a translocal refraction, so as to float identity and belonging in variable relation? These are some of the problematic things the occurrent arts can contrive to do: so many ways of transitioning through history—and living beyond biography. Immanence: many lives (in expressive potential).

Notes

INTRODUCTION

1. Deleuze and Guattari, *A Thousand Plateaus*, 11.

2. Deleuze and Guattari are emphatic in their assertion that conversation and debate are the death of philosophy: "Communication always comes too early or too late, and when it comes to creating, conversation is always superfluous" (*What Is Philosophy?* 28). On the difference between interaction and relation, see chapter 2 below and Massumi, *Semblance and Event*, chapter 2.

3. One such collaboration was *HUMO: Huge + Mobile: The Art of Urban Intervention*, a weeklong "guerilla art" master class with public-space interventions involving large-scale image projection on buildings and urban infrastructure. The event, held in Linz, Austria, on February 3–7, 2003, was organized as part of the "Interfacing Realities" master-class series sponsored by the European Union's Culture 2000 program and cosponsored by V2: Institute for Unstable Media (Rotterdam) and Ars Electronica Center (Linz). The master class was conceived and directed by Rafael Lozano-Hemmer; my role was as conceptual consultant, coteacher of certain preparatory sessions, and participant in the projections. For an account of the project, see Massumi, "Urban Appointment." Another collaboration was *Levels of Nothingness: A Libretto of Color for Voice*, an interactive color–voice performance with public participation, featuring the actress Isabella Rossellini. The event— held during the New York Guggenheim Museum's 50th Anniversary Celebrations, on September 16–21, 2009—was conceived and directed by Rafael Lozano-Hemmer; my role was as author of the script of the voice performance (a polyphonic dialogue of conceptual characters composed of quotes from philosophers and researchers on color, synesthesia, the body, and space). The titles for both *Levels of Nothingness* and *Amodal Suspension* arose from our discussions in the context of regular studio visits through the years.

4. Whitehead, *Process and Reality*, 5.
5. On the immanent relation of philosophy and non-philosophy, see Deleuze and Guattari, *What Is Philosophy?* 41, 93, 109, 218.
6. Ruyer, *Neofinalism*, 129.
7. In fact, this ventriloquist approach represents a longtime practice, going at least as far back as *Parables for the Virtual*—for example, in chapter 2 on Ronald Reagan and chapter 4 on Stelarc. It is not uncoincidental that in those two chapters practices of mime/mimicry (Reagan) and of various forms of ventriloquism/puppetry (both Reagan and Stelarc) figure explicitly. Erin Manning and I also adopted the transductive approach to philosophical writing from art in the essays making up part 1 of our coauthored *Thought in the Act*.
8. On "immediation," see Manning, Munster, and Thomsen, Immediations.

1. FORM FOLLOWS FORCE

1. Lynn, *Animate Form*, 15.
2. See Lynn, *Archaeology of the Digital*; and Carpo, *The Digital Turn in Architecture*.
3. What is formalizable is less the figure itself than the field of transformation within which it operates. That field is formalizable in terms of parameters defining what Lynn, in design terms, calls a "performance envelope." See Lynn, *Animate Form*, 13, 25. "In architecture today, there is an explosion of new geometries available to designers, yet these are being understood critically as just another set of shapes that look a little like shapes we have seen before. . . . Topological surfaces are not merely shapes or figures, as most architects, theorists, and historians persist in understanding them, and there is a big difference between framing questions of geometry in terms of shape and performance" (understood in terms of "flow"). Lynn, "Geometry in Time," 165.
4. "Why Tectonics Is Square and Topology Is Groovy," in Lynn, *Folds, Bodies and Blobs*, 169–86: the title says it.
5. Lynn, *Animate Form*, 15–16.
6. Eisenman, "Diagram: An Original Scene of Writing," in *Diagram Diaries*, 29.
7. See Galofaro, *Eisenman*.
8. All quotations in this paragraph are from Eisenman, "Diagram."
9. On "following" process, see Deleuze and Guattari, *A Thousand Plateaus*, 409, 431.
10. What is ultimately "anterior" is a kind of outside—a constitutively open field—that is more radically open than any exterior defined as such relative to a given, structurally bounded interior. The in-

foldings of this absolute outside constitute "an inside that lies deeper than any interior world" (a monad of virtuality). Deleuze, *Foucault*, 96.

11. The architect works in an indefinitely open field of contributory factors: "The architect's studio encompasses partners, architects and designers, not to mention broader project teams that also include clients, officials, engineers, other design specialties, renderers, and the manufacturing and building trades. Architecture can be understood as a nexus between design media and a complex and collaborative team of authors," Lynn, *Archaeology of the Digital*, 14. The confluence ("nexus") of growth factors is fusionally expressed, as folded into the continuity of the architectural design's becoming. As the emphasis above on the tools indicates, and later on the discussion of the role of contextual elements, the growth factors are not limited to human part-"authors."

12. On resemblance as produced by a play of difference, see Deleuze, *Difference and Repetition*, 116–22. See also Massumi, *Semblance and Event*, 123–24, 128–29.

13. "A phenomenon of force is both a fact and *more-than-fact*, a given and *more-than-given*, for force directs itself, beyond its present existence, toward a state it itself will produce." Ruyer, *Le monde des valeurs*, 142.

14. This bipolar definition of nature, as the given (the also-ran) and the surpassing of the given (a running-ahead-of-itself), is derived from Whitehead. See Massumi, *What Animals Teach Us about Politics*. The two poles roughly correspond to the Spinozist distinction between "natured nature" and "naturing nature." See Massumi, *Ontopower*, 37–39, for a discussion of this distinction in which natured nature is construed as the dedicated preparation of given "nature" for uptake into a particular domain of practice.

15. Lynn, *Animate Form*, 102–19.

16. Logically, it is a fuzzy subset rather than a classical intersection.

17. For Lynn on intensity, see *Folds, Bodies and Blobs*, 113, 117, 139.

18. See Lynn, "Geometry in Time."

19. "I actually love the term [virtual]." Greg Lynn, interview with Eva Prinz.

20. On the history of the "three-body problem," Poincaré's mathematical investigations of it, and its relation to chaos, see Diacu and Holmes, *Celestial Encounters*. For Lynn on this question, see *Animate Form*, 16.

21. For Lynn on anexactness, see *Folds, Bodies and Blobs*, 41–42, 70, 83–84, 118, 136, 213–14.

22. See *Animate Form*, 108–9.

23. For Lynn on proto-formalism, see "Forms of Expression: The

Proto-Functional Potential of Diagrams in Architectural Design," in *Folds, Bodies and Blobs*, 223–33.

24. The "cinematic" nature of architectural design is also something Lynn makes explicit and embraces: his 1998–99 studio at the Columbia School of Architecture experimented with importing organizational models from the film industry (complete with field trips to Hollywood). It is not coincidental that the animation software used in topological architectural design was originally developed to generate special effects for film.

25. Processual qualities that may (or may not) be expressed as personal character traits are what Deleuze and Guattari term "conceptual personae" or "rhythmic characters." See *What Is Philosophy?* 61–83, and *A Thousand Plateaus*, 317–19.

26. The blob modeling software adopted by Lynn in his early work was Meta-Balls, part of Wavefront Technologies Inc.'s Explorer 3Design program.

27. Lynn, *Folds, Bodies and Blobs*, 166.

28. Lynn, *Animate Form*, 142–63.

29. Lynn, "Architectural Curvilinearity," 14.

30. Bernard Cache, "A Plea for Euclid," *ANY (Architecture New York)* 24 (1999): 54–59, reprinted in Cache, *Projectiles*, 31–59.

31. Lynn, "Architectural Curvilinearity," 14.

32. Although Lynn does use the term "compliant" as a synonym for "pliant" in "Multiplicitous and Inorganic Bodies" and "The Folded, the Pliant and the Simple," both in *Folds, Bodies and Blobs*, 33–62, 109–34.

33. Lynn, 229.

34. Lynn speaks of this in terms of "pacts" and "productive alliances" produced by "continuously transforming internalization of outside events" and "external forces" into the design process, enabled by the topological approach. Lynn, 39–42.

35. Massumi, "Interface and Active Space" (the incident reported here occurred at a re-presentation of this paper in another context).

36. The most extended critique of metaphorical thinking as a denial of the primary ontological status of multiplicity is Deleuze and Guattari's *Anti-Oedipus*. See also Deleuze and Guattari, "One or Several Wolves?" in *A Thousand Plateaus*, 26–38.

37. These broad-stroke criticisms of metaphor do not apply to accounts of metaphor, such as Lakoff and Johnson's, that consider the process of metaphor itself as fundamentally generative, even if it settles into cliché, seeing the play of resemblances that seems to underlie its operation as in fact produced by the very movement of metaphor, understood as a dynamic relation that creates its own terms and with them the system of transitive connection which then may

settle into a symbolic structure. See Lakoff and Johnson, *Metaphors We Live By.*

38. Already-constituted form approached metaphorically or imitatively is taken as a design device only in one project, *The Ark of the World* (2002–3): "The design is inspired by the form, texture and color of the indigenous tropical flora and fauna [of Costa Rica]." Lynn and Rashid, *Architectural Laboratories,* 40. The imitative gesture was undertaken to echo the program of the proposed building (an ecology museum).

39. Lynn, "The Renewed Novelty of Symmetry."

40. Lynn, *Folds, Bodies and Blobs,* 41.

41. Another architect often accused of biomorphism is Frederick Kiesler, a pre-digital proponent of curvilinearity in architecture. Kiesler responded to the perception of biomorphism in his work by making a distinction between "biotechnics" and "biotechnique." The latter refuses any founding resemblance, which means refusing not only metaphor but *imitation* of pregiven form or function: "The new designer will learn to understand the methods by which nature builds to meet her purposes (biotechnics): but he will not imitate her methods. . . . The Biotechnical approach tries to develop the possibilities of specific actions contained in any nucleus of human physiology. These potentialities remain at first undiscovered. Only with time are they individually or collectively developed until finally they are consciously demanded. The result will be entirely new functions within the old framework of what was considered 'human nature,' sustained by inventions." Kiesler, "On Co-Realism: A Definition and Test," 67. Kiesler's open field of virtuality was the human body itself, exfoliating in a taking-architectural-form of its own untapped potential. This task was approached through pre-computation analog methods (distinguished from imitative methods in that they fundamentally concern the invention of differences rather than the reproduction of the given).

42. Lynn, *Animate Form,* 10.

43. Lynn, 34.

44. Spuybroek, *NOX.*

45. Arakawa and Gins, *Architectural Body.* Elsewhere, Arakawa and Gins provocatively equate this reanimation, this reintensification of life by architectural means, with a promise of immortality, or "reversible destiny" (the ultimate continuing problem). See Arakawa and Gins, *Making Dying Illegal.*

46. Lynn explicitly criticizes Husserl's "phenomenological reduction" for "canceling out variation" and "eliminating difference" through the construction of an ideal "eidetic" form (*Folds, Bodies*

and Blobs, 66, 207–9). His aversion, however, seems to extend beyond phenomenology in the strict sense to anything that might be described as phenomenological in the most extended senses of the term. The thought of Alfred North Whitehead, which was in abeyance during Lynn's formative years and does not figure on his theoretical radar, offers a nonphenomenological philosophy of experience that suggests potential convergences between work like Lynn's and that of Spuybroek and Arakawa and Gins, especially in dialogue with Deleuze (whose work Lynn was deeply engaged with from early in his career).

47. See in particular "Multiplicitous and Inorganic Bodies" (33–62) and "Body Matters" (135–56) in *Folds, Bodies and Blobs.*

48. Cited in Manning and Massumi, *Thought in the Act,* 39. Gilles Deleuze also ties the definition of the body to concepts of folding: "the body is flection." See *The Logic of Sense,* 284.

49. Lynn, *Folds, Bodies and Blobs,* 149–51.

50. Lynn, 139.

51. On the concept of the shape of enthusiasm, see Manning, "The Shape of Enthusiasm," in *Always More Than One,* 184–203.

52. Bergson, *The Two Sources of Morality and Religion,* 111 (translation modified).

53. James, *Essays in Radical Empiricism,* 153.

54. Erin Manning analyzes events of bodying on the abstract cinematic surface in *Always More Than One,* chapter 3, "Waltzing the Limit," 41–73. She proposes the term that is taken up here of "becoming-body" for these events.

55. Lynn, *Folds, Bodies and Blobs,* 150–54.

56. In other words, the abstract body of architecture is a "semblance" in the sense developed in Massumi, *Semblance and Event.*

57. Lynn discusses how the topological *extrusion* of nine tubular pseudopods in his Stranded Sears Tower project engenders multiple "affiliations" between the architectural surface and "local events—adjacent buildings, landforms, sidewalks, bridges, tunnels, roads and river's edge—that would have been repressed by a more rigid and reductive geometric system of description." The topological design process yields "now supple and flexible internal order of the bundled tube that is differentiated by" its generative infolding of "the [virtualized] external forces of the river's edge, the city grid, and the vectors of pedestrian and transportation movement. The bundled tube is a possible paradigm for a multiplicitous monument." See *Folds, Bodies and Blobs,* 55.

58. On perception as a generative transductive relation operating across the membrane of the skin to processualy couple what are essentially "transindividual" open fields, see Simondon, *L'individuation à la*

lumière des notions de forme et d'information, 233–61. On topology: "The topological conditions are what can be called form"; "transductive thought establishes a topology of the real" (45, 119).

59. Lynn discusses the example of hunger in *Folds, Bodies and Blobs*: "Hunger is a unifying gesture that renders thousands of tiny perceptions visible as an abstract expression. Gestures are rigorous, precise modes of organization that render imperceptibly minute and multiple desires as unified perceptions. Bodies are expressed, stabilized, organized and unified through the play of a multiplicity of tiny forces" (150). Lynn's use of the words "tiny perceptions" is an allusion to Leibniz's similarly multilevel theory of the body as a nested hierarchy of an indefinite multiplicity of "monads" peaking in a "dominant," integral expression. In *Difference and Repetition* Deleuze refers to the proto-actors whose expressive subgestures are doubled by these tiny perceptions as "larval subjects" (78–79, 97, 118–19, 215). See also Deleuze, *The Fold*, chapter 7, "Perception in the Folds," 85–99.

60. What I have been describing I have called elsewhere "bare activity."

61. The origin of the stadium wave is a topic of much controversy among sports fans. The first organized wave seems to have occurred in 1981 in Oakland at a baseball game, but there are reports of unled waves occurring as far back as the early 1960s. The leader of the 1981 wave claims personal responsibility as the inventor. But it is of the nature of body-events not only to have a multiplicity of formative factors but also to be irreducible to a single origin. For it is the field conditions and its abstract ripeness for the effect that is the nonlocal origin of the event, and field conditions tend to come in distributed multiples. Although stadium waves may not be officially led and organized, they must still always be seeded by a nucleus of proto-wavers whose performed enthusiasm takes, or not. See Williams, "It's Settled."

62. Lynn emphasizes the "affiliative" or "alliance" oriented nature of architectural process, as opposed to the filiative relation of assignable origins. See *Folds, Bodies and Blobs*, 44–45, 47, 53–54.

63. Lynn, *Intricacy*, n.p.

64. Spuybroek, *The Sympathy of Things*. On Vision Machine, see Massumi, "Building Experience."

65. As Spuybroek remarks, "Expressionism directly relates force to form." *Sympathy of Things*, 15.

66. See Delanda, "Materiality."

67. Borasi and Zardini, *Other Space Odysseys*, 25–59.

68. This is how Lynn explains the derivation of final form and function from a single variational matrix through serially repeated topological deformation, speaking specifically of a project to design a

cutlery set for Alessi: "I define *deformation* as the method by which a change creates something more specific in something that was previously more generic [i.e., singular-multiple]. Each deformation moves away from a simple generic thing to something that has more traits [emergent determination] *without ever stepping out of its internal logic* [generative matrix of virtual forces], never adding or subtracting elements [which, topologically speaking, would constitute a "cut" marking the limit of the figure's self-varying]. Working in this way I could start to *blur the boundaries* between common flatware elements and *rediscover and invent new functions*—things like fish forks and cheese knives and so on. We ran through countless deformations of these elements, then started to *develop them continuously*, from dessert forks to salad forks, table forks, serving forks, meat forks, all the while *fusing elements*—adding a bit of spoon quality to the dessert forks, taking some traits away and adding others to table forks, and then going more toward a knife, and on and on [cross-contamination between types, blurring boundaries at the level of the formal whole]." Lynn, "Machine Language," 61; emphasis and bracketed comments added. This matrixial approach is made possible by the use of infinitesimal calculus to drive the geometry. In calculus, *"the one and the many are equivalent* . . . because calculus drives the model, if any one of the elements moves, the change trickles through the whole thing" (62–63). On the cutlery project (Flatware, 2005), see Lynn, *Greg Lynn*, 203–6.

69. Lynn, "Machine Language," 60.

70. Lynn, 59, 62. See also quote in note 57 on the topological blurring of boundaries between parts and the cross-contamination between types on the level of the whole.

71. Lynn, *Intricacy*, n.p.

72. Lynn.

73. Lynn.

74. It is a contention of Whitehead's process philosophy, and the basic tenet of his aesthetic philosophy, that all "activity belongs to the individual actualities." This qualifies his process philosophy as what might be an *elementalism*. Whitehead also employs the vocabulary of fusion: "The qualities shared by many individuals are fused into one dominating impression." See *Adventures of Ideas*, 213. A concept of sympathy as a kind of symbiosis constitutive of dynamic form can be grounded in this concept of fusion: "The whole heightens the feelings for the parts, and the parts heighten the feelings for the whole, and for each other." This symbiosis drives what Whitehead terms "progress." For a development of an allied concept of sympathy applied to animal life and its evolution, see Massumi, *What Animals Teach Us about Politics*.

75. Lynn, *Intricacy*, n.p.
76. Lynn and Rashid, *Architectural Laboratories*, 60; Lynn, *Predator*, 134.
77. Lynn, *Intricacy*, n.p.
78. Lynn and Rashid, *Architectural Laboratories*, 60. The crucial distinction between assembly and fusion—or between the concreteness of structuring aggregation and the emergence of dynamic form on an abstract surface doubling the concrete surface of the assembly—should be taken as a conceptual warning to "assemblage theory."
79. Lynn and Rashid, 53.
80. Lynn, "Color," in *Greg Lynn*, 118.
81. The decorative dimension, understood in this way, is one form that the immediate self-reference included in every expression may take. As Peirce remarked, an expression does not just express. In the same stroke, it "expresses its expressing something." See *The Essential Peirce*, vol. 2, 408. For further discussion of this in the context of the integral expression of a multiplicity of "partial subjects," see Massumi, "Collective Expression," *The Principle of Unrest*, chapter 3. On unmediated self-reference, see also Massumi, *Semblance and Event*, 44.
82. Lynn, "Color," in *Greg Lynn*, 120.
83. Lynn and Rashid, *Architectural Laboratories*, 80–81; Lynn, *Greg Lynn*, 186–87.
84. On surface effects, see Deleuze, *Logic of Sense*; in particular 103–4: "The skin has at its disposal a vital and properly superficial potential energy. And just as events do not occupy the [concrete] surface but rather frequent it, superficial energy is not *localized* at the surface, but is rather bound to its formation and reformation."
85. Lynn, *Folds, Bodies and Blobs*, 41–44. It should not be forgotten that the abstract surfacing of the body envelops a multitude of sub-bodies organized into strata (organs, cells, organelles, etc.), sandwiched between each of which is an abstract surface proper to each in-between, or interstratum. This constitutes an "interior" milieu—which is not really one in any rigid sense, given that "impenetrability is a difficult notion" and the envelope of the skin and the in-betweens of its enveloped strata are more on the order of membranes than barriers (Whitehead, *Adventures of Ideas*, 206–7, 225). The "exterior milieu" that folds into the surface from outside is similarly stratified and populated by multitudes of bodies. Bodying understood as a surface effect, developed in this chapter, is akin to what Deleuze and Guattari call "corporeality": "a *corporeality* (materiality) that is not to be confused either with an intelligible, formal essentiality or a sensible, formed and perceived, thinghood. This corporeality has two characteristics: on the one

hand, it is inseparable from passages to the limit as changes of state, from processes of deformation or transformation that operate in a space–time itself anexact and that act in the manner of events (ablation, adjunction, projection . . .) [i.e., topological transformations]; on the other hand, it is inseparable from expressive or intensive qualities, which can be higher or lower in degree, and are produced in the manner of variable affects (resistance, hardness, weight, color . . .). There is thus an ambulant coupling, *events-affects*, which constitutes the vague corporeal essence and is distinct from the sedentary linkage, 'fixed essence-properties of the thing deriving from the essence,' 'formal essence-formed thing.'" See *A Thousand Plateaus*, 407–8. By vague, they do not just mean lacking determination but rather being determined in such a way as to dynamically envelop a multiplicity of potentials. This is the sense in which Spuybroek speaks of an "architecture of vagueness." See Lars Spuybroek, "The Structure of Vagueness," in Spuybroek, *NOX*, 352–59; and Massumi, "Building Experience," 329–30.

86. Simondon, *L'individuation à la lumière des notions de forme et d'information*, 275–76.

87. "Future Primitives," 23rd Biennale of Interiors, Kortrijk, Belgium, 2012.

88. Lynn and Rashid, *Architectural Laboratories*, 34, 47

89. Lynn and Rashid, 17.

90. Speaking of the 5900 Wilshire Restaurant Pavilion Model (2008), "Our project is a new gateway to the multibuilding office complex that includes a cafe with outdoor seating under a shaded trellis. As we began thinking about the context of Wilshire Boulevard it became clear that we needed a presence on the boulevard that addressed the speed of the cars as well as the movement of pedestrians. The restaurant is only a few thousand square feet, but spanning above it is a vast luminous ceiling that provides shade during the day and is arrayed with hundreds of dynamic lights at night. We can determine the color and intensity of the lights to produce varying images, moods, and patterns across the site. During the day the trellis produces dappled light through the undulating shaded roofscape and at night it becomes a luminous glow reflected off the metallic surfaces of the building." Lynn, "Machine Language," 59.

91. See note 65.

92. See notes 34 and 59.

93. Simondon, *Du mode d'existence des objets techniques*, 57.

94. Lynn, "Machine Language," 59; Lynn, *Greg Lynn*, 173–75.

95. Lynn, "Machine Language," 62.

96. Lynn, *Greg Lynn*, 181, 183, 185. For the *Alessi Coffee Piazza*, which

uses similar procedures, the matrix can produce fifty thousand permutants. See Lynn, interview with Mark Rappolt.

97. On filiation, alliance, and involution, see Lynn, *Folds, Bodies and Blobs*, 47.

98. Lynn, *Greg Lynn*, 175.

99. Lynn, 173.

100. Greg Lynn, "Introducing Composites, Surfaces and Software," in Lynn and Gage, *Composites, Surfaces, and Software*, 13.

101. Greg Lynn, "From Composites to Cooking in a Bag," in Lynn and Foster, *Composites, Surfaces, and Software*, 20.

102. In 2015, Lynn was named chief creative officer of Piaggio Fast Forward, a company designing lightweight high-performance vehicles. See http://www.piaggiofastforward.com/.

103. Lynn, "Introducing Composites, Surfaces and Software," in Lynn and Gage, *Composites, Surfaces, and Software*, 9.

104. Lynn, 11.

105. Lynn, *Greg Lynn*, 173.

106. Greg Lynn, "NOAH: New Outer Atmospheric Habitat," in Borasi and Zardini, *Other Space Odysseys*, 24–29; "Greg Lynn and Giovanna Borasi Meet in Venice, Los Angeles, in the Fall of 2009," in Borasi and Zardini, 37–54.

107. Greg Lynn, "A New Style of Life," in *Greg Lynn*, 298–301; Greg Lynn, "New City," in Borasi and Zardini, 30–35 (design for a futuristic virtual city).

2. RELATIONAL ARCHITECTURE

1. All of the projects discussed in this essay are documented on the artist's website, http://www.lozano-hemmer.com/.

2. Lozano-Hemmer, "Relational Architecture," 56.

3. Lozano-Hemmer. "Real and Virtual Light of Relational Architecture," 307.

4. These ungraspable movements occurring at inhuman scales have more recently been dubbed "hyperobjects." See Morton, *Hyperobjects*. But objects, processually, are precisely what they are *not*.

5. Michotte, *The Perception of Causality*, 204.

6. Kaufman, *Perception*, 378.

7. "Plus qu'unité": Simondon, *L'individuation à la lumière des notions de forme et d'information*, 25, 27, 31–33. See also Manning, *Always More Than One*, and on touch hinging more on "reaching-toward" than contact, see Manning, *Politics of Touch*.

8. Michotte, *The Perception of Causality*, 204; emphasis added.

9. Baudrillard, *Simulacra and Simulation*.

10. Simondon, *L'individuation à la lumière des notions de forme et d'information*, 24–32.

11. Simondon, 148–51, 211, 224–28.
12. Bakhtin, *Art and Answerability*, 299; emphasis added.
13. Marcel, "Blindsight and Shape Perception: Deficit of Visual Consciousness or of Visual Function?" For more discussion of this, under the concept of the "feedback of higher forms," see Massumi, *Parables for the Virtual*, 198–99.
14. Bargh, "The Automaticity of Everyday Life," 24. For more on nonconscious affective modulation and blindsight, see de Gelder et al., "Non-Conscious Recognition of Affect in the Absence of Striate Cortex." See also Massumi, *Ontopower*, chapter 3.
15. Bargh, Chen, and Burrows, "Automaticity of Social Behavior."
16. Whitehead, *Process and Reality*, 182.
17. Peirce. *The Essential Peirce*, vol. 1, 44.
18. Peirce, 42.
19. Peirce, 42. On suchness as an autonomous, infra-phenomenal dimension of reality (Peirce's Firstness), see Massumi, "Such As It Is."
20. Peirce, *The Essential Peirce*, vol. 2, 480.
21. Peirce, *The Essential Peirce*, vol. 1, 44.
22. Peirce, 44.
23. Peirce, 54.
24. Bergson, *Matter and Memory*, 23–24, 74–75, 120. On "incipient action," see also Massumi, *Parables for the Virtual*, 128–29. Also on incipient action and the related concept of "preacceleration," see Manning, *Relationscapes*, 3–29.
25. James, *Essays in Radical Empiricism*, 161; Massumi, *Semblance and Event*, 1–3; Massumi, *Ontopower*, 44–49, 74–78, 131–32.
26. Whitehead, *Adventures in Ideas*, 181.
27. Whitehead, 182.
28. For more on priming and nonsensuous perception, see Massumi, *Ontopower*, 66–67, 107–16, 129–34.
29. Lozano-Hemmer, "Real and Virtual Light of Relational Architecture," 307.
30. On the concept of the occurrent arts, see Massumi, *Semblance and Event*. On the event as medium, see 81–83. The concept of the event as medium is closely allied to Whitehead's notion of the "world as medium" (the world of process, in process, converging into the "actual occasion"). See Murphie, "The World as Medium"; and Brian Massumi, "Immediation Unlimited."
31. An allied concept of processual neighborhood as a "zone of proximity" that is a degree of contraction of a "zone of indiscernibility" (rather than a structured context or gestalt ground) is used by Deleuze and Guattari in connection with their concept of becoming. See *A Thousand Plateaus*, 272–73, 293, 306–7.

32. Bakhtin, *Art and Answerability*, 274.

33. On abstract cultural-political surfaces and the composition of events of expression, see Manning, *Relationscapes*, 119–42. See also the discussion of abstract surfaces in chapter 1 above. The cultural domain is like the stadium wave, but more multitudinous in its elements, more populated.

34. Readers familiar will easily associate this with Bergson's cone diagram of the virtual contracting punctually into the actual in *Matter and Memory*, 211.

35. See Manning, Munster, and Thomsen, Immediations.

36. Lozano-Hemmer, "Real and Virtual Light of Relational Architecture," 310.

37. Whitehead, *Process and Reality*, 105. See also Debaise, "Une philosophie des interstices."

38. Evens, *Sound Ideas*, 15.

39. Lozano-Hemmer's project *Atmospheric Memory* (2018) plays explicitly with this idea.

40. Evens, *Sound Ideas*, 15–18. The movement of the uncontracted "ground" rising into implication with what comes to stand out from it complicates any cut-and-dried figure–ground dichotomy in a similar way to the body in relation to its kinesthetic ground, as discussed earlier. On the rising of the ground into what emerges from it, and the descent of the emerged back into the formative potential of the ground for another iteration, see Deleuze, *Difference and Repetition*, 274–75. The rising and falling of the ground in the expressive event makes it a "groundless ground": it takes the shape of an event, with whose passing and rhythmic replacement by another it becomes co-substantial. This makes it, at the limit, a virtual ground, similarly to the topological figures discussed in chapter 1 as the passing-in-between forms of process's formative ongoing.

41. Vološinov, *Marxism and the Philosophy of Language*, 85. The controversy surrounding the authorship of Vološinov's works and whether it should be attributed to Bakhtin is not relevant to this discussion. The works are cited as published.

42. Vološinov, 93.

43. Vološinov, 96.

44. Vološinov, 76.

45. Vološinov, 81.

46. Vološinov, 118.

47. The organizing force that is residually harbored in the archive is the *anarchive*: the incipiency of an expressive movement that will crest in a new variation, to make a difference. This is a differential formative force that moves processually through the archive. At the

limit, the Archive is the Anarchive (just as, at the limit, the ground is dynamically groundless). See Murphie and SenseLab, *The Go-To How-To Book of Anarchiving*. The *Amodal Suspension* project is an instantiation of the anarchive.

48. Vološinov, *Marxism and the Philosophy of Language*, 116.

49. Blanchot, *The Space of Literature*, 26, 47, 50; Blanchot, *The Infinite Conversation*, 159, 242, 329. See also Deleuze and Guattari, *A Thousand Plateaus*, 77, 105.

50. During the Yamaguchi *Amodal Suspension* installation, close to ten thousand messages were sent. The project drew over four hundred thousand unique visitors from ninety-four countries. Visitors requested over 6.3 million server documents.

51. This coincident two-way movement is the rise and fall of the groundless ground of the event described in note 40.

52. On the cosmic dimension of cultural becoming, analyzed in relation to rhythm and music, see Deleuze and Guattari, *A Thousand Plateaus*, 343–50.

53. On internal, ulterior, and immanent limits, see also chapter 1, "Capital Moves," in Massumi, *The Principle of Unrest*.

54. Vološinov, *Marxism and the Philosophy of Language*, 99.

55. Vološinov, 103, 105.

56. Vološinov, 96, 100.

57. In chapter 1, the adjective "elemental" was used to refer to the multiplicity of isolatable elements that enter in the dynamic unity of a fusion. In this chapter, the connotation of the "elemental" shifts to designate the conjugation (in something like the grammatical sense of the word) to which the fusion itself belongs, by which the multiplicity of disparate elements comes to hold together in the singularity of an event.

58. Vološinov, *Marxism and the Philosophy of Language*, 70, 94.

59. Vološinov, 153.

60. Vološinov, 153.

61. Vološinov, 70.

62. Vološinov, 70–71.

63. Vološinov, 73, 81.

64. "Media, *all* media, information, *all* information, act in two directions: outwardly they produce more of the social, inwardly they neutralise social relations and the social itself." Baudrillard, *In the Shadow of the Silent Majorities*, 66. Of course, this diagnosis holds only as long as there are segregable "outward" and "inward" spheres for mediation to move between.

65. Vološinov, *Marxism and the Philosophy of Language*, 110.

66. Vološinov, 145.

67. Vološinov, 102.

68. Deleuze, *Logic of Sense*, 141, 152.

69. Vološinov, *Marxism and the Philosophy of Language*, 144.

70. Vološinov, 134–35.

71. Vološinov, 154.

72. Vološinov, 135.

73. Vološinov, 80.

74. Vološinov, 119–20, 125.

75. Vološinov, 137. Quasi-direct discourse, carried to the limit, is what Deleuze and Guattari, following Pasolini, analyze as "free indirect discourse." See *A Thousand Plateaus*, 80, 84.

76. Vološinov, *Marxism and the Philosophy of Language*, 158.

77. Vološinov, 158.

78. Vološinov, 158.

79. Vološinov, 158.

80. Vološinov, 159.

81. Vološinov, 159.

82. Rifkin, *The Age of Access*.

83. Deleuze and Guattari, *What Is Philosophy?* 87.

84. Attali, *Noise: The Political Economy of Music*.

85. *Merriam-Webster's Collegiate Dictionary*, s.v. "adventitious."

86. Simondon, *L'individuation à la lumière des notions de forme et d'information*, 292–316.

87. Peirce, *The Essential Peirce*, vol. 2, 403–4.

88. Peirce, 389.

89. Peirce, *The Collected Papers of Charles Sanders Pierce*, vol. 4, 551.

90. Massumi, *Ontopower*, chapter 2; *Principle of Unrest*, chapter 1, esp. 48–56; and *99 Theses on the Revaluation of Value*, theses 49–68.

3. MAKING TO PLACE

This essay is based on a series of conversations with the artist held in Sydney in July and August 2012.

1. Simryn Gill, unpublished text, 2012.

2. Gill.

3. Gill.

CONCLUDING REMARKS

1. Lapoujade, *Les existences moindres*, 51.

2. Massumi, *Semblance and Event*.

Bibliography

Arakawa, Shusaku, and Madeline Gins. *Architectural Body*. Birmingham: University of Alabama Press, 2002.

Arakawa, Shusaku, and Madeline Gins. *Making Dying Illegal: Architecture against Death*. New York: Roof Books, 2006.

Attali, Jacques. *Noise: The Political Economy of Music*. Translated by Brian Massumi. Minneapolis: University of Minnesota Press, 1985.

Bakhtin, M. M. *Art and Answerability: Early Philosophical Essays by M. M. Bakhtin*. Edited by Michael Holquist and Vadim Liapunov. Translated by Vadim Liapunov. Austin: University of Texas Press, 1990.

Bargh, John A. "The Automaticity of Everyday Life." In *The Automaticity of Everyday Life*, edited by Robert S. Wyer, 1–63. Mahwah, N.J.: Lawrence Erlbaum Associates, 1997.

Bargh, John A., Mark Chen, and Lara Burrows. "Automaticity of Social Behavior: Direct Effects of Trait Construct and Stereotype Activation on Action." *Journal of Social Personality and Social Psychology* 71, no. 2 (1996): 230–44.

Baudrillard, Jean. *In the Shadow of the Silent Majorities; or, The End of the Social*. Translated by Paul Foss, Paul Patton, and John Johnston. New York: Semiotext(e), 1983.

Baudrillard, Jean. *Simulacra and Simulation*. Translated by Sheila Glaser. Ann Arbor: University of Michigan Press, 1995.

Bergson, Henri. *Matter and Memory*. Translated by Nancy Margaret Paul and W. Scott Palmer. Mineola, N.Y.: Dover, 2004.

Bergson, Henri. *The Two Sources of Morality and Religion*. Translated by R. Ashley Audra and Cloudesley Brereton with the assistance of W. Horsfall Carter. London: Macmillan and Co., 1935.

Blanchot, Maurice. *The Infinite Conversation*. Translated by Susan Hanson. Minneapolis: University of Minnesota Press, 1993.

Blanchot, Maurice. *The Space of Literature*. Translated by Ann Smock. Lincoln: University of Nebraska Press, 1989.

Borasi, Giovanna, and Mirko Zardini, eds. *Other Space Odysseys: Greg Lynn, Michael Maltzan, and Alessandro Poli*. Montreal / Baden: Canadian Centre for Architecture / Lars Müller Publishers, 2010.

Cache, Bernard. *Projectiles*. London: Architectural Association, 2011.

Carpo, Mario, ed. *The Digital Turn in Architecture: 1992–2012*. West Sussex, U.K.: John Wiley & Sons, 2013.

Debaise, Didier. "Une philosophie des interstices: Whitehead et la question du vivant." *L'art du comprendre* 18 (2009): 125–37.

De Gelder, Béatrice, Jean Vroomen, Gilles Pourtois, and Lawrence Weikrantz. "Non-Conscious Recognition of Affect in the Absence of Striate Cortex." *NeuroReport* 10, no. 18 (December 1999): 3759–63.

Delanda, Manuel. "Materiality: Anaexact and Intense." In *NOX: Machining Architecture*, edited by Lars Spuybroek, 370–77. London: Thames and Hudson, 2004.

Deleuze, Gilles. *Difference and Repetition*. Translated by Paul Patton. New York: Columbia University Press, 1994.

Deleuze, Gilles. *Foucault*. Translated by Paul Bové. Minneapolis: University of Minneapolis Press, 1988.

Deleuze, Gilles. *The Logic of Sense*. Edited by Constantin V. Boundas. Translated by Mark Lester and Charles Stivale. New York: Columbia University Press, 1990.

Deleuze, Gilles, and Félix Guattari. *Anti-Oedipus*. Translated by Robert Hurley, Mark Seem, and Helen R. Lane. Minneapolis: University of Minnesota Press, 1983.

Deleuze, Gilles, and Félix Guattari. *A Thousand Plateaus*. Translated by Brian Massumi. Minneapolis: University of Minnesota Press, 1987.

Deleuze, Gilles, and Félix Guattari. *What Is Philosophy?* Translated by Graham Burchell and Hugh Tomlinson. London: Verso, 1994.

Diacu, Florin, and Philip Holmes. *Celestial Encounters: The Origins of Chaos and Stability*. Princeton, N.J.: Princeton University Press, 1999.

Eisenman, Peter. *Diagram Diaries*. London: Thames and Hudson, 1999.

Evens, Aden. *Sound Ideas: Music, Machines, and Experience*. Minneapolis: University of Minnesota Press, 2005.

Galofaro, Luca. *Eisenman: An Office in the Electronic Era*. Basel: Birkhäuser, 1999.

Kaufman, Lloyd. *Perception: The World Transformed*. Oxford, U.K.: Oxford University Press, 1979.

Kiesler, Frederick. "On Co-Realism: A Definition and Test." *Architectural Record* 86, no. 3 (September 1939): 63–69.

James, William. *Essays in Radical Empiricism*. Lincoln: University of Nebraska Press, 1996.

Lakoff, George, and Mark Johnson, *Metaphors We Live By*. Chicago: University of Chicago Press, 1980.

Lapoujade, David. *Les existence moindres*. Paris: Minuit, 2017.

Lozano-Hemmer, Rafael. *Amodal Suspension. Relational Architecture No. 8*. 2003. http://www.lozano-hemmer.com/amodal_suspension.php. Project website: http://www.amodal.net/index.html.

Lozano-Hemmer, Rafael. *Displaced Emperors: Relational Architecture No. 2*. 1997. http://www.lozano-hemmer.com/displaced_emperors.php.

Lozano-Hemmer, Rafael. "Real and Virtual Light of Relational Architecture: An Interview with Rafael Lozano-Hemmer." In *Uncanny Networks: Dialogues with the Virtual Intelligentsia*, ed. Geert Lovink, 304–13. Cambridge, Mass.: MIT Press, 2003.

Lozano-Hemmer, Rafael. "Relational Architecture." *Performance Research* 4, no. 2 (Summer 1999): 52–56.

Lozano-Hemmer, Rafael. *Re:Positioning Fear. Relational Architecture No. 3.* 1997. http://www.lozano-hemmer.com/repositioning_fear .php. Project website: http://archive.rhizome.org/artbase/2398/fear/.

Lozano-Hemmer, Rafael. *Vectorial Elevation. Relational Architecture No. 4.* 1997. http://www.lozano-hemmer.com/vectorial_elevation.php.

Lynn, Greg. *Animate Form.* Princeton, N.J.: Princeton Architectural Press, 1999.

Lynn, Greg, ed. *Archaeology of the Digital.* Montreal: Canadian Centre for Architecture, 2013.

Lynn, Greg. "Architectural Curvilinearity: The Folded, the Pliant, and the Supple." *Folding in Architecture*, special issue of *Architectural Design* 102 (1993): 14.

Lynn, Greg. *Folding in Architecture*, special issue of *Architectural Design* 102 (1993).

Lynn, Greg. *Folds, Bodies and Blobs: Collected Essays.* Brussels: La Lettre volée, 1998.

Lynn, Greg. "Geometry in Time." In *Anyhow*, edited by Cynthia Davidson, 164–73. New York: Anyone Corporation / MIT Press, 1998.

Lynn, Greg. *Greg Lynn: FORM.* Edited by Mark Rappolt. New York: Rizzoli, 2008.

Lynn, Greg. Interview with Eva Prinz. *Index Magazine*, 2005, http://www .indexmagazine.com/.

Lynn, Greg. Interview with Mark Rappolt. *Icon Magazine* 5 (September 2003), http://www.iconeye.com/.

Lynn, Greg. *Intricacy: A Project by Greg Lynn.* Philadelphia: Institute of Contemporary Art / University of Pennsylvania, 2003.

Lynn, Greg. "Machine Language," *Log* 10 (Summer–Fall 2007): 61.

Lynn, Greg. *Predator.* Design Document Series 15. Seoul: Damdi Publishing, 2006.

Lynn, Greg. "The Renewed Novelty of Symmetry." *Basilisk* 1 (1995), http://www.basilisk.com/R/renw_d_novlty_symmtry_576.html.

Lynn, Greg, and Mark Foster Gage, eds. *Composites, Surfaces, and Software: High-Performance Architecture.* New Haven, Conn.: Yale School of Architecture, 2010.

Lynn, Greg, and Hani Rashid. *Architectural Laboratories.* Rotterdam: Nai Publishers, 2002.

Manning, Erin. *Always More Than One: Individuation's Dance.* Durham, N.C.: Duke University Press, 2013.

Manning, Erin. *Politics of Touch: Sense, Movement, Sovereignty.* Minneapolis: University of Minnesota Press, 2006.

Manning, Erin. *Relationscapes: Movement, Art, Philosophy*. Cambridge, Mass.: MIT Press, 2009.

Manning, Erin, and Brian Massumi. *Thought in the Act: Passages in the Ecology of Experience*. Minneapolis: University of Minnesota Press, 2014.

Manning, Erin, Anna Munster, and Bodil Marie Stavning Thomsen, eds. Immediations. 2 vols. London: Open Humanities Press, forthcoming.

Marcel, Anthony. "Blindsight and Shape Perception: Deficit of Visual Consciousness or of Visual Function?" *Brain*, 121, no. 8 (August 1998): 1565–88.

Massumi, Brian. "Building Experience: The Architecture of Perception." *NOX: Machining Architecture*, edited by Lars Spuybroek, 322–31. London: Thames and Hudson, 2004.

Massumi, Brian. "Immediation Unlimited." In Immediations, edited by Erin Manning, Anna Munster, and Bodil Marie Stavning Thomsen. London: Open Humanities Press, forthcoming.

Massumi, Brian. "Interface and Active Space: Human–Machine Design." In *Proceedings of the Sixth International Symposium on Electronic Art*, 188–92. Montreal: ISEA, 1996.

Massumi, Brian. *99 Theses on the Revaluation of Value: A Postcapitalist Manifesto*. Minneapolis: University of Minnesota Press, 2018.

Massumi, Brian, *Ontopower: War, Powers, and the State of Perception*. Durham, N.C.: Duke University Press, 2015.

Massumi, Brian. *Parables for the Virtual: Movement, Affect, Sensation*. Durham, N.C.: Duke University Press, 2002.

Massumi, Brian. *The Principle of Unrest*. London: Open Humanities Press, 2017.

Massumi, Brian. *Semblance and Event: Activist Philosophy and the Occurrent Arts*. Cambridge, Mass.: MIT Press, 2011.

Massumi, Brian. "Such As It Is: A Short Essay in Extreme Realism." *Body and Society* 22, no. 1 (March 2016): 115–27.

Massumi, Brian. "Urban Appointment: A Possible Rendez-Vous with the City." In *Making Art of Databases*, edited by Joke Brouwer and Arjen Mulder, 28–55. Rotterdam: V2 Organisatie / Dutch Architecture Institute, 2003.

Massumi, Brian. *What Animals Teach Us about Politics*. Durham, N.C.: Duke University Press, 2014.

Merriam-Webster's Collegiate Dictionary. 10th ed. Springfield, *Mass.: Merriam-Webster*, 1998.

Michotte, Albert. *The Perception of Causality*. London: Methuen, 1963.

Morton, Timothy. *Hyperobjects: Philosophy and Ecology after the End of the World*. Minneapolis: University of Minnesota Press, 2013.

Murphie, Andrew. "The World as Medium." In Immediations, edited by Erin Manning, Anna Munster, and Bodil Marie Stavning Thomsen. London: Open Humanities Press, forthcoming.

Murphie, Andrew, and SenseLab. *The Go-To How-To Book of Anarchiving*. Montreal: SenseLab, 2016.

Peirce, C. S. *The Collected Papers of Charles Sanders Pierce*. Vols. 3–4. Edited by Charles Hartshorne and Paul Weiss. Cambridge, Mass.: Harvard University Press, 1933.

Peirce, C. S. *The Essential Peirce: Selected Philosophical Writings*. Vol. 1. Edited by Nathan Houser and Christian Kloesel. Bloomington: University of Indiana Press, 1992.

Peirce, C. S. *The Essential Peirce: Selected Philosophical Writings*. Vol. 2. Bloomington: University of Indiana Press, 1998.

Rifkin, Jeremy. *The Age of Access: How the Shift from Ownership to Access Is Transforming Capitalism*. New York: Penguin, 2000.

Ruyer, Raymond. *Le monde des valeurs*. Paris: Aubier, 1948.

Ruyer, Raymond. *Neofinalism*. Translated by Alyosha Edlebi. Minneapolis: University of Minnesota Press, 2016.

Simondon, Gilbert. *Du mode d'existence des objets techniques*. Paris: Aubier-Montagne, 1969.

Simondon, Gilbert. *L'individuation à la lumière des notions de forme et d'information*. Grenoble: Millon, 2005.

Spuybroek, Lars, ed. *NOX: Machining Architecture*. London: Thames and Hudson, 2004.

Spuybroek, Lars. *The Sympathy of Things: Ruskin and the Ecology of Design*. 2nd ed. London: Bloomsbury, 2016.

Vološinov, V. N. *Marxism and the Philosophy of Language*. Translated by Ladislav Matejka and I. R.Titunik. Cambridge, Mass.: Harvard University Press, 1986.

Whitehead, A. N. *Adventures of Ideas*. New York: Free Press, 1967.

Whitehead, A. N. *Process and Reality*. New York: Free Press, 1978.

Williams, Doug. "It's Settled: Where the First Wave Started." *ESPN*, March 1, 2013, http://espn.go.com/blog/playbook/fandom/post/_/id/18888/its-settled-where-the-wave-first-started.

Index

BRIAN MASSUMI is author of numerous
works across philosophy, political theory,
and art theory, including *The Politics of
Everyday Fear* (Minnesota, 1993) and
99 Theses on the Revaluation of Value
(Minnesota, 2018). He is coauthor, with
Erin Manning, of *Thought in the Act*
(Minnesota, 2014).